ELAINE BLACK YONEDA

D1518975

RACHEL SCHREIBER

ELAINE BLACK YONEDA

Jewish Immigration, Labor Activism,
and Japanese American Exclusion
and Incarceration

TEMPLE UNIVERSITY PRESS
Philadelphia | *Rome* | *Tokyo*

TEMPLE UNIVERSITY PRESS
Philadelphia, Pennsylvania 19122
tupress.temple.edu

Library of Congress Cataloging-in-Publication Data

Names: Schreiber, Rachel, author.
Title: Elaine Black Yoneda : Jewish immigration, labor activism, and
  Japanese American exclusion and incarceration / Rachel Schreiber.
Description: Philadelphia : Temple University Press, 2022. | Includes
  bibliographical references and index. | Summary: "This book tells the
  story of Elaine Black Yoneda (1906-1988), daughter of Russian Jewish
  immigrants to the United States and Communist labor activist, who spent
  eight months during World War II in a concentration camp, not in Europe,
  but in California"—Provided by publisher.
Identifiers: LCCN 2021015260 (print) | LCCN 2021015261 (ebook) | ISBN
  9781439921555 (cloth) | ISBN 9781439921562 (paperback) | ISBN
  9781439921579 (pdf)
Subjects: LCSH: Yoneda, Elaine Black, 1906–1988. | Social reformers—United
  States—Biography. | Civil rights workers—United States—Biography. |
  Radicals—United States—Biography. | Communists—United
  States—Biography. | Labor movement—United States—History. | Japanese
  Americans—Evacuation and relocation, 1942–1945. | Japanese
  Americans—Civil rights. | LCGFT: Biographies.
Classification: LCC HQ1413.Y66 S37 2021 (print) | LCC HQ1413.Y66 (ebook)
  | DDC 303.48/4092 [B]—dc23
LC record available at https://lccn.loc.gov/2021015260
LC ebook record available at https://lccn.loc.gov/2021015261

Printed in the United States of America

9 8 7 6 5 4 3 2 1

I dedicate this book to my two grandmothers, Genia Zalesky and Clara Schreiber. I see some of Elaine in each of them— Grandma Genia's Russian- and Yiddish-tinged English rings in my ears as I imagine how Elaine's voice might have sounded, and Savta Clara's determined devotion to her family and her ideals is a powerful match for Elaine's values. Their lives spanned years of the twentieth century similar to Elaine's, and all three women stand together in my mind as role models and inspirations for the experiences of emigration and immigration that shaped the twentieth-century Jewish experience.

Contents

Acknowledgments   ix

Introduction   1

Part I: Russia and New York City   19

Part II: Los Angeles   31

Part III: San Francisco   57

Part IV: Manzanar   109

Part V: San Francisco and Penngrove   153

Postscript   177

Notes   181

Bibliography   203

Index   209

Photo gallery follows page 98

Acknowledgments

In 2009 I was commissioned by the Contemporary Jewish Museum in San Francisco to produce a visual body of work for their upcoming exhibition *California Dreaming: Jewish Life in the Bay Area from the Gold Rush to the Present*, which focused on the history of Jewish life in the state.[1] Then director Connie Wolf approached me with her concern that the exhibition would be overly focused on the "rich and famous"—wealthy business owners, philanthropists, politicians, and so on. She wanted to ensure that the stories of important and interesting—but lesser known—Jewish Californians would be included. I began my research for what ultimately became a body of landscape photographs of sites around the state, each one tied to a historic Jewish Californian who, though not famous, made an important contribution. It was in Fred Rosenbaum's book *Cosmopolitans: A Social and Cultural History of the Jews of San Francisco* that I first read about Elaine Black Yoneda, in one brief paragraph devoted to her.[2] Thus began my many years of research on this fascinating woman and the incredible life that she led. After the *California Dreaming* exhibition, Bernice Yeung took an interest in the story and encouraged the inclusion of a short text on Elaine to be published in *Hyphen* magazine. After that, the idea for a biography took hold in my mind. My journey from that first encounter to this present book could not have happened without support from a wide range of people; here I acknowledge just a few of those individuals.

Librarians and archivists are always a historian's best friends. I am grateful to Catherine Powell, director of the Labor Archives at San Francisco State University, and Frances Kaplan, reference and outreach librarian at the California Historical Society, for their assistance. Catherine Powell and Molly Haigh in the Library Special Collections at University of California, Los Angeles went above and beyond to obtain image scans while their universities were shuttered because of Covid-19. Research support has been graciously extended by my institution, Parsons School of Design at The New School. Francesca Gambino, Hannah Leffingwell, and Kurt Pelzer provided valuable research assistance.

Numerous historians and scholars were generous with their time, particularly Ben Kobashigawa and Arthur Hansen. I will forever be grateful to Ken Kann, who connected me with Tom Yoneda, Elaine's son. Speaking with Tom on multiple occasions, sharing memories and going through old photos, was an amazing experience, and I am deeply grateful for his generosity. And I thank Moses Leggese, who assisted with photographic research.

I want to express my appreciation for the anonymous readers who peer-reviewed this manuscript. "Reader 1" in particular is the most generous reader I've encountered—their corrections and comments pointed me in the right direction where I'd been astray and helped me see how to more fully articulate the major points and themes, always in the spirit of support and encouragement to see a full-length study of Elaine come into being. I am grateful too to my editors and the entire team at Temple University Press. Aaron Javsicas has been enthusiastic about the project from the start, and Shaun Vigil has provided attentive and thoughtful support for publishing a book in the midst of a global pandemic. I could not imagine that the book cover could be designed by anyone other than the incredible Lucille Tenazas, who was excited about being involved in the project from the moment I told her about it.

Friends, family, and colleagues too numerous to name helped bring this project to fruition. The dedicated staff in the dean's office at Parsons enabled me to turn my attention to this project when needed. The amazing women of my writers' group, which has now been meeting for thirteen years and in the Zoom age meets across multiple international time zones, patiently read the book and offered productive comments and encouragement. They are Kim Anno, Nicole Archer, Paula Birnbaum, Irene Cheng, Jeanne Finley, Tirza True Latimer, Amy Lyford, Jordana Moore Saggese, and Jenny Shaw. Mary P. Ryan read an early draft and, moreover, provided support and feedback throughout the conceptualization of this project. My entire family has been deeply supportive of the project from the start.

My husband and partner in all things, David Gissen, encouraged me to use our four-month adventure in Vienna, Austria, as a kind of writing residency—without that time, this book would surely not have been completed. He provided a shoulder to cry on the day I finished my first draft and wrote the details of Elaine's passing, which had me in tears. Side by side with David, all things are possible.

ELAINE BLACK YONEDA

Introduction

Elaine Black Yoneda: *Jewish Immigration, Labor Activism, and Japanese American Exclusion and Incarceration* is a biography of Elaine Black Yoneda (1906–1988), Communist labor activist and daughter of Russian Jewish immigrants, who spent eight months during World War II living in a concentration camp—not in Europe, but in California. Elaine's path to the Manzanar War Relocation Center wends through a multigenerational history of labor activism commencing in Russia, continuing on the East Coast of the United States, and culminating in California, where Elaine and her family became involved with the racially and ethnically diverse radical community of Los Angeles. It was there that Elaine met the love of her life, Japanese American Communist organizer Karl Yoneda. When Karl and their three-year-old son Tommy were required to go to Manzanar, Elaine insisted on accompanying them.

Sadly, the xenophobic fervor that swept the United States after the bombing of Pearl Harbor has recently emerged yet again in this country, rendering Elaine's story prescient of current events. The anti-Asian discrimination and violence that proliferated alongside the Covid-19 pandemic is yet another instance in our history of the construction of a racial panic. The early and erroneous ascribing of the spread of the virus to travelers from China only confirmed this society's all-too-easy willingness to blame a racialized other for its own inability to adequately respond to a crisis. But perhaps the most poignant and uncanny example that relates to Elaine's story was the recent repurposing of a military base in Oklahoma that had been used to incarcerate Japanese Americans during World War II to detain Latin American children separated from their families at the border.[1] The contemporary relevance of such topics reminds us of our historic and contemporary anti-immigrant rhetoric, laws, and policies. Studying the history of Japanese American exclusion and incarceration is critical for a full understanding of the dangers posed by such actions.

Elaine Black Yoneda focuses on this chapter of Elaine's life, but it also explores in depth the labor activism that occupied Elaine in the 1930s and narrates her overall life story. The book examines the culture and work of the Communist Party of the United States of America (CPUSA) and labor activity on the West Coast that, by virtue of its interracial makeup, differed qualitatively from the better-known history of labor organizing on the East Coast, particularly in New York City. Elaine worked for the International Labor Defense (ILD), an organization sponsored by the CPUSA, which provided legal aid for arrested strikers on the local level and contributed to national civil- and labor-rights causes such as the campaign to free Tom Mooney, who had been falsely accused of planning a bombing at a Preparedness Day Parade in San Francisco in 1916. The ILD also defended the Scottsboro Nine, a group of African American men who were falsely accused of raping two white women in Alabama in 1931. During a period of heightened possibilities for women in the CPUSA, and during a decade of intense labor activity that was matched by equally violent antiunion suppression, Elaine's accomplishments were impressive—she was the only woman on the executive committee of the 1934 General Strike in the San Francisco Bay Area, and she would eventually become the vice president for the Pacific Coast region of the ILD. And while Elaine was able to rise to prominence within the party, she certainly experienced sexism within the organization and in the broader activist community.

Elaine's activism might have continued into the 1940s, but the events after the attack on Pearl Harbor changed the course of her family's life. *Elaine Black Yoneda* delves into the ways that the Yonedas' time at Manzanar defies commonly held ideas about Japanese American exclusion and incarceration. For one, Elaine was part of a small but not insignificant number of non-Japanese Americans, mostly spouses in interracial marriages, in the camps. Second, and what is perhaps most surprising, Elaine and Karl joined others—many of them Japanese Americans—in publicly supporting the U.S. decision to exclude Japanese Americans from the coast. Communists such as Karl and Elaine felt that the urgent need to fight fascism super-seded all other concerns, and they vowed devotion to the Allied cause. In this, they sided with nonradical assimilationist Japanese Americans who were eager to demonstrate their patriotism and, in fact, assisted with the plans for removal. In camp, Elaine and Karl were criticized and harassed for their cooperationist stance and accused of being spies. The accusation had merit—Karl did inform the Federal Bureau of Investigation (FBI) and the War Relocation Authority of "anti-American" and pro-Axis activities at camp before enlisting in the U.S. Army and leaving camp. Internecine camp politics among the incarcerated reflected divisions that had existed within the Japanese American community before the war and would ultimately result in a violent revolt at Manzanar, after which Elaine and Tommy returned to San Francisco.

After the war, the Yonedas settled for about a decade in Sonoma County, where they joined a community of radical leftist chicken ranchers and settled into a routine of hard agricultural work and moderate local activism. Although somewhat quiet during the repressive McCarthy era, they were active later in the century in the campaigns for reparations and redress for Japanese American incarceration and the work to designate Manzanar a national memorial site. Their efforts brought once again to the fore questions of Elaine and Karl's cooperationist stance during exclusion and incarceration. Unfortunately, Elaine would not live to see the culmination of the campaign, dying just a few months before the signing of executive apologies and the order for the reparations that she had worked to secure.

Elaine Black Yoneda offers a view from very close to the ground of a woman who was not highly ideological—she herself admitted that she only read Karl Marx and other theorists in a cursory way—but who supported the rank and file every day. Elaine was a high school dropout, but she was a natural public speaker and tenacious advocate who was unafraid to confront authorities. With no formal legal training, she defended oth-ers—and herself—in courtrooms and was often asked why she did not go to law school. Elaine had an extreme distaste for seeing people's rights violated, and that simple fact drew her into activism more than any theo-retical or philosophical adherence to class struggle. Oddly, her aversion to the violation of civil rights did not carry over into her reactions to the events resulting from Executive Order 9066 (EO 9066), which led to Japanese American exclusion and incarceration. She would later regret her capitu-lation, while also averring that it was a confusing time and that she had done what she thought best for her family.

Elaine Black Yoneda is a work of biography that can be situated within what some have called the new biography or feminist biography. Biography as a form fell out of favor with a generation of gender and labor historians as part of a reaction against history as a chronology of individual great men that was not adequately attentive to the masses. But recent theorists of biography claim the value of telling the life stories of marginalized individuals in order to illuminate the ways in which they challenged dominant discourses, occupied roles of their own self-fashioning, and managed all such efforts within their own specific times and places.[2] Gender historians in particular have relied on biography to reclaim the contributions of women like Elaine Yoneda, whose lives give evidence of the intertwining of the personal and the political and who counter received ideas about how gender might proscribe work, family, and everyday life.[3]

Critics of biography claim that the biographer artificially seeks to produce a coherent, truthful narrative where one doesn't really exist, that a lucid thesis cannot be devised from one person's life story. New biographers dispute this claim by allowing for the contradictions that sometimes crop up when telling a life story and acknowledging that individuals' lives are not lived in pure coherence.[4] Biography allows the historian to be attentive to the messiness of real life. Furthermore, focus on an individual life provides "a counterweight to abstract causation and 'conceptual' history, using primary sources and the personal perspective to explore, relativize, confirm or correct existing understandings and interpretations of the past," as Renders, de Haan, and Harmsma write.[5] Themes do emerge and the recounting of specific experiences exposes the ways that people responded to and found agency within the larger contexts in which they lived.

Elaine Yoneda's life experiences exemplify these aspects of the new biography. The fact that a Jewish woman spent time in a concentration camp on U.S. soil during World War II exposes the profound contradictions of the rhetorics employed to express the necessity of incarcerating Japanese Americans precisely in order to fight a very analogous system of racial classification in Europe. Here, she volunteered to go; there, she would have had no choice. There, she would have been included in a racialized group that the state asserted was a threat to the future of that society; here, her husband and son were thus assigned, while she was not. Indeed, the circumstances that pushed her parents from Russia were due to their need to escape violence based on that very identity while the pull to this country was based on the promise of a society free from such persecution. Here, Elaine clearly enjoyed a sense of privilege—which must be emphasized—by virtue of the construction of Jewishness as whiteness, and yet that construction was only, at this point in time, a recent phenomenon in U.S. history. Upon their arrival in New York City, her parents, as Russian Jewish working-class immigrants, would have been very much understood to be "not white," but, as scholar Karen Brodkin has demonstrated, through distinctly U.S. processes of race-making, this would shift by midcentury.[6] While Elaine definitely relied on her self-presentation as a well-dressed, confident, and assertive white woman to achieve some of her objectives as an activist, in other ways she was always cognizant of her status as a foreigner. Her parents eschewed religious observance, as she did in turn, and yet her cultural identification with being Jewish is evident throughout her life—in her friendships and shared use of Yiddish with other Jewish activists, in her memories that foreground her mother's Jewish cooking as central to a sense of home, and later to her connections to Northern California Jewish organizations. For Elaine, as for many second-generation Jewish Americans, the privileges of whiteness commingled with the histories of, as well as first-hand experiences of, discrimination. As Brodkin describes, Jewish Americans experienced the "racial middleness" of both belonging and marginality.[7] The mutual attraction between Elaine and Karl was surely due in part to their shared experiences as immigrants and outsiders—a fact that contributed to their colocation in the Boyle Heights neighborhood of Los Angeles and therefore to the circumstances under which they met.[8]

Elaine's negotiation of her own status as an immigrant; her encounters with anti-Semitism, white supremacy, and anticommunism; and the construction of her husband and child as threats to national security are only revealed through a full accounting of her story, from birth to death. The ways in which Jewish emigration from Russia, labor activism in the United States, and West Coast racism against Japanese Americans come together within one person's lifetime expose aspects of the U.S. past that would not emerge in a sweeping or synthetic study of any one of these histories. More than a mere timeline of milestones, *Elaine Black Yoneda* is a book that gives texture and nuance to these experiences, exploring the intersecting and at times contradictory political and social forces that shaped Elaine's life and that of her family.

To accomplish its aims, *Elaine Black Yoneda* draws on the biographic methodologies of feminist scholars whose innovations were to demonstrate the value of being attentive to lacunae, to engage different kinds of looking and reading, and to investigate any piece of archival information—even when seemingly insignificant—as sources that can be richly mined.[9] Such a methodology recognizes that it is a privilege to appear in the archives, a privilege not regularly afforded to people of all genders, races, abilities, and socioeconomic backgrounds. The Yonedas did not have the luxury of stable housing or geography—of course, their greatest disruption happened during World War II. In addition, as an interracial couple they faced significant housing discrimination both before and after the war and therefore they moved between rented apartments quite regularly. It is reasonable to assume that valuable archival materials were misplaced or discarded along the way. Historians of marginalized subjects must not assume that a lack of readily available information on a subject reflects the relative importance of their subject, nor that it limits the ability to tell a person's life story.

Gender bias emerges even between the records of Karl and Elaine—though they worked hand in hand for decades, his archive is far more extensive than hers.[10] Elaine's archive is uneven—the Manzanar experience is a focus. Clearly it was a defining event in her life and in U.S. history, and after the war she spent considerable effort on the campaign for redress and reparation. Relative to that, little record exists of her years working for the ILD, except where she appears in stories written by and about her in the ILD publication the *Labor Defender* and on the occasions that she appeared in other newspapers of the day.

Two invaluable primary sources of information on Elaine are the oral histories conducted with her while she was alive. *Elaine Black Yoneda* mines these rich documents to assemble not only factual information such as the chronology of events in Elaine's life but also her point of view and interpretation of her own experiences. Reading both what is in the transcripts and between the lines of the oral histories' pages exemplifies the previously discussed feminist methodological approach that a historian must use when scant additional primary sources are available. Both oral histories were produced within important scholarly institutional frameworks. The first is the 1974 oral history conducted by Arthur Hansen and Betty Mitson for the Japanese Americans Project of California State University at Fullerton's Oral History Program. This project was founded and overseen by Hansen, one of the key historians of Japanese American exclusion and incarceration. This oral history is limited in scope to the topic of Japanese American exclusion and incarceration, which was the aim of the project at the university. Elaine provides detailed descriptions in it of the events that transpired at Manzanar and, as might be expected, occasionally refers back to her life before the war. The second oral history was conducted a few years later by Lucy Kendall for the California Historical Society's Women in California collection in 1977 and 1978. The collection, held at the California Historical Society and at the Bancroft Library of the University of California, Berkeley is a crucial archive that documents feminist perspectives on California history. Kendall probes Elaine's memory, asking her to examine such topics as her sexual relationships, motherhood, and the status of women in the Communist Party in order to assess Elaine's perspective on her own role in women's history.

Arthur Hansen has also written extensively on the critical importance, as well as the methodological shortcomings, of oral histories of marginalized subjects but also very specifically on those of Japanese Americans who experienced exclusion and incarceration.[11] Hansen urges the oral historian to be mindful of race, gender, and ethnicity as they affect the relationship between interviewer and subject. Nevertheless, Hansen asserts the great value of oral histories to practices of history that seek to bring complexity to our understanding of the ways in which individual historic actors experienced events, often quite distinctly from one another. As Hansen writes, oral histories help us to see the "ample scope for subcultural diversity and individual differences (even during a time of extreme crisis when the expectation would be minimal normative deviation)."[12] Embedded in both oral histories are critical perspectives in which the interviewers adeptly circle back to unclear points or direct Elaine to reconsider various questions.

In addition to these two primary sources, two books have greatly informed this study. A previously published biography of Elaine written by Vivian McGuckin Raineri appeared under the title *The Red Angel: The Life and Times of Elaine Black Yoneda, 1906–1988*.[13] Produced by the Elaine Black Yoneda Memorial Book Committee of the San Francisco Bay Area Labor History Workshop shortly after her death, this earlier biography was, in its author's own words, "originally conceived as a self-published project to say something about Elaine's life and to record the impressions and tributes that her friends, relatives, and co-workers wanted to express."[14] As a result, *The Red Angel* reads as a vanity publication that records, but doesn't question or interpret, Elaine's perspective on events. By contrast, *Elaine Black Yoneda* contextualizes Elaine's memories, drawn from oral history transcripts, letters, and other primary documents, published articles, and *The Red Angel* in relation to broader historical research about those events. Although *The Red Angel* is not a memoir or autobiography, in many ways it reads like one since the purpose of the book was, to put it simply, to present Elaine's point of view. In this way, it is similar in perspective to Karl's published memoir, *Ganbatte: Sixty-Year Struggle of a Kibei Worker*.[15] *Ganbatte* provides an important resource for information on Elaine, told from the perspective of her husband, and written while she was still alive.

Additional primary sources consulted for this book include articles by and about Elaine published in the labor press during the 1930s and unpublished materials such as letters between Elaine and Karl and other family members, drafts for unpublished articles, photographs and other images and ephemera, transcripts of radio addresses, and more. Elaine's testimony to the Commission on Wartime Relocation and Internment of Civilians, given in Los Angeles in 1981 during the campaign for redress and reparations, is published in full in *Only What We Could Carry: The Japanese American Internment Experience*, a collection of primary source documents related to the history of Japanese American exclusion and incarceration.[16] Finally, this book draws on my interviews with several historians, most of whom knew Elaine and Karl, as well as my interview with their son, Tommy Yoneda, eighty years old at the time of the interview.[17]

The research for this interdisciplinary book further draws on a range of secondary literature to provide historical context and to allow for analysis of events that extends beyond Elaine's point of view. Too broad to fully recount here, the most relevant in content and methodology are studies of interracial and interethnic social and political formations and movements in early twentieth-century U.S. history, particularly in California; the role of women in the CPUSA, primarily in the 1930s; and the study of the exclusion and incarceration of Japanese Americans during World War II, as well as the postwar movement for redress and reparation.

While previous scholarship on the histories of immigrants, underrepresented communities, and social labor movements tended to focus on one group or another, more recent scholarship illuminates the importance of intersectional analyses that examine how such groups lived and worked in relation not only to the dominant culture, but alongside one another. Even more specifically, a number of these studies focus on the ways that, on the West Coast of the United States, and particularly in Los Angeles, nondominant groups lived and worked in coalition far more than on the East Coast, where patterns of settlement and labor activism tended to emerge from groups composed of similar affinities. Allison Varzally's book *Making a Non-white America: Californians Coloring outside Ethnic Lines, 1925–1955* not only offers an excellent example of a study that looks at the cross-racial and cross-ethnic engagements of various groups in shared space but also is particularly germane to this book. Varzally's focus is on Los Angeles, largely on the Boyle Heights neighborhood where Elaine was raised once the family settled in Los Angeles. Varzally studies interracial marriage, hetero-social environments, and even the specific ways that the exclusion and incar-ceration of Japanese Americans affected families that included Japanese Americans and non-Japanese Americans. Varzally's work has provided sig-nificant data for this study of Elaine and moreover provides methodologi-cal insights into how one fashions an analysis that seeks to study across racial and ethnic lines. Similarly, Mark Wild's *Street Meeting: Multiethnic Neighborhoods in Early Twentieth-Century Los Angeles* examines how a mix of immigrant, interethnic, and interracial groups found community with one another and in response to the ways that dominant groups used urban development as a tool to carve their own spatial boundaries.[18] Wild's focus within the book on interracial Socialist and Communist labor organizing includes the period when Elaine's parents moved to Los Angeles, became engaged with these groups, and ultimately drew Elaine into the work as well.

Several studies explore the role of women in the CPUSA during the 1930s, the period in which Elaine was most deeply involved. Rosalyn Baxandall's chapter, "The Question Seldom Asked: Women and the CPUSA," is an impor-tant and early study that notes both women's contributions and the ways in which they were limited by gender discrimination.[19] Elsa Jane Dixler's doc-toral dissertation, "The Woman Question: Women and the American Com-munist Party, 1929–1941," provides a useful overview of the primary source data, as well as an analysis of just how high into the ranks women were—and were not—allowed to rise.[20] The most comprehensive work on women's roles in the party is Kate Weigand's book *Red Feminism: American Communism and the Making of Women's Liberation.* Weigand covers the broad sweep of women's engagement in U.S. Communism, contextualizing the rise of wom-en's roles in the party during the 1930s. As she demonstrates, women's increased roles occurred in tandem with and in relation to the Comintern's purposeful prioritization of racial and gender inequity in labor in the Unit-ed States, particularly as the Great Depression enabled Americans to once again embrace Communism after the Red Scare of the late 1910s had driven radical politics underground.[21]

The literature on the history of the Japanese American incarceration and exclusion during World War II is far too extensive to fully review here. Scholars have thoroughly documented the events as they unfolded after the bombing of Pearl Harbor, life in the camps themselves, and the subsequent movement for redress and reparations.[22] A range of studies have focused on the history of West Coast racism that enabled the military and the federal government, bolstered by economic interests and the media, to violate the rights of U.S. citizens on a scale that, within U.S. history, can be compared only with the theft of the lands and the rights of Indigenous Peoples.[23]

Although, as said, the scholarly literature on this topic is extensive, nevertheless aspects of this history that deserve further exploration remain, for example, a number of topics that appear within Elaine's story, such as the recounting of the Manzanar Revolt and the history of non-Japanese Americans in the camps. This is not to say there is no scholarship on these topics; but that these details are lesser known. Arthur Hansen's writing on the Manzanar Revolt offers important correctives to the ways that the incident has been previously told.[24] Representations in the contemporaneous press of a "riot" at Manzanar influenced historians' analyses of these events for many years, until Hansen reframed the eruption of violence at Manzanar in December 1942 as an expression of the resistance to incarceration. To my knowledge, Paul Spickard is the only scholar to publish an article devoted to the policies on interracial families in the camps.[25] In addition, the histories of the discord within the Japanese American community between those who "cooperated" with U.S. authorities in plans for exclusion and those who committed acts of resistance in the camps are not widely known.

Numerous biographies and memoirs document a diversity of individuals' experiences of exclusion and incarceration. *Elaine Black Yoneda* might sit on a shelf next to these works in particular to fill in the picture of all the ways that this history affected people's lives and how people responded to exclusion and incarceration. The list would include *From Kona to Yenan: The Political Memoirs of Koji Ariyoshi*; *Enemy Child: The Story of Norman Mineta, a Boy Imprisoned in a Japanese American Internment Camp during World War II*; *Nisei Naysayer: The Memoir of Militant Japanese American Journalist Jimmie Omura*, and any number of other works.[26]

Although a work of fiction, it is worth mentioning *No-No Boy* by James Okada.[27] Written in 1957, the novel centers on a young Japanese American man who was incarcerated in a camp during World War II and subsequently arrested for refusing to sign the loyalty oath administered by the War Relocation Authority, which was required in order to serve in the U.S. Army. After the war, Okada's protagonist faces ostracization in his home community for his choices. The story is based to some extent on his own life: Okada and his family were incarcerated in Idaho during the war. The War Relocation Authority administered the loyalty oath in 1943, after Elaine, Karl, and Tommy had left Manzanar. People in the camps, including Karl and Elaine, had argued from the start of exclusion that the government should discern loyal Japanese Americans from others.[28] The oath was implemented to gauge loyalty as a path to allowing those incarcerated to return home and also in preparation to enroll male camp incarcerees in the U.S. military draft that had been put into place in 1940. A small but significant number of people answered "no" to two questions on the Application for Leave Clearance— these "no-no boys" were imprisoned at Tule Lake Relocation Center.[29] *No-No Boy* has had an interesting and circuitous publishing history. Initially rejected by numerous publishers, the book was eventually released in 1957 in a very small print run and was essentially unnoticed throughout Okada's lifetime, likely owing to the challenges the narrative posed to dominant Japanese American assimilationist discourse. The book was reissued in the late 1970s after Okada's death and sold well. More recently it has been at the center of a publishing controversy. Penguin Classics, which reissued the book, was challenged for copyright infringement and ultimately withdrew its advertising for the publication.[30]

No-No Boy highlights an important, though lesser known, aspect of the history of Japanese American incarceration in its history of active resistance. The mainstream Japanese American agenda, put forward by members of the Japanese American Citizens League and others, was to demonstrate patriotism, assimilation, and cooperation. In 1957 fiction may have been the only acceptable form in which to narrate such a story, and, even then, the book's reception at the time of its initial publication indicates the challenges of presenting this perspective. Since the time of Japanese American exclusion and incarceration, representation of its history within popular culture has lacked complexity and been fraught with ideological underpinnings.

A stark example is the copious photographic record of life in the camps. The photographers commissioned by the Farm Security Administration (FSA) to document the effects of the Great Depression overlapped temporally with Japanese American exclusion and incarceration, and several among them photographed the camps, including Ansel Adams, Clem Albers, Dorothea Lange, and Toyo Miyatake.[31] Adams and Lange photographed extensively at Manzanar, and in fact one of Lange's best-known images from the work is a portrait of Karl Yoneda. It's worth noting that, in the original exhibitions of this portrait, Karl is not identified by name but rather presented as an archetypal "incarceree." This universalizing tendency, which has been critiqued extensively in scholarship on the work of the FSA photographers, essentially demonstrates the flattening of the broad diversity of people's experiences of exclusion and incarceration.[32]

Somewhat similarly, *Farewell to Manzanar* by Jeanne Wakatsuki Houston and James D. Houston is perhaps the best-known popular memoir not only about Manzanar but also about the Japanese American exclusion and incarceration more broadly.[33] Wakatsuki was only seven years old when she was incarcerated at Manzanar; her account of events is told through the eyes of a small child. Though elements of social and cultural history are added to her memories of the camp, the fact that a young child's recollections of this experience stand as the iconic perspective in our popular collective memory exemplifies the overly general approach to this history. In telling Elaine's life story in a straightforward manner, *Elaine Black Yoneda* seeks to contribute a counternarrative that fleshes out this history with nuance and specificity.

Tracing the popular and scholarly literature on the topic of Japanese exclusion and incarceration, a reader will note that the use of specific language and terms has changed over time. Early on, the usage "Japanese evacuation and internment" was unquestioningly employed by historians. In accordance with the more recent work of scholars of Japanese American history, I choose the terms *exclusion* and *incarceration* to describe the events resulting from EO 9066. Historian Roger Daniels clearly articulates why the older terms of *evacuation* and *internment* are inappropriate. *Internment* is a legal process with its own history and usage in the United States, one that can be "applied to nationals of a country with which the United States [is] at war." The term is therefore incorrect when discussing U.S. citizens.[34] Furthermore, the manner in which Japanese Americans were removed to camps was extralegal. *Evacuation* implies relocating people for their own safety, and *internment* does not connote the full force of imprisonment. In addition, I describe members of this population as "Japanese Americans" to emphasize the fact that those who were subject to EO 9066 were *Americans*. Though some, particularly Issei (first-generation Japanese American immigrants), may not have been citizens, that fact owed to racist legislation that barred nonwhites from naturalization processes. They had been living in the United States for decades, and in most cases their children were citizens.

For similar reasons, I have chosen the term "concentration camp," rather than "internment camp," when referring to Manzanar and other camps. *Concentration* is apt because the intention was to group a population of people together in a controllable, proximate location. Currently, the United States is once again concentrating groups of immigrants and migrants near our borders—at the time of this writing, even in the very facilities of former Japanese American concentration camps.[35] The government and media use sensational language to fabricate the view that these immigrants are a threat to national security. The connection to the unjust exclusion and incarceration of Japanese Americans, which the U.S. government has officially identified as a grave mistake, must be emphasized.

Of course, in the context of World War II, "concentration camp" takes on special meaning, in that it connects these camps to those in Europe. The allusion is, on one hand, purposeful—it reveals the hypocrisy of the U.S. government's and military's derision of what was happening in Europe during World War II while building concentration camps of their own within the United States. On the other hand, as Elaine and Karl themselves stated, "concentration camps" were not the same as Nazi "death camps," the latter existing for the express purpose of genocide. Scholars of European history, too, differentiate concentration camps that existed in Europe from death camps—that is, not all concentration camps in Europe and Russia were death camps. Roger Daniels traces the fraught history of the usage of "internment camps" rather than "concentration camps," demonstrating that it was only after the liberation of Nazi camps in Europe that the U.S. government objected to the use of "concentration camp" to describe the sites of Japanese American incarceration operated by the War Relocation Authority, because that would clearly create an association between the U.S. government and the Third Reich.[36] So strong was the refusal to use this term that the Manzanar Committee had to fight hard to allow the use of "concentration camp" on the memorial plaque at the site, as is discussed in Chapter 29. The term "concentration camp" is used throughout this book to honor that effort, in addition to offering linguistic clarity.

A few comments are warranted about the use of words to describe those who supported exclusion and incarceration. In this book, I use *cooperationist* as a broad term to describe those who did not oppose exclusion and incarceration. The reasons for cooperation were varied. Communists and leftists like Elaine and Karl were expressly antifascist; based on this ideology they were cooperative with the U.S. and Allied forces' fight against the Axis powers. By contrast, members of the Japanese American Citizens League (JACL)—whom many criticize for aiding and abetting the unjust work of the military—were eager to assimilate into U.S. society and believed their cooperation would demonstrate their patriotism. Others may have cooperated simply out of fear or from lack of the means to act otherwise—it is worth remembering here that those Japanese Americans who had the ability and resources to relocate to the Midwest or East Coast of the United States to avoid incarceration and the seizure of their property did so, for example. *Coopera-*

tionist admittedly employs too broad a stroke to capture this diversity; nevertheless, it is useful at times in this narrative to group them in this way.

Similarly, it is simplistic to describe all those who opposed exclusion and incarceration as pro-Axis, pro-Japan, and anti-American. More dangerous still, to do so risks diminishing the importance of those who actively resisted racist and unconstitutional U.S. policies and actions. Unfortunately, though, throughout Elaine's oral histories and Karl's memoirs, both of them simply describe anyone who opposed exclusion and incarceration as pro-Japan. Where such generalizations appear in their quotations, they remain verbatim in this book. To return the nuance and differentiation that belongs to this group, and to acknowledge the important work of resistance, when not making direct quotations, I use the words *resistance* or *rebels*.

Historians choose words deliberately and in so doing situate their analysis within an ideological perspective. The historiographic record of Japanese American exclusion and incarceration is replete with language that obfuscates the great injustices committed against them; I endeavor to be attentive to this and to offer my corrective. At the same time, out of respect for the linguistic choices of the historical actors themselves, I have attempted to balance the choices made by those who spoke the words with the context provided by the histories in which they were spoken.

This book is organized spatially, divided into five parts that correspond to the places in which Elaine's life was situated during particular periods. Geography is an important aspect of Elaine's story, for her life and outlook were shaped not only by the influence her parents brought with them from Russia and New York City but also by the particular features of California's racial and ethnic politics and communities. The first part, set in Russia and New York City, briefly explores Elaine's early life story, including background on her parents and what led them to emigrate from Russia. The biographical information presented in it, particularly about Elaine's parents Molly and Nathan, sets the stage for understanding the potent environment of radical politics of Elaine's youth. Her father and mother arrived in the United States in 1904 and 1905, respectively, and Elaine was then born in 1906. A brother, Al, was born a few years later. The family first came to New York City, settling in Brooklyn. As Socialists fleeing anti-Semitism, Elaine's parents raised her and her brother in a secular home that was focused on labor rights. The chapters reveal the character of labor culture in both Russia and New York City, which contrast with that of California—whereas the two former locations saw mostly single-ethnic unions, California would become known for its interracial and interethnic activism.

Part II traces the family's move to California, first to a few locations near San Diego before finally making Los Angeles their home, where they became involved in the multiracial and multiethnic radical community. At first, Elaine expressed little interest in her parents' politics but eventually experienced a political awakening after witnessing police brutality at a number of labor demonstrations. Elaine was drawn into the work of the ILD. She began at this time to understand the power of her voice through her work with the ILD, and she was quickly recognized by those around her as a powerful speaker and leader. Elaine married, and subsequently left, her first husband, Ed Russell, with whom she gave birth to a daughter, Joyce. Through her labor work, she met Karl Yoneda, who would become her lifelong partner. She and Karl faced much opprobrium for their interracial union, which was founded on their mutual devotion to labor rights.

San Francisco is the setting for Part III. Elaine was promoted within the ILD and moved to San Francisco in 1933, at the start of a wave of intense labor activity throughout the state. This period marks the most active for Elaine's professional life; her rise within the ILD exemplifies the possibilities for women within the CPUSA. The spatial reach of her activity throughout Northern California is explored, as are her friendships with other women activists. Elaine played a key role in the 1934 San Francisco General Strike, perhaps the pinnacle of this intense era of strike culture. Stories of Elaine's various interactions with antiunion employers, judges, and vigilantes paint a vivid picture of the conflicts throughout California during this time and Elaine's resourcefulness in responding to them. Karl followed Elaine to San Francisco, and they moved in together. In 1939 Elaine gave birth to their son, Tommy.

Part IV opens in December 1942 with the bombing of Pearl Harbor. In the immediate aftermath, Elaine and Karl shared the uncertainty of the Japanese American community about what these events would portend. It may be surprising that Elaine and Karl were among those who did not oppose exclusion, claiming that the most urgent matter was opposition to fascism and a victory for the Allies. Karl left for the Manzanar Relocation Center; shortly after, notice was given that Tommy must go as well and Elaine insisted on accompanying them. This section details the family's eight months at Manzanar, exploring daily life in camp, and examines camp politics. There, Elaine and Karl were from the start subjected to threats for their cooperationist stance. Throughout this time, Karl sought permission to enlist in the U.S. Army. He was eventually accepted into the Military Intelligence Service and sent to Burma as a translator and propagandist.

After Karl's departure from the camp, heightened threats of violence were directed at Elaine and Tommy, and they were eventually granted permission to leave. The Manzanar Revolt is recounted and analyzed from a variety of perspectives. While Elaine and Karl saw this event as being perpetrated by profascist thugs, recent scholarship understands the revolt as an expression of resistance to exclusion and incarceration.

The concluding section of the book, Part V, traces the period of Elaine's story after World War II, in San Francisco and Penngrove, Sonoma County, through to the end of Elaine's life. With Karl overseas, Elaine and Tommy returned to San Francisco, where she worked in war industries until the end of the war. Karl was serving in Burma when he learned of the bombing of Hiroshima, the city of his birth and where his mother was living at the time of the devastation. It would be months before he would learn that she had survived. After Karl returned, he and Elaine bought a small chicken ranch in Penngrove, north of San Francisco—at the time the region was often described as the country's "egg basket"—joining a community of radical leftists who'd been raising chickens there since before the war. They found the work to be difficult and unsatisfying, but they were eager to bring some stability to Tommy's life, and so they stayed until he completed high school. In that community, they participated in various labor-related causes but not to the same extent as they had before the war. After Tommy went to college, Elaine and Karl moved back to San Francisco. Elaine worked office jobs within some of the unions she knew from before the war, and they remained there until Elaine died in 1988. After Elaine's death, she was memorialized by many of the people whom she had supported and defended throughout her life, in tributes from the International Longshore and Warehouse Union, the San Francisco Board of Supervisors, the Northern California Communist Party, and others.[37]

Throughout this latter period, Elaine and Karl were active in the campaigns to designate Manzanar a federally recognized memorial site and for redress and reparations to Japanese Americans. In the course of this work, debates resurfaced about their cooperationist stance on exclusion and incarceration and the rightful characterization of those who opposed these U.S. policies and actions. Elaine and Karl did express regret for their acquiescence, but they continued to insist on the wrongfulness of the behavior of those at Manzanar who perpetrated violence there.

Elaine Black Yoneda lived an extraordinary life, spanning most of the years of the twentieth century. Her life story illuminates the experience of immigrant labor activism throughout a period marked by major wars, the flowering of a radical labor movement followed later by its deep suppression, and worldwide conflict during which a nation that decried genocide abroad did so while acting unconstitutionally toward a racialized group of its own citizens. In the face of all these events, Elaine was a powerful figure, always vocally advocating for what she believed in and tenacious in her devotion to and love of family and friends. Her story productively complicates our idea of what it means to be American, while also offering stark and specific reminders of this nation's history of, and propensity for, xenophobic actions and policies.

PART I

Russia and
New York City

1

Minsk, the late nineteenth century. A match factory opens, and industrialization reshapes Russian life. The work of producing matches is difficult, noxious. By hand, workers dip flat strips of treated wood into a gelatinous substance composed of white phosphorous, gum Arabic, and other ingredients and then lay them out to dry. Once dried, the wood is cut into thin match strips. Before the phosphorous dries, it emits fumes that, settling into the laborers' lungs, lead to lifelong debilitating respiratory illnesses.[1] Another omnipresent danger is that a match factory, especially when built of wood, is prone to explosive fires and, as with all early industrial factories, fire protection and methods of egress were woefully inadequate. Women and children, the most vulnerable of workers, are regular laborers in this volatile and poisoned space. Despite all these dangers, such enterprises lured people from the countryside in large numbers with their promise of more stable futures. The work is plentiful, and all members of the family can take part in earning wages.

As was happening in many cities around the world throughout this period, the opening of the match factory in Minsk led to major demographic shifts in the region as scores and scores of people abandoned the rural life and economy of past generations in pursuit of better economic circumstances. For Jews in Belarus and surrounding areas, the opportunity to leave behind life in the shtetls, the small villages throughout eastern Europe, held strong appeal. In addition to the instabilities and poverty of the rural economy, Jews in the Pale of Settlement, the region within Russia where Jews were relegated by decree to live and work for more than one hundred years until the revolution of 1917, lived with the ongoing threat and reality of pogroms, during which bands of anti-Semitic marauders would subject them to random and ongoing waves of state-sanctioned violence.

Though urban centers offered more security and relief from the harsh conditions of shtetl life, industrial labor posed its own challenges. Working conditions were grim, and labor laws to protect workers from the no-holds-barred, profit-driven motivations of factory owners did not exist. And so, alongside this shift toward urban life and mass production came growing adherence to Marxism and a wave of movements for workers' rights. Radical labor movements formed in tandem with mass industrialization and urbanization, as laborers sought to improve their situations.

Among those who saw in Minsk the opportunity for a better life were two families: the Kvetnays and the Buchmans. The four parents who oversaw these two households scarcely could have imagined, though, that the relatively short move from the countryside of Belarus to Minsk would put in motion events that would set two of their children, Molly and Nathan, on a path to even more significant changes. For Molly and Nathan, who met in the match factory at the ages of eight and eleven, respectively, would first become childhood sweethearts and then abandon the religious life of their parents, adopt Communism as their guiding ideology, and eventually raise two children, Elaine and Al, a world away in California.[2] Elaine herself would eventually share her parents' politics and raise a family of her own.

Though it would take some time before Elaine espoused her parents' politics, she eventually embraced the cause of workers' rights and made their defense the core of her work. Elaine's professional life would be completely enmeshed in her family life—through her affiliations with the CPUSA, she would find her lifelong partner, fellow Communist organizer Karl Yoneda. Their life story includes major historical moments in California history and throughout its geography, including the San Francisco General Strike of 1934, the history of Japanese American exclusion and incarceration, the period after World War II when Californians grappled with their past and present racism, and the pursuit of reparations and redress for Japanese Americans.[3] But her story had begun before she was born, when her parents met in that match factory in Minsk.

Elaine Black Yoneda was born Elaine Rose Buchman in 1906 in New York City to Molly Kvetnay and Nathan Buchman, who had recently immigrated to the city. Molly and Nathan were part of the great wave of immigration from eastern and southern Europe that filled cities in the northeastern and midwestern United States with industrial workers prior to the 1920s, when immigration from Europe was severely restricted. Like most Russian Jewish immigrants, the Buchmans came seeking economic opportunity and to escape the pervasive anti-Semitism that their families had endured for generations. And, as with other Russian Jewish immigrants, they brought with them to the United States the radical labor politics they had imbibed at an early age as child laborers. Though strongly identified as Jewish, they eschewed the prescriptive religious ways of their parents. In America, they raised Elaine and her younger brother, Al, in a home that was completely secular but deeply steeped in Socialist and Communist politics and values and infused with Yiddish-language laborite culture.

Having met as children while working at the match factory in Minsk, Molly and Nathan had been drawn into the nascent labor movement that was a regular feature of factory life there. As Molly and Nathan grew, they joined the ranks of other workers who opposed the deplorable conditions in which they worked. They quickly became active in the Jewish labor movement. Jews constituted a significant proportion of industrial labor and were a working class with their own identity. At the height of Jewish population in the period, more than five million Jews lived in the Russian Pale of Settlement, the largest concentration of Jewish population in the world prior to World War I. Like the Kvetnays and Buchmans, most had lived in small shtetls until the middle to late nineteenth century, when the population shifted to urban centers. Life in the shtetl had been hard, not only because of severe poverty but also because the concentration of Jews in small villages rendered them vulnerable to the rampant pogroms that brought waves of violence to their communities. While not entirely immune from such violence in larger cities, the burgeoning urban areas did offer increased security—economic and physical—and so, many Russian Jews migrated to the cities within the Pale, including Minsk, Bialystok, Vilnius, and others.[4]

Jewish identification was the strong shared sentiment that led to the formation of the *Bund*, or General Jewish Workers' Union, which began in 1897 and spread throughout the Jewish communities of Russia and Poland. Though affiliated in some ways with larger Socialist movements, Jews maintained strong ties with one another in the face of continuing discrimination even within the labor movements. The *Bund* conducted its business in Yiddish; the linguistic dimension was critical to the group's cohesion. As Gerald Sorin writes, the *Bund* was "the first and most important *Jewish* social democratic party," and it eventually developed the "idea of an autonomous Jewish movement combining class war with loyalty to the Jewish people—indeed, to Jewish peoplehood."[5] Cultural ties, rather than religious practices, connected the community, as many had moved away from the strict observances of their parents and grandparents.[6] This form of identity-based labor organization would lay the groundwork for early twentieth-century unionism on the U.S. East Coast that often centered on national or ethnic groups as well. Members of the *Bund* came to see that life in Russia would always be bound by limitations from the state-sanctioned anti-Semitism under which its members lived. Seeking more freedoms in America, *Bund* members helped initiate an era of Jewish migration that would eventually shift the locus of world Jewish population from Russia to the United States.

Molly and Nathan were both members of the *Bund*. Pressed into industrial work at very early ages, they had both experienced firsthand the challenging double blow of economic privation and systemic discrimination that Russian Jews faced. Eventually they were both blacklisted from working in the factory for their participation in a labor strike and their agitation for better working conditions after a factory fire.[7] They began to set their sights on a life in America, where they had heard from others who had emigrated from their community of possibilities for better economic opportunity and religious and ethnic tolerance. Additional incentive for migration came when Nathan received word that he was to be conscripted into the czar's army—a prospect he very much wanted to avoid, both because he disagreed with the imperial project and because surviving day-to-day life in the army, particularly for Jewish conscripts, would be arduous.[8] And so, Nathan and Molly planned to move their lives to New York City, epicenter of U.S. Jewish immigrant life and culture. Like many Jewish Russian immigrants, gender determined the order of immigration—Nathan came first to America and Molly followed later, after Nathan had found stable employment and a place to live.[9]

2

Nathan and Molly's move to America could not have been easy. In 1904 a steamship ticket cost about $34 (nearly $1,000 in today's dollars)—a tidy sum for an industrial laborer. Steerage class promised a grueling voyage lasting anywhere from thirteen to twenty days, and arrival at Ellis Island presented its own challenges, with its chaotic environment and endless supply of swindlers looking to take advantage of green immigrants.[10] Nevertheless, Nathan made the trip in 1904, at age twenty-one, and sent for Molly a year later.

Of course, Jews were not the only group to immigrate *en masse* to the United States in this period, searching for economic opportunity and freedom from oppression. A large number of people poured into New York City and other U.S. cities at the turn of the century, until the U.S. government restricted open migration from Europe and Russia in the 1920s. Similarly, a range of groups emigrated from Asia to the West Coast of the United States, though the numbers were not nearly as large. Significant immigration from China occurred prior to the passage of the Chinese Exclusion Act in 1882. Japanese immigration grew around the turn of the century, first to Hawai'i and then to California. But even by the 1920s, immigrants to the United States from Japan numbered under 300,000; by comparison 30 million had come to the northeastern United States from Europe.[11] One aspect of Jewish migration that set it apart from other groups was that Jews did not intend to return. That is, other groups, such as Italians, viewed migration to the United States as a short-term means of improving one's economic position, always with the anticipation of returning to the Old Country—whether they did or not. But largely because of the anti-Semitism from which Jews were attempting to escape, Jewish families did not generally plan to return.

Molly arrived in 1905 and in 1906, within a short year, gave birth to a daughter, Elaine Rose. At the time, the Buchmans lived in a tenement building at Avenue D and 12th Street in Manhattan, but they moved quite a bit during this period.[12] The first few years that Molly and Nathan were in America were spent casting about for the best place and means of making a living. After a stint working for a barber, Nathan brought the family to Pennsylvania, where his brother had settled.[13] Nathan took a job in the coal mines, but the work was dirty and physically demanding, so he didn't stay long. The Buchmans relocated again, joining some other family members who had emigrated to Connecticut, where Elaine's younger brother Al was born. Eventually the family returned to New York City, settling in the Brownsville neighborhood of Brooklyn, where many other Jewish families lived and where Elaine spent the majority of her childhood, until her teenage years.[14]

Members of Nathan's family were spread throughout New York City. Nathan's parents, along with a great aunt and uncle, lived on the Lower East Side of Manhattan—another New York City neighborhood that was home to many Jewish immigrants—and a sister lived in the Bronx along with her family. Nathan's parents, Reuben and Rachel, were Orthodox Jews, in contrast to the secularism that Nathan and Molly had adopted as Socialists. Despite not being observant, Nathan and Molly's Jewish identification continued to be strong. They spoke Yiddish at home—a language that Elaine would continue to speak throughout her life—and they maintained social and political affiliations primarily with other U.S. Jews. As historian Tony Michels has shown, this social formation was decidedly new, unique in many ways to New York City—a laborite culture that was religiously secular but thoroughly Jewish. Language continued to be the strong point of identification, and American Yiddish culture thrived in the period.[15]

Nathan and Molly were, however, thoroughly ideologically opposed to religion, which put them at odds with Nathan's parents. Despite these deep differences between Molly and Nathan and all of their parents (Molly's parents, who had remained in Russia, were also Orthodox Jews), Elaine was always aware of the deep respect her parents had for her grandparents and their practices. Nathan and Molly did bring the children to gather with other family members at his parents' home on the Lower East Side during Jewish holidays, but Nathan would not set foot in a synagogue. Reciprocally, his parents would not come to Brownsville for meals since Molly and Nathan did not keep a kosher kitchen.

Nathan's deep opposition to an enforced religious upbringing and Judaism was made clear to Elaine and Al. He told Elaine and her brother that their youth should be free of religious instruction—they could decide later, after they turned eighteen, if they wanted to be religious and, if so, they could at that point choose any religion they wished.[16] As a small girl, Elaine had played hooky from school because she wanted to join a friend to go to the synagogue and hear the shofar being blown. Although most of her classmates, who were Jewish, were not required to go to school on the Jewish High Holy Days, Elaine's parents did require her and Al to go. But Elaine had been told by friends that the sound of the shofar was like nothing else they had ever heard, and so, out of curiosity, she joined her friends and went to the synagogue. When her father found out that not only had she skipped school but she had done so to attend synagogue, she was severely reprimanded—in fact, she later stated that it was the only time her father had ever physically punished her. He reminded Elaine that he had told her she was to have nothing to do with religion until she was eighteen. At that point, if she wanted to become religious, he would gladly help her, even if her choice was to become a nun. Perhaps Nathan's response was simply rhetorical—it's hard to imagine that he would really accept such a life for his daughter. Elaine had been asking him about the unusually dressed women they would see when they passed the church on Flatbush Avenue, and he had explained to her what nuns were, so it was a reference that was at hand.[17]

In Brownsville, Nathan worked as a barber once again and eventually he opened his own shop, which boasted four chairs, large by the standards of the day.[18] Molly, a "beautiful, . . . tall and stately" woman in Elaine's young eyes, was a model in a shirtwaist factory.[19] Although Elaine's parents were active in the trade union groups, as shop owners they were not themselves union members. Their jobs afforded them means that were not the norm for Russian Jewish immigrants to New York City—they may not have been wealthy, but Elaine and Al were never hungry. Nathan and Molly were able to provide for their children and they were able to increase their wealth over the next few years. Nathan insisted on paying union wages in the barber shop and later to his employees when he owned a dry-goods store. Nathan taught Elaine Socialist lessons, as when she asked why the other barber shop, down the street, often had its windows broken. "People don't really like that man," Nathan explained to his small daughter. "He is against the workers. He accumulates all the wealth he can and he doesn't want to pay his workers a fair wage."[20] By contrast, Nathan displayed a union card prominently in the window of his shop, though not required to do so, and he explained to young Elaine that the card was why his windows were never broken.

When Nathan and Molly immigrated to the United States, they brought with them the radical politics they had been exposed to in the match factory and as members of the *Bund*. In New York City, they encountered a circle of Yiddish-speaking Socialists, many of whom had come from Russia and Germany and had begun to establish a community during the late nineteenth century. New York was, as Tony Michels puts it, "a laboratory for political and cultural innovation" that not only brought together this secular Jewish community through shared language but also in turn informed eastern European Jewish socialism at the turn of the century.[21] Nathan and Molly were part of a wave of Russian Jewish immigrants that arrived during the first decade of the twentieth century and brought with them new ideas that infused the movement. The Buchmans sent Elaine to a Socialist Sunday school. They also brought both children along to rallies and on May Day parades in New York City. As in Russia, the trade union movement in New York City was organized along ethnic lines. Elaine recalled a protest by a bakers' union, which featured a block-long challah.[22] Although the nature of their activism would change as the family later moved west, Nathan and Molly's strong devotion to workers' causes would remain a regular feature of the Buchman family. In New York City, this affiliation largely centered on the culture and language they shared with other Jewish immigrants.

3

In 1911 Molly and Nathan devised a plan for Molly to take the children back to Russia for about two years to live with her parents. Although the family was on its way to a somewhat sound financial footing, with the family abroad Nathan could build up a larger nest egg before bringing everyone back again. Molly had also vowed that she would return, to assuage her parents' fears that she had left in order to distance herself from them.[23] In late summer 1911 the circumstances were right for the journey. It just so happened that they were able to make use of the passport of a woman who resembled Molly and also had two small children—Elaine and Al had to memorize their new names and be ready to answer to them when face to face with any authorities. Because there was a warrant for Nathan's arrest in Russia for having evaded conscription, Molly could travel there only if she could hide her identity.[24] The expenses were set aside for the trip. Molly and Nathan formally married at city hall on the way to the ship, with Elaine and Al in tow.[25] Though they had effectively considered themselves to be married since their arrival, this legal formality would ensure the ease of the family's return. Molly, Elaine, and Al set off to the Kvetnay home in the shtetl of Mozyr, near Minsk, where her parents had returned after Molly had left.[26]

Elaine had fond memories of the time spent with her grandparents. Farm life was fun for a small girl—and so different from New York City. There was space to run around and, despite the external threats of anti-Semitic violence, the day-to-day life was bucolic. The house did not have running water but was still considered to be a comfortable, middle-class home. There were plenty of cousins around to play with, and the children went on horse-drawn carriage rides and enjoyed their grandmother's home-baked treats. Women and men would go on different days to swim nude in the river by the house and do the washing.[27] Elaine's grandfather would also pick up a special Turkish treat—halvah—on his trips to town, and the children loved it.[28] Additionally, Elaine's grandparents doted on her and gave in to all her childish desires, much to Molly's chagrin, for she began to feel that Elaine was acting like a spoiled little girl.[29]

Elaine became fluent in Russian on the trip and everyone spoke Yiddish at home—in fact, she refused to use English, and Molly feared that she would forget the language.[30] She was quite curious about her surroundings, and so she earned the nickname "*Vos is dos*?"—Yiddish for "What's this?"[31] Molly's parents were observant Orthodox Jews, but there Molly drew the line—she and the children did not accompany them to the synagogue for the Sabbath, and they did not participate in the observances at home.[32]

Sadly, the trip was interrupted after only nine months, when a pogrom struck the small shtetl during the High Holy Days. The children were gathered and hidden on top of the big oven in the kitchen. The stove was not lit because of the holiday. Elaine recalled being told "to lie still and not even cough if it choked us."[33] On this occasion, the Kvetnay home escaped the violence only because it was located a few houses away from the other Jewish homes, with some non-Jewish homes between them, and so the pogrom had stopped short of their farm. This event, combined with the fact that the imminent outbreak of World War I was evident to all, convinced Molly that she should end the trip early and return to New York City with the children.[34] The decision to leave was surely based primarily on concern for the physical safety of the family. But it symbolized more for Molly, in that it confirmed the rightness of the decision that she and Nathan had made to emigrate. For one, there was the fact of ongoing anti-Semitism and violence faced by Russian Jews. And also, the political and religious differences between her and her parents had come to the fore in the crisis. In response to the pogrom, Molly's parents passively asked, "Why did God let this happen?" Meanwhile, the *Bund* was preparing for armed self-defense.[35] For Molly and Nathan, the religious climate of the Kvetnay household, with its attendant reluctance to act against injustice and its passive acceptance of what was seen as God's will, was decidedly not how they wanted to raise their children. For Elaine's part, the trip taught her this lesson in a visceral way. She always remembered that, while farm life was bucolic in some ways, the privations and threats that her grandparents seemed to tolerate were unacceptable. Throughout her life, she would equate religion with an incapacity to act and a source of disunity among groups, and she would always disavow any religious practice or identification.

PART II

Los Angeles

4

The family returned to New York City, where Nathan had set up his new barber shop in Brownsville. But soon after their return, the Buchmans began planning a move to California, which they carried out in 1920. Eventually they would settle in Los Angeles, after first briefly living in and near San Diego.

Nathan's two sisters were living in Southern California. His parents joined them on the move, and the entire family was closer together. Just before Elaine's fourteenth birthday, the family first moved to Lemon Grove, a small town outside San Diego. One of Nathan's sisters lived there and had two children similar in age to Elaine and Al.[1] Nathan once again opened a barber shop. Nathan and Molly continued to feel that Elaine was spoiled— she could be stubborn and incorrigible if she didn't get her way. They assigned her chores in the home that she disdained, and she exhibited no interest in taking lessons on the piano they had brought with them all the way from New York.

Life in Lemon Grove differed significantly from life in Brooklyn. Elaine attended a rural high school, where she was the only Jewish student.[2] There, anti-Semitism greeted Elaine. One day at school, during lunch, Elaine had some cookies that her mother had baked, and she shared them with her friends. When her classmates asked her what the cookies were called, Elaine said that she didn't know what they were called in English, but that they were called rugelach, and the friends asked what language it was. Elaine replied that it was Yiddish, the language of Russian Jews. The children accused Elaine of saying she was Jewish only to provoke an argument. She couldn't possibly be Jewish, they explained, because Jews are stingy and she had shared her cookies. The comment led to a larger fight.[3] Elaine recalled that this was her first direct experience with anti-Semitism; while she had been in Russia during a pogrom, that experience was abstract relative to directly having friends her age express a biased stereotype. When Elaine asked her parents why her friends held these views, they explained that stereotypes were a means of keeping people divided. Elaine argued with her classmates about the meaning of being Jewish. Both at home and at school, Elaine was rebellious and strong-minded.[4]

Lemon Grove would not be the family's last stop in their transition to California, nor would San Diego, to which they next relocated, where they would once again be amid a sizable Jewish community. Nathan had been seeking a way to quit being a barber, as he had developed a case of rheumatism that made standing for hours on end very difficult. In San Diego, he was able to buy a small dry-goods shop. As he had done in New York, he paid union wages to his employees. In California, though, Nathan's employees included people from diverse backgrounds. A Mexican American woman was the store's buyer and would work with Nathan for many years. Elaine tagged along on buying trips and began to learn some Spanish. As historian Allison Varzally has shown, on the West Coast in this period racial and ethnic groups who were not accepted as members of the white community mutually supported each other across racial and ethnic lines, in contrast to the single-ethnic business models the Buchmans would have experienced in New York City.[5] Molly worked as well in San Diego; together with a friend she ran a candy and ice-cream shop in the lobby of a local theater, where Elaine would make herself large chocolate sundaes.[6] The family might have stayed in San Diego, but Nathan continued to have ambitions for more affluence. In 1923 he had the opportunity to purchase a larger dry-goods store, on Whittier Avenue in Los Angeles, and so the family moved once again.[7]

The store on Whittier Avenue was in the east Los Angeles neighborhood of Boyle Heights, home to the largest Jewish population west of Chicago for the first half of the twentieth century and home to nearly one-third of Los Angeles's Jewish population.[8] The neighborhood was distinctly multiethnic, home also to communities of Japanese, Mexican, and African Americans. By 1930, the neighborhood's diversity had increased to include immigrants from China, Armenia, Italy, India, and more. Overall, the neighborhood was notable for the ways in which these groups coexisted in relative harmony. Anti-Semitism and racism were certainly a part of life in greater Los Angeles and California more broadly at this time. Though such discrimination did spill into the neighborhood at times, overall, children who went to school there in this period recalled later that the public schools were very mixed and few problems arose.[9]

The Buchmans lived in an apartment at the back of the dry-goods store and, for the first time, Elaine and Al each had an individual bedroom.[10] The store had a library section, where Elaine worked. Molly worked in the store as well, in the clothing department. A proficient seamstress, Molly designed and sewed clothes for Elaine and Al. Influenced perhaps by her mother's predilection in this area, Elaine developed during these years a love for fashion that stuck with her throughout her life, though she herself never did learn to sew. She took great pleasure in the shop's offerings, which included silk stockings from Paris, hats, and a wide array of fabrics.[11]

Nathan and Molly continued to be key members in left-wing groups wherever they lived. In 1919 Nathan and Molly had left the Socialist Party to become members of the newly formed Communist Party of the United States (CPUSA). Later they would be asked to leave the party, because as shop owners they were considered to be part of the bourgeoisie—a fact that was ironic to them given their humble background.[12] Regardless, they continued their work with CPUSA members. They sought support for Soviet Russia and better relations between that country and the United States and were active in the Trade Union Education League (TUEL). The TUEL was not itself a labor union but rather a group that brought together radicals from a range of individual trade unions with the aim of making the American union movement more militant. Molly and Nathan also hosted in their home Ella Reeve Bloor, described by some as the "best-known Communist woman in the United States" in the period.[13] The Buchman home was a regular meeting place for various causes, groups, and meetings.[14]

The character of the organizing work that Molly and Nathan found in Los Angeles differed from the milieus with which they had been familiar in Minsk and New York City in a key way—in Los Angeles, activism regularly crossed ethnic and racial lines. California activism in general, and in Los Angeles in particular, was distinguished from those in the northeastern United States in that its nonwhite neighborhoods tended to be very mixed— Boyle Heights was exemplary in this way. This demographic makeup carried over into labor activism and unionism in the region. Although there were single-ethnicity interest groups, such as a women's council on which Molly served that consisted mostly of Jewish immigrants from Russia, or the Japanese American Citizens League, members of these groups regularly interacted with others and joined forces. Allison Varzally has demonstrated how groups that were "subject to similar restrictions in employment, housing, and education tended to cluster in many of the same residential and economic places. In these shared spaces, they did not simply coexist but actively intermingled. Minorities argued, fought, allied, collaborated, and then revised their notions of community to accommodate these complex interactions."[15] Jewish Americans were part of these interracial and interethnic organizations. Though in many ways accepted as white, Jews faced housing discrimination and other social restrictions that led to their settlement in the mixed neighborhoods of Los Angeles.[16] There, they organized, socialized, and were educated alongside diverse residents.

5

Much to Molly and Nathan's disappointment, they could not engage Elaine in politics while she was a teenager; moreover, she was disdainful of their interests. She did read some of the copious books on class struggle that her parents brought to the house, but she locked herself away in her room to do her schoolwork during meetings, despite being invited to join in.[17] As she was nearing the completion of high school, she increasingly sought avenues of rebellion from her parents. Just as she was heading into her senior year, she told her parents that she had decided to study to be a nurse after high school, which met with her parents' firm disapproval. They pushed her to go to college, to become a doctor, or anything else—but "they didn't want their daughter carrying bed pans."[18] Unfortunately for Elaine, she needed her parents to sign a form to complete her application to nursing school, and they refused. Ever defiant, Elaine quit high school instead and enrolled at the Woodbury Business College in courses in secretarial training, where she studied shorthand, bookkeeping, and other business courses.[19] After her studies, she professed a deep dislike for keeping books and other administrative tasks, but these skills would eventually serve her well.

She graduated early and landed a job at the stately Darby Hotel on West Adams Boulevard in Los Angeles, performing administrative and clerical tasks. The position exposed her to a world she had not previously known—opulent interiors, a private restaurant, and art exhibitions. She was proud of the fact that her fashion sense was an asset in this position, for the hotel owners wanted staff to keep up a certain appearance. A self-described clothes-horse, Elaine attended to all the details of her outfits, ensuring that gloves, shoes, and hat all matched the dress: "If I had a lilac dress[,] . . . I had lilac shoes. And if it was brown, it was brown shoes."[20]

However much she disclaimed any sympathy with her parents' politics, glimmers of class consciousness began to emerge in her experience at the Darby. The wastefulness she saw around her made her uneasy. Because no other eateries were nearby, she was provided with lunch every day at the hotel restaurant, and so she saw that in the dining room, fresh fruit was put out on each table every day, and even if it wasn't eaten, the next day it would be replaced, lest the guests see day-old fruit on the tables. She and one of the servers in the restaurant remarked to one another how wasteful the practice was, when there were poor people in the city who did not have enough to eat.[21] As well, the owners of the hotel kept two separate sets of books. Elaine became aware of their practice when she was asked to be the bookkeeper, and she was disgusted with how the rich hotel owners hid their profits in this way.[22]

Elaine's parents continued to urge her to develop an interest in politics. In early 1924, they encouraged her to attend meetings of the Young Workers' League (YWL), a group formed to develop young people's awareness of class issues and introduce them to Communist thinking. The YWL membership represented the diversity of the Boyle Heights neighborhood.[23] Although Elaine was not very interested, she agreed to attend a meeting. There she met Edward Russell, another attendee who was present out of family obligation and, like Elaine, had little interest himself in the topics under discussion. Ed's family was Irish American and also active unionists. The two began dating and soon married. Their attraction owed, in many ways, to their like-mindedness. They were both children of immigrant families active in labor unionism, but both at that time eschewed their parents' politics. As Elaine reported, "neither one of us was too interested. And maybe that was our mutual interest at the time."[24]

Similar to Elaine, Ed was raised in a family of left-wing activists. But unlike Nathan, Ed's father was a member of the rank and file—a machinist whose membership in the Industrial Workers of the World (IWW) and the Machinists' Union caused him at times to be the target of antiunion violence. Following in his father's footsteps, Ed also worked as a machinist. Ed's upbringing differed from Elaine's in that Ed's family had definitely gone through periods of scarcity. This, coupled with the fact that Ed had witnessed the challenges his father had faced for his activism, meant that Ed had more of a firsthand understanding of the working-class politics and Communist theories presented at the YWL. Elaine was cognizant of the relative privilege of her upbringing—"I was a spoiled brat," she recalled. "I had whatever I wanted."[25] While neither Elaine nor Ed was particularly active politically, Elaine recognized that Ed's understanding of the labor movement and its aims were keener than hers.

Ed and Elaine married at City Hall in Los Angeles in early 1925. Molly and Nathan were not thrilled; it's unclear whether they were upset that Elaine had quit her job to marry Ed or whether they did not approve of Ed—who was evidently a bit of a ruffian and already showing a tendency toward strong drinking, as was true and widely known of his father. Certainly, the couple's parents shared a social circle. They also may have been displeased because Ed and Elaine continued to insist that they were not interested in the movement; that they wanted only to set up a home and live a quiet life.

Elaine had little experience as a homemaker—having been the rebellious child, she had never learned to cook, although Molly was by all accounts an excellent cook. Ed taught Elaine how to iron his shirts. Ed expected Elaine to take care of the laundry and to have dinner ready when he got home from work.[26] At first, she was not entirely opposed to Ed's traditional gender expectations, but she was somewhat restless and it was not long before her malaise at being a housewife became apparent. Tensions had been part of their marriage from the start, and they would only increase over the next few years. Elaine's awareness of Ed's drinking was growing, and it was obvious that he had trouble maintaining consistent employment. He lost his job as a machinist and was occasionally driving a milk truck, and so the couple had to move back in with Elaine's parents in order to make ends meet. Elaine helped out some in her parents' store, and then in 1926 she worked in a larger department store in downtown Los Angeles. In July 1927 Elaine gave birth to a daughter, Joyce. Molly supplemented Elaine's housekeeping, making clothes for Elaine and Joyce.[27]

Elaine and Ed's economic fortunes continued to swing up and down. By 1929, when the stock market crashed, Ed was back at work, as a machinists' foreman in Hollywood film studios. Once again, Elaine lived a life of relative privilege in comparison with many around her. Ed had the opportunity to work overtime, which was very lucrative. Ed, Elaine, and Joyce moved out of the Buchman home into their own place in a bungalow court and enjoyed an active social life. Ed was a member of the Fraternal Order of Elks and Elaine was an "Elkette." The membership was a surprising choice in light of the order's exclusionary policies—membership was limited to "white male citizen[s] of the United States" and women were barred as well. While these policies excluded Elaine and other friends of theirs from joining, the couple overlooked the strictures because they enjoyed the opportunity for social engagements that came along with Ed's membership.[28] They continued to attend some left-wing events, such as concerts of the workers' chorus, but without engaging in the discussions of political readings that went hand in hand with the entertainment.[29] Still, they were not unaffected by the events of the day. In 1927 Nicola Sacco and Bartolomeo Vanzetti had been executed. Many on the left believed the two anarchists to be innocent; their conviction and subsequent execution were understood to reflect anti-immigrant and antiradical bias. The entire Buchman household was in mourning, including Elaine and Ed, who were "very distressed."[30]

Elaine and Ed's social circle continued to include those whom they'd met at the YWL and other left-wing activists who were part of their families' orbits. As the Depression unfolded after 1929, Ed would engage in debates with his friends about what it would take to improve the lot of working people. Ed and Elaine's friends, themselves involved in Communist rallies and other events, couldn't believe that Ed, whose father had been a longtime Wobbly (as IWW members were known), didn't see the necessity of being part of the trade union movement. Ed continued to feel trepidation about participating in demonstrations, rallies, and other public left-wing events for fear of losing his job, which would be likely to happen if his employer were to learn of his involvement in such activities. Elaine disputed her friends' claims of government censure and police brutality directed against young Communists—she insisted that their behavior at protests must be provoking the authorities in some way. Though they spent time with these friends, they continued to keep a distance from the public events and did not profess allegiance to their friends' causes.

6

On the evening of February 28, 1930, Elaine dressed up for an evening on the town with Ed and friends—dinner and a movie at the recently opened Tower Theater, after having dropped off two-year-old Joyce at her parents'. Elaine continued to be a clotheshorse.[31] She chose her outfit carefully, as usual: "a cocktail gown of layers of georgette with rhinestone trimming, rhinestone belt," the color of her shoes "blending in" with the rhinestones of the dress. Ed and Elaine had agreed to meet up with some friends, including their friend Meyer Baylin, who worked as a full-time organizer, after the friends had spent the day at a protest.[32] They would meet downtown and continue their evening from there. Little did Elaine know, as she dressed and prepared for the evening, that the events of that evening would redirect the entire course of her life—politically, professionally, and personally.

Elaine and Ed arrived at the plaza where they were to meet Meyer, his wife Vera Baylin, and other friends. But when they arrived, they could see immediately that there was a problem. No one was on the street, and the square had been turned upside down—Elaine could see that "there must have been some sort of a struggle there."[33] Finally they came upon Vera, who was a bit frantic—she had heard that there had been some arrests at the demonstration. It was about 5:30 or 6:00 in the evening, already dark in February, and she asked Elaine and Ed to help her find Meyer. Their search led them to the third floor of a building on First Street, to the office of the ILD, which supported union members and labor activists when arrested or harassed by the police. Not finding Meyer there, they next went to an office on the first floor of the same building, which was the Communist Party headquarters. There they found a group of about twenty-five people, including Meyer, and a group of Japanese American men. Those who had gathered had been part of the demonstration. Some had fought off the police who had come to break up the demonstration; others had been detained but escaped by jumping off the police wagon.[34]

As the group chattered excitedly about the events that had just transpired and their improbable escape from arrest, Elaine tugged at her friends to get on with their evening; she did not want to miss their dinner reservation. Years later, Elaine would reflect on her actions to that point in the evening: "At the height of the Depression I was worried about dinner reservations."[35] But Meyer held them back, eager to ascertain who was present and had made it back to the party headquarters. Elaine urged him one more time to get going, but just at that moment the door burst open and in came the red squad, headed by William "Red" Hynes.

Hynes and his cronies were known among leftist circles in Los Angeles as perpetrators of extralegal violence against suspected Communists, anarchists, and other radicals. Initially formed as bomb squads to respond to the anarchist violence of the earlier part of the century, Hynes's and similar groups continued to work legitimately under the auspices of the police, but their brutal suppression of free-speech rights clearly exceeded legal bounds. Hynes and his squad in Los Angeles were the typical "red squad"; their tactics were later repeated in police forces around the United States in attempts to squelch radical activity.[36]

As they broke into the office, the squad began to bully the people assembled there. They demanded that one older woman sit down, and when she did not, they forcefully pushed her into the chair, in such a way that the wooden chair collapsed and she fell to the floor. At that point, they demanded the names of those present. Elaine was aware of the trouble that could ensue for her and Ed—particularly the fact that Ed's employment would be imperiled. Quick on her feet, Elaine stated that she was Elaine Black, and Ed followed suit by giving his name as Ed Black. The source of this name was

Ed's workplace nickname—Blackie—which he was called because he was what was called black Irish. The name Elaine Black would stick for years, long after she would cease to be Elaine Russell. The officers regarded Elaine and Ed, dressed as they were (Ed, too, was dressed for the evening, in a starched shirt), and concluded that they had not been part of the day's events. They released them but admonished them to not fraternize with "red Russian Bolsheviks again."[37]

The evening turned out to be pivotal for Elaine in a number of ways. First, she witnessed for herself the police brutality Meyer and others had described to her. Seeing it firsthand lit a spark that would eventually become a fire—her great passion for defending activists who were unfairly treated. The evening was the beginning of Elaine's turn toward her parents' politics and of her own awareness of how her interests to that point had been petty and superficial. She continued to be contrarian, but now rather than rebelling against her parents and all that they stood for, her renegade spirit would turn to support for unionism and the rights of workers to advocate for themselves. Second, though she wouldn't have been aware of the fact when she stepped into its office, the ILD would become not only the source of her employment but the cause to which she would dedicate herself fully for most of the next decade and, by extension, to similar causes, for the rest of her life.

Finally, that evening was the first time she laid eyes on the man who would become the great love of her life: Karl Yoneda. Karl had been among the group of Japanese American men also present at the ILD headquarters. Like Elaine, he had provided a pseudonym: Karl Hama, a name he used regularly for his work as a Communist activist. Though it would be some time before they would see each other again, and even longer before they would become a couple, they both would always remember seeing one another that night for the first time.

While the events of February 28 initiated a change in Elaine's commitments, it was her participation in the downtown Los Angeles protest of March 6, 1930 that would seal the deal and lead Elaine's life down a new path. Communist Party leadership in Moscow, as well as the CPUSA, had declared March 6 International Unemployment Day. Planning for the day had been conducted across the United States by the Trade Union Unity League (TUUL), an umbrella organization of Communist unions. The TUUL had been formed in 1929 as a successor to the TUEL, which had been marginalized by the American Federation of Labor (AFL), the national association of labor unions. Unlike the TUEL, the TUUL did seek to form unions that would compete with existing industrial unions. Elaine and Ed's friends, as well as Karl and his circle of activists, were all involved in the TUUL. The TUUL assembled people from various left-wing groups who were frustrated by the lack of governmental recognition of the extent of unemployment after the crash of the stock market in 1929. They regularly sent organizers to places in U.S. cities where people who were jobless congregated, to enlist participants. In what turned out to be a massive international day of protests, demonstrators in all major cities in the United States gathered to demand unemployment insurance and other benefits, including health care, food programs, and housing assistance.[38]

During the course of the evening of February 28, Meyer and others had urged Elaine to attend future protests, including the March 6 event. Elaine had initially expressed some of the same reserve that she had about the protest on February 28 that had preceded their dinner plans, dismissively stating, "if I can find a babysitter[,] . . . I will come down and watch it."[39] She did find someone to watch Joyce and, as usual, she dressed carefully for the day, donning a carefully matched ensemble that was "the height of fashion at the height of the Depression."[40] She set out to a spot near city hall where the events were already underway, and the first thing she saw was an older woman being harassed by the police for no apparent reason, her arm violently twisted behind her, then dragged away and thrown into a patrol car. Elaine recognized some of the men perpetrating this incident as those she had seen on February 28 working for Hynes's red squad. Seeing this woman mistreated in this way seemed to push Elaine over the edge. She now understood even more clearly that her friends had been right all along—that the police were harassing protesters unprovoked, impinging on their ability to exercise free speech, the right to protest, and their quest to improve the lives of workers. After the events of that day, Elaine went to the ILD office and offered to serve as a witness for garment worker Lillian Silverman, the woman she had seen brutalized by the police.

When Elaine walked into the ILD office to offer her services as witness, those present were initially suspicious of her. Why would a well-dressed woman, who was clearly not in need of relief or help herself, be showing up, out of the blue, to offer her support? Yet they noted her contact information and, on the day of the trial, Elaine appeared to serve as witness. Silverman was charged with rioting, disturbing the peace, and refusing to cooperate with the police.[41]

Elaine was shocked by what transpired during her first time in a courthouse—though it would be far from her last. Here again was Red Hynes, who told the judge and jury, under oath, that Elaine was a "well-known

Communist and getting Moscow gold." Elaine was shocked that Hynes would state this and other falsehoods. Elaine would later recall sardonically that it was not until one year later that she would join the Communist Party! While Hynes was prescient in his assumption of her politics, his courtroom accusation was factually inaccurate.[42] It was the second time her path crossed that of Hynes, and there would be many more.

Also in the courtroom that day was Leo Gallagher, another figure who would appear throughout Elaine's professional life, and who would eventually defend Elaine in court. Gallagher was an attorney who had studied at Yale Law School and at the University of Innsbruck and had settled in Los Angeles in 1923. He devoted himself to defending cases that involved violations of free speech and the right of assembly. Gallagher's first association with the ILD was in 1925; he would later be retained to defend a number of key cases, including a retrial in 1932 for Tom Mooney, who had been falsely accused, but convicted, of planning the bombing that occurred at the 1916 San Francisco Preparedness Day parade. Known to be a brilliant debater, Gallagher's style was boisterous and loud, fiery and full of passion. So much so that there were times when the ILD staff wondered whether he might be a liability.[43] Carey McWilliams, a left-wing writer for the *Nation*, wrote about Gallagher and lauded his ability to expose specious applications of laws such as the Criminal Syndicalism Act, which were increasingly being used by authorities to squelch radical voices.[44] About Gallagher's courthouse style, McWilliams wrote, "every trial in which he is involved . . . is converted into a frontal attack on the whole farcical business of pretending to 'try' radicals with impartiality."[45] This is not to say that Gallagher always prevailed—though he did win at times, the climate for suppression of workers' rights could be quite strong.

Indeed, on this day, the judge's sympathy was clearly with the prosecution, which Elaine found very disturbing. The judge went on to question Elaine about her politics, interrogating her for possible allegiance to Russia, and asking about Ed. These lines of inquiry were the last straw for Elaine—she finally "got on her high horse" and told the judge to subpoena her husband if she had questions for him.[46] Further, she understood that asking about the Soviet Union had no bearing on what she had witnessed on March 6—scores of people peacefully demonstrating, seeking only food, shelter, and employment. In the end, Elaine was shocked. The jury convicted Silverman, although the case was later overturned on appeal. The ILD staffers who were present at the trial immediately saw that Elaine had a talent for speaking publicly and for standing up to authority figures. She was sharp and undeterred by aggressive questioning. For Elaine, the entire experience led her to join the ILD, which she did on April 1, 1930. She began to become somewhat more active, occasionally attending meetings, and Ed became involved as well.

Elaine's involvement with the ILD continued to increase. Eventually, people in the ILD office learned that Elaine was a skilled office worker and asked her to interview for an open position they were seeking to fill. Elaine was offered the job, and though the pay of $10 per week was slightly less than what she was making at the grocery store, she accepted because she could see that the work would be more interesting.[47] Initially she was hired simply to answer phones and help with the clerical work. The atmosphere in the office was stressful, as there were constant emergencies to deal with. The main focus of the ILD was to bail out workers and activists who'd been arrested, to defend them at trial, and to raise funds to cover the associated expenses. Every week, the office would receive a call informing the staff of someone's arrest, and immediately the staff would spring into action to assist in the situation. The funds came from donations that the staff procured in amounts ranging from $5 to $100, sometimes more.[48] Also, the red squad conducted regular raids on the ILD offices. Elaine recalled that on these occasions, the police would "make a shambles of the place." The atmosphere was so stressful that "you either fell by the wayside or grew with the situation." Elaine grew, and grew.[49]

7

Elaine was quickly promoted from her initial position as office worker to district secretary. In that position, her job was to notify district organizers Ida Rothstein and Lillian Goodman when there were arrests and then head to the jail to learn what amount had been set for bail.[50] The job could be very stressful—it required one to be assertive and be a confident speaker who would not be easily intimidated. Elaine excelled at these skills and handled the pressure well. She was adept at a range of tasks. She soon became involved in the full range of ILD work, on both local and national levels. At the national level in the 1930s, the ILD worked primarily on three cases: support for Harlan County, Kentucky, miners; the campaign to release the Scottsboro Nine; and the Free Tom Mooney campaign.

In Harlan County, Kentucky, the United Mine Workers of America sought to unionize miners there who had been experiencing wage cuts and terrible working conditions. Organizing activities had turned into violent skirmishes between the miners, local authorities, and the National Guard who'd been called in to assist authorities. Unionization efforts eventually failed, but the events became a symbolic touchstone within the CPUSA and other labor organizations for the violence perpetrated on workers seeking to exercise their right to organize.

The Scottsboro Nine was a group of young African American men who had been falsely accused of raping a white woman in Alabama. The case was rushed to trial, and all but the youngest one of them was sentenced to death, despite ample evidence that they were innocent. The case went through a range of appeals at the behest of not only the ILD but also the National Association for the Advancement of Colored People, all the way to the Supreme Court, where it led to a landmark decision involving the composition of juries (the original jury had been all white).

Tom Mooney's case was a cause célèbre of the radical labor movement, after his conviction for the Preparedness Day bombing in San Francisco in 1916. Little evidence supported his conviction but, in the furor over anarchist violence and bombings in this period, Mooney and another falsely accused man named Warren Billings became the scapegoats for the rage. Initially sentenced to be hanged, Mooney's sentence was commuted to a life sentence by President Woodrow Wilson as a result of public pressure from around the world. Pressure continued over the next two decades—Mooney served twenty-two years in prison before eventually being pardoned in 1939, largely because of Free Tom Mooney campaigns such as those mounted by the ILD.

Of these three campaigns, the Mooney campaign would become a focus of Elaine's work for the next decade. Elaine would eventually move to San Francisco and from there could visit Mooney, who was being held at San Quentin, just outside the city. Elaine visited him regularly and arranged for visits from national dignitaries. Through this work, she would personally get to know him, as well as his mother, in the coming years.

Alongside this national work, and before relocating to San Francisco, Elaine demonstrated her moxie in the local, everyday work of the ILD: bailing out arrested workers and raising money for the bail fund, visiting jailed workers and providing support to their families, and organizing protests and other events.

Shortly after Elaine started to work for the ILD, the Los Angeles office organized a Southern California conference, to be attended by AFL members and others, to advance the three national cases that the ILD was focusing on. Among the speakers would be Sam Darcy, the head of the Communist Party in California. Darcy, whose parents had also immigrated to New York from Russia, had been one of the key organizers of the International Unemployment Day protest on March 6, 1930, where Elaine had witnessed Lillian Silverman's experience of police brutality. Darcy was prominent in California labor politics; his top billing for the event would surely draw a crowd. The ILD sought a hall large enough to accommodate everyone and, with financial support from local unions, it secured use of the Los Angeles Philharmonic Hall. They paid the entire $400 rent in advance—a significant sum—to ensure there would be no problems later.[51] The ILD printed leaflets that were distributed widely to publicize the event and informed the media.

News of the event apparently had reached the red squad in addition to the intended audience. Elaine arrived at the hall early to set up and noticed that several hundred people had already showed up—by the end of the evening, the number of attendees would reach 2,000.[52] But immediately she knew there was a problem, for the hall was dark—the lights had not been turned on. When she went inside, she was met by Red Hynes, who told her, "There's not going to be any meeting." Elaine protested that they could not be disturbing the peace as it was an indoor meeting, that they had a constitutional right to free assembly, and that they had lawfully paid rent for the space. Undeterred, Hynes began to shove Elaine. At this point, she figured that she would be better off outside on the street than inside the dark lobby at Hynes's mercy, so she went outside. There she found that hundreds of cans of tear gas had been used to disband the gathered crowd; chaos and screaming were everywhere.

Elaine headed away from the hall toward Hill Street, eager to get away. On the corner, she saw the same group of red squad members who had appeared at the Communist Party headquarters the first night she had seen Karl. They were beating a man whom Elaine recognized as a needle trade worker, and Elaine immediately ran over and put herself between them and the worker. She had assumed that the men would not beat a woman, but she was wrong. She sustained several blows before being arrested and thrown into the patrol car—her first arrest. She had earlier witnessed the sadistic manner of these men, and now she was experiencing it firsthand.[53]

When she got to the station, the police asked for her name, but Elaine refused to share it, infuriating them further. She was conscious of the fact that the others who'd been arrested would hear how she responded, and she thought it best for no one to provide their names or personal details. Hynes was called into the room where Elaine was being held. "So," he said, "you won't say who you are." He dragged her into another room, where they were beating Ed. Hynes said, "You are going to be like that if you don't answer our questions! You are a flag waver!" So Elaine replied that her name was Betsy Ross. For her address, she gave the address of the ILD office.[54]

Elaine was one of eight people who were arrested that evening. The case later became known in the media as the Betsy Ross case. All were put in jail—in addition to charges of disturbing the peace and refusing to move, charges of criminal syndicalism were included. Because the latter was a felony, the court had the right to hold them for seventy-two hours before allowing bail to be posted. Six women were put into one solitary confinement cell. In the next cell, a woman was being held who apparently was going through withdrawal from drugs or alcohol; she spent the night banging her shoes on the steel walls and howling in ways that Elaine had never heard before.[55] Eventually they were put into individual cells. All were held for seventy-two hours and were bailed out on amounts ranging from $500 to $1,000.[56]

Four of them, including Elaine, decided to defend themselves in court; Leo Gallagher would defend the others. All of them knew to ask for a jury trial and were well versed in asking questions of potential jurors to rout out the plants invariably put there by the prosecution. Unfortunately, they had used up all their challenges when a juror who seemed to be one of the plants took the stand. Later, when there was a hung jury, Elaine witnessed that particular juror using hand signals to indicate to the prosecution that four jurors were holding out. Eventually, this juror seemed to have persuaded the others and the verdict was returned—all were found guilty. The judge, whom Elaine had determined to be sympathetic, immediately granted a motion for appeal and eventually the charges were dismissed.[57]

Elaine's ability to use the courtroom as a forum was evident in the defense she had mounted. Despite the problems with the planted juror, Elaine convincingly argued that the group's right to assembly had been violated—particularly in that the site was a private hall that they had rented. Elaine's first arrest and experience in prison opened her eyes even further to the mistreatment of Communists and labor activists and deepened her commitment to the ILD and the larger movement. It would not be the last time Elaine was arrested, nor the last time she would appear in a courtroom with Leo Gallagher. And those around her continued to see her capacities as a committed advocate for workers.

Elaine's growing responsibilities at the ILD and in the movement coincided with, or perhaps even precipitated, a deepening strain on her relationship with Ed. Ed had been laid off from his job in the film industry, for new technologies in sound film displaced the previous need for machinists. He joined the newly formed Unemployed Council and continued to look for work. The couple's changed economic circumstances forced them out of their home and back, yet again, to Molly and Nathan's home in Boyle Heights. Ed's drinking was increasingly a problem. Much to her consternation, Elaine began to learn that Ed was also a gambler and a fixture at local speakeasies. The challenge of their economic circumstances in this period and Ed's behavior led to frequent fights and a series of temporary separations for the couple.[58]

In addition, Ed's traditional gender expectations created strains in the relationship. He saw Elaine as the homemaker, not the central breadwinner, and he did not easily accept the reversal. For Elaine's part, she had found her way into this marriage before she had become engaged with the ILD. Increasingly, she found her work with the ILD to be fulfilling; by contrast, she had never actually been drawn to domestic responsibilities such as cooking, housekeeping, or parenting. Ed was jealous of the attention Elaine was receiving from the movement when his involvement in unionism had been relatively stronger, for example, when Elaine was selected to go to the Party District School for one month of training. Ed felt that he should have been the one to be chosen.[59] Overall, he seemed to experience her professional successes as an affront that highlighted his own weaknesses. That her successes also disrupted his normative expectations of acceptable roles for husband and wife surely exacerbated the situation.

The final break occurred on Joyce's fifth birthday, in July 1932. Elaine hosted a district meeting at home because of all the raids that had been happening at the ILD office. Ed appeared, likely drunk, and was very disruptive. He demanded that Elaine iron a shirt for him, to which she replied that since he had taught her to iron, he very well could iron the shirt himself—couldn't he see that she was working? But Ed continued to interrupt the meeting. In a fit of anger, Elaine got up, gathered all of Ed's clothes, threw them outside onto the front yard, and told him to leave. This would turn out to be their final separation, leading to their divorce.[60]

As her marriage was ending, Elaine's work with the ILD was simultaneously becoming more central to her world. Elaine's very first day of employment at the ILD office on February 9, 1930, was just one day prior to a major demonstration organized by the Communist Party's Unemployment Council, which was to include a march to city hall.[61] There were several arrests, and some of the protesters were brutally beaten. Elaine swung into action with the rest of the staff to identify the jails where arrested protesters had been taken. Among those arrested was Karl Yoneda, still using the name Hama to conceal his identity, but no one could find the station to which he had been taken. The next day, Karl was featured in reporting on the demonstration in the *Los Angeles Times*, in a series of three photographs showing him being beaten and dragged away by the police under a headline that read "Police Have Dampening Influence on Red Demonstration on Main Street."[62] Three full days after the protest, Hynes phoned the ILD office and, using a racial epithet, told them to come pick up Karl, stating "he's going to die anyway."[63] Elaine immediately set off for the Georgia Street prison, along with ILD staffer Anna Kanatz, to post bail for Karl. Karl was brought from his cell to the front desk and would later recall that he was "relieved and elated" to be greeted there by Elaine's "cheerful" face.

8

Karl Yoneda had been working with the ILD and participating in protests for a few years by that time, ever since returning to California and joining the Communist Party in 1927. Karl was born Goso Yoneda in California in 1906, the same year that Elaine was born in New York City. He had returned to the U.S. in 1926 after thirteen years spent in Japan. Like Elaine's parents, Karl's parents migrated to the United States in search of economic opportunity. Karl's parents Hideo and Kazu Yoneda were part of a major wave of Japanese immigration to the United States. For centuries, Japan had barred emigration, but once it opened trade with the wider world in 1854, it became difficult to continue its isolationism. Meanwhile, Hawai'i negotiated with the Japanese government to allow contract workers to come from Japan to work on plantations there. Besides, the American West was experiencing a shortage of labor in low-paying jobs such as farming, railroads, mining, and other fields after passage of the Chinese Exclusion Act. Hideo first left his home in a remote mountain area of the Hiroshima Prefecture in 1895 and took a job as a contract worker for a sugar plantation in Hawai'i. In 1903 he went back to Japan to marry and returned to Hawai'i with his new wife, Kazu. Soon he joined a mass exodus of plantation workers, fed up with conditions in Hawai'i, for greater opportunity on the mainland. Karl was one of the very first Japanese Americans to be born in the United States in that wave of immigration. His parents settled in Glendale, near Los Angeles. While labor conditions were better there than they had been in Hawai'i, the Yonedas worked constantly. Both parents worked in landscaping, and his mother also took in laundry and mending, which she completed in the evenings, but still the family barely made ends meet. In 1913 Hideo took Karl and his brother Hitoshi back to Japan; Kazu and Karl's sister joined them one year later. It was common for this first generation of Japanese immigrants, or Issei, to have their children, or Nisei, educated in Japan so that they would maintain Japanese language and culture, even if they did return to the United States. In this way Karl was a typical Kibei—a Nisei child of Issei parents who was sent to Japan for education—although the Yonedas were atypical in that the whole family went back to Japan, and Karl's parents would not ultimately return to the United States.[64]

Karl remained in Japan for thirteen years, until the age of twenty. Hideo, who suffered from tuberculosis, had died in 1915. Karl was eager to please his mother and did initially pursue the education that his parents wanted him to have. While in high school in Japan, he became interested in the rights of workers, both within his small sphere and also in the country at large. He joined a student strike in 1921 against his dormitory authorities and engaged in a newspaper boys' strike after the paper he worked for added to the delivery routes but did not increase wages. While in Japan, Karl was appalled at the practice of burning rice fields in order to increase the prices for the large companies who profited from rice production.[65] A voracious reader, Karl devoured writings by Bakunin, Pushkin, Engels, Marx, Tolstoy, Voltaire, and others. Karl would continue throughout his life to be involved in newspapers, eventually as a printer and editor. By 1922, he had dropped out of school entirely to join the labor movement, participating in newspaper strikes and publishing a progressive monthly, for which the government fined him for failing to register it.[66]

Eventually, Karl received notice that he was being conscripted into the Imperial Japanese Army. In parallel to Elaine's father Nathan, Karl fled the country rather than join an army whose agenda was at odds with his Socialist beliefs. He was scheduled to report for duty on January 10, 1927, and so in late November 1926, he boarded the S.S. *Shunyo Maru* in steerage class as it set sail for San Francisco, California. After sixteen days at sea, he was relieved and excited to sail through the Golden Gate. The next thing he did was to throw his Socialist and labor books overboard, for fear of how they'd be received as he passed through border control.[67] But as he disembarked at Pier 25 in San Francisco, his feelings of relief turned to apprehension when his cousin Saiji Okumura, who had agreed to come and receive him, did not show up because he was busy with the planting season in Southern California.[68]

A woman explained to him that he would be sent to the Immigration Detention House on Angel Island in the San Francisco Bay. Fearful thoughts occupied Karl's mind: "Would I be sent back [to Japan] to face a court martial as a deserter? What will the villagers think of my mother who had borrowed money for my steamship ticket that made it possible for me to run away from the emperor's army?"[69] Most of the others from the *Shunyo Maru* who were sent to the detention center were women, all from steerage class, and Karl could not understand why he was being sent there too. Karl was a U.S. citizen; he held his worn birth certificate stating Los Angeles as his place of birth, but he was not allowed to proceed until a family member came to retrieve him.[70]

During the first half of the twentieth century, 85,000 Japanese immigrants to the United States were processed through Angel Island.[71] The largest group to be processed there was from China, followed by those from Japan, and then those from other Pacific Rim countries. Angel Island has sometimes been described as the Ellis Island of the West Coast, although there were two key differences. First, the number of immigrants who came to the United States through Angel Island was minuscule in comparison with the number who came through New York City. Second, Ellis Island had no detention center. If one did not have the necessary paperwork to be allowed through easily, one could be detained at Angel Island for weeks or months.

Karl was placed in a cell with nine other Japanese men, who had come into the United States over the Mexican border and were awaiting deportation back to Japan. All the men could talk about was how they would again try and come to the United States, for they had no prospect of employment in Japan.[72] When January arrived, Karl contemplated his imminent twenty-first birthday and imagined how he might direct his life in a way that would "better the lot of humanity."[73] He also spent his time reading whatever literature he could get his hands on and writing Japanese poetry. He wrote a poem about Angel Island, describing how, though he was born in the United States, "America does not want me here." He wrote too about the mix of languages he was hearing, indicating the diversity of immigrants coming through the center, noting that they are "voices of sorrow, nostalgia, rage, and passion." The poem was written to mark his twenty-first birthday and seems to indicate the monotony of the passing of time as he awaited the next chapter in his life.[74] Finally, in January, after the season's harvest was complete, Karl's cousin Okumura came to Angel Island to vouch for Karl.[75] That still did not suffice for the authorities, and it wasn't until the end of February, after further investigation and testimony from Karl's sister Emi in Los Angeles, that he was released. It is unclear why Emi had not been able to do so earlier, but Karl was relieved to finally be done with the ordeal.[76]

In Los Angeles, Karl joined his family members in their work as gardeners and housecleaners, two of the only occupations open to Japanese immigrants. Karl made plans to finish high school and initially dreamed of going on to college. But his plans did not come to fruition, as once again he was drawn into the labor movement. A friend he had made at the boardinghouse where he stayed, Einosuke Yamaguchi, enlightened Karl about the economic, social, and political discrimination experienced by Japanese immigrants in the United States. Discrimination even came from within the labor movement itself, as the American Federation of Labor had supported the Asia Exclusion Act of 1924 (Johnson-Reed Act) and had been unwilling to organize other groups of Asian immigrants and African Americans. Only the Communist Party had expended energy to help nonwhite workers. Yamaguchi brought Karl to meetings of the Los Angeles Japanese Workers' Association (JWA), a Communist organization, and the TUEL.[77]

Karl joined the CPUSA in 1927, after being inspired at a May Day meeting by the "feeling of ease among the JWA members and hundreds of whites, Mexicans, and Negroes, men, women, and children" who were present.[78] He signed up after an appeal for new members, using the name Karl Hama for the first time. The inspiration for his new name came from Karl Marx. Until that point, Karl had been living in the United States under various other pseudonyms for fear of being found out by the Japanese government. Karl continued his engagement with the TUEL and the JWA and was elected propaganda director to the latter, which gave him the opportunity to make use of his Japanese language writing and editing skills. He also got involved in the newly formed ILD in 1928. He was elected literature agent and also volunteered to help recruit Japanese workers into the organization.[79] Karl was active in many Los Angeles protests, including those that had initiated Elaine into the movement.

When Elaine appeared at the courthouse in 1930 to bail Karl out, Karl was delighted to see her. He recalled that he had seen her before with her husband Ed, whom he knew to be a machinist and member of the Labor Sports League, but it was not until he saw Elaine in the police station that the two would exchange words. Elaine and Anna took the bloodied, beaten Karl to the office of Dr. Toshio Ichioka, a physician who offered free services to members of the Japanese Unemployed Council. Later, Karl learned that a French sailor had come to Karl's aid as he lay on the street that day and that afterward the sailor was deported back to France.[80]

Karl was charged with disturbing the peace—a laughable charge, for he had been standing silently holding up a sign that read "Our children need food"—a fact documented in the newspaper photographs that featured him. The image, which depicts a calm and self-possessed man standing with a picket sign, is deeply at odds with the idea that Karl could be disturbing the peace.[81] Leo Gallagher defended Karl in court, but to no avail. Karl was sentenced to ninety days. Many other unemployed activists were in the prison with him, and they regularly received messages and visits from members of the ILD, the TUUL, and the CPUSA. As Karl had done on Angel Island, he whiled away the days writing poetry in Japanese. Among the poems he wrote this time was "Who Is Elaine Black?" One can already sense his attraction to her, as he describes her "big smiling eyes and youthful gestures." The poem notes that Elaine helps workers of all races and nationalities. Finally, he concludes, "She is always at the jail door with bail money if you are arrested/ You may forget her name but not her warm and friendly words."[82]

Whether he yet realized it or not, Karl's infatuation with Elaine had clearly begun. He was released early, after seventy-five days in prison, for good behavior. He was then appointed by the Southern California ILD District Office to the post of district literature agent. His job was to promote ILD publications. It also meant that he worked in the same office as Elaine. Seeing Elaine in action as an organizer and a public speaker, Karl once again committed his thoughts about Elaine to poetry, in the poem "Comrade Elaine Black." His composition becomes even more sentimental and somewhat sexually charged. He describes her calm demeanor as she performs in the courtroom, noting "how great she looks, her young body concealed in a black dress." He praises her for juggling the work for the ILD alongside motherhood and concludes with a few lines that are clichéd but indicate the attention he is paying to her appearance:

> *Your lips represent proletarian emancipation and . . .*
> *Your wavy hair signifies a banner of revolutionary triumph . . .*

He concludes the poem by identifying Elaine as a "comrade and eternal revolutionary companion."[83] During the next three years, Karl and Elaine spent increasing amounts of time together. As Elaine's relationship with Ed was waning, Karl became a regular presence in her life. In addition to working together at ILD meetings and fundraisers, they enjoyed picnics with one another, attended lectures and meetings together, and saw each other at social events.[84]

Elaine's mother Molly was reluctant to approve of their relationship at first—although she and Nathan had raised their children to oppose racism, and Elaine and Ed were involved in numerous cross-ethnic left-wing groups, the idea of her daughter being involved in an interracial relationship was hard for her to accept. That Ed was not Jewish but Irish had not been an issue for Nathan and Molly. Though from a different national, cultural, and religious background, Irish and Jewish were both generally constructed and understood as white, and clearly the Buchmans did not place importance on their children marrying someone of the same religion. Their concerns over Elaine's relationship with Karl reveals the ways that whiteness still cohered in such a way that even the multiethnic milieu of Boyle Heights was not free from racial hierarchies.

The generational shift between Elaine's attitudes and those of her parents was evident in other families in Boyle Heights, and Los Angeles more broadly. Parents in such neighborhoods accepted the heterogeneity of the geography and even expressed its positive effects, but interracial relationships were another matter. Among the youth who had grown up in the same public schools and been involved in their integrated social environments, some would boldly abandon their parents' conventional ideas about marriage and family, as historian Allison Varzally has shown. And it was within leftist circles that the first challenges to conventional norms would arise. As Varzally writes, "In the 1930s and 1940s progressive circles included those of diverse backgrounds who mingled comfortably, shared a frustration with the status quo, and embraced tolerance as a social ideal. In the mixed environment of labor unions and civil rights organizations, interracial marriages appeared more acceptable and customary."[85] Elaine and Karl's generation led the way for what would eventually be acceptance of relationships like theirs.

Indeed, after some time, Molly and Nathan embraced Karl as they got to know him and saw how very different he was from Ed. But in these early days, Elaine and Karl were themselves aware as well that they would face challenges in their relationship because of how others would perceive them. Both recognized that, as was the case with Elaine's parents, prejudice against interracial unions was common all around them—in fact, they could not legally marry in California, or in numerous other U.S. states, at that time. Elaine had doubts about whether, in addition to the battles she fought through her work with the ILD, she was "prepared to fight on another front—

mixed marriage."[86] Karl wondered whether they would be able to marry and live together and what it would be like to visit his mother in Hiroshima.[87]

But as Varzally noted earlier, they also "shared a frustration with the status quo" and within their relationship treated each other as equals. Karl was different from Ed in so many ways, not least of which was the fact that Elaine and Karl had met *through* Elaine's work with the ILD; her strong presence as an activist was central to Karl's attraction to her. With Ed, she was constantly under pressure to be a mother and homemaker while working as an activist. With Karl, the two were far more on an equal footing; absent from their relationship were the gendered expectations that Ed apparently clung to and part of what attracted Karl to Elaine was her professional success. As the poem he wrote evidenced, he understood the challenges she faced as a working mother.

At the time, the ILD's activity in Northern California was increasing, as unemployment soared in the San Francisco Bay Area and radical activity there increased. The San Francisco District Office was growing, and there was need for a new district secretary. Elaine was tapped for the position and numerous colleagues encouraged her to take it.[88] Elaine was torn—she was flattered by the offer, which clearly represented a step forward in her career. Of course, there was the question of caring for Joyce—by this time, Ed had moved to Las Vegas and the couple was divorced, but part of the agreement was that Joyce would remain in Los Angeles where Ed could see her regularly. In the end, Elaine decided to accept the position. She felt she needed a "change of scene."[89] Her growing feelings for Karl were confusing too; she didn't know where their relationship was headed. In San Francisco, she assumed that she would be able to focus on her career. She and Karl agreed that, with some time apart, they could each consider what the future would hold for their relationship.[90] Molly and Nathan agreed to take Joyce—they would, in fact, continue to be surrogate parents for Joyce for most of her childhood and adolescence. In April 1933, Elaine left for San Francisco.

In San Francisco, Elaine quickly busied herself with the ILD's efforts to free Tom Mooney, as well as the daily activities. Meanwhile, in Southern California, Karl felt the void left in his life by Elaine's absence. Also, he had never fully recovered from the police beatings he had endured at the earlier protest. Dr. Ichioka had given him a clean bill of health physically, but he nevertheless remained exhausted and suffered from some depression. Overall, he needed a break. Karl's sister lived on a farm outside San Diego; the lease was actually in Karl's name. His sister had married a Japanese national, which resulted in the loss of her U.S. citizenship, and this rendered her ineligible to sign the lease herself. As Karl considered where he could go for a quiet restful period, a cabin on the farm came open, and Karl jumped at the chance to spend time there. It was a mostly restful retreat, although Elaine was constantly on his mind. "Would we be reunited someday in a more personal way? When? How?" he wondered.[91]

His sister took good care of him, and he helped around the farm when he felt up to it. His two Issei brothers-in-law, who did not share his politics, were less sympathetic. They did not approve of the radical life he had been leading. Most of all, they disapproved of his relationship with Elaine, dispensing opprobrium for their union from yet another direction. The brothers-in-law attempted to bribe Karl into accepting funds to go to college and to buy a car if he would agree to a match with a Japanese American woman. If he were to reject their offer, they threatened, they would contact his mother and tell her that Karl was "a jailbird, Bolshevik troublemaker consorting with a white woman who already had a child."[92] Karl took a gamble. He refused their offer and figured he'd deal with the consequences if they told his mother. Later that year, he would learn that they had indeed told his mother, who had responded by writing that "if Goso [Karl] is happy, I will be too. I welcome Elaine." Further, she thanked Buddha and God and expressed her hope that the couple would one day have a son. Her wish would come true in another six years.[93]

Karl and Elaine would not, in the end, be apart nearly as long as either of them had anticipated. In May the editor of the *Rodo Shimbun*, the Japanese-language Communist weekly published in San Francisco, had been issued an order of deportation by the U.S. government for radical activity.[94] After the editor had left, Karl received an urgent message from the paper asking him to come to San Francisco and take over the position. Karl was perfectly suited for the job—the paper was read both in the United States and Japan, and so the editor needed strong skills in both languages, and Karl could draw on his experience working with newspapers as an editor and as a writer. Upon hearing this news, his spirits were lifted, not only for the professional opportunity it represented, but of course also because it meant that he would once again be close to Elaine.[95]

Karl borrowed bus fare from his sister and set out for San Francisco. When he arrived, he went straight to the ILD office, only to learn that Elaine was at a Free Tom Mooney demonstration. Though he did not know how long she would be, Karl sat in the office and waited for her. As soon as she arrived at the office and saw him, her face lit up. They both immediately knew that whatever reservations each had had about being together were inconsequential. From that day, Karl and Elaine decided to live together.[96]

PART III

San Francisco

9

Karl and Elaine's decision to move in together was not easily to put into practice. As an unmarried interracial couple, securing housing proved to be a daunting challenge, one that would plague them for years. Inquiring at one for-rent sign after another—with white as well as Japanese American landlords—they were turned away.[1] Their lack of financial stability exacerbated the situation; both worked for organizations that operated on a shoestring and could not always pay on time. They knew that marriage might ease the situation. It mattered little to the two of them whether they married or not, but marriage could not be simply accomplished either. Antimiscegenation laws in California prevented them from marrying in the state. They briefly considered going to Washington state or New Mexico, where they could marry, but they did not have enough money to travel to either place.

Finally, after staying with generous friends in an overcrowded household, they found a landlord willing to rent them a place for $20 per month at the corner of O'Farrell and Laguna Streets, at the edge of the Fillmore District.[2] The neighborhood was similar in many ways to Boyle Heights in Los Angeles. Known before World War II as one of the most diverse neighborhoods in California, the district was home to a significant number of African Americans, as well as Japanese, Mexican, Filipino, and Jewish Americans. Furthermore, its commercial districts employed and catered to an interracial crowd. A portion of the neighborhood would develop and become known locally as "Japantown" for the predominance of Japanese American residents and shops there.[3] In these ways, the location must have felt very familiar to Elaine and Karl. The apartment itself was in a worn-down building that had survived the 1906 earthquake and fire, on the fourth floor, though the toilet and bath were on lower floors. The couple was delighted, and they moved in together on October 1, 1933. Elaine could finally devote herself to the work of the ILD. She and Karl invested themselves wholly throughout this decade in the work of the Communist Party.

The 1930s was an important period for labor organizing in the United States, and for the CPUSA in particular. In the 1920s radical activity had been suppressed. The nation's first Red Scare had taken hold after World War I and the Bolshevik Revolution of 1917, putting an end to the intense labor activism of the 1910s and instigating xenophobic limitations on immigration. After the crash of the stock market in 1929, unemployment numbers soared in the United States, and workers once again were receptive to the message of the Communist Party, which promised an organized and robust voice for the unemployed. As the Great Depression unfolded, labor organizing took on renewed import and appeal.

In 1933, shortly after winning the presidency on a bid based largely on federal support for economic recovery, Franklin Roosevelt proposed the National Industrial Recovery Act, which was then passed by Congress. The bill guaranteed workers' rights to collective bargaining and the right to organize and prohibited employers from forcing workers to pay dues to any particular union. After the bill's passage, as labor historian David Selvin writes, "Union fever swept across the land in a contagious epidemic. . . . In a major, unprecedented upsurge of unionism, the labor movement in little more than half a year added some 400,000 members."[4] A new age of American unionism had dawned.

America's left wing had suffered in the 1920s not only from state suppression, but also from internecine battles, largely between Communists and Socialists as each party struggled for dominance. By the 1930s, the CPUSA had emerged as dominant, just in time for conditions to be ripe again for labor organizing. The expansion of the CPUSA in this period owed much to its adoption of the Popular Front strategy that was emphasized by the Russian and German branches of the International. Under this strategy, the party expanded its work to bolster a broader range of people, efforts, and ideologies, even if not oriented to full-scale revolution. The Popular Front included fighting fascism, which was on the rise globally, and support for workers' rights regardless of those workers' politics or party affiliations. In the United States, it was through the Popular Front that the CPUSA could state its support for Roosevelt's New Deal. The CPUSA also shifted in this era beyond the white male membership base that had previously been its mainstay, adding to its ranks numerous immigrants, African Americans, and women. The expansion helped the party grow in California, a state with a diverse population and a strong history of cross-ethnic and cross-racial organizing.

The party also increased its numbers in the U.S. South, in line with its focus on the civil and labor rights of African Americans. Described as a push for Black people's self-determination and commonly referred to as the Black Belt theory, the CPUSA saw its African American membership increase in this decade, and the party placed significant emphasis on a number of prominent legal cases involving the violation of civil rights of African Americans—often, of African American men being falsely accused of raping white women, two prominent examples being the Scottsboro Nine and the defense of Festus Lewis Coleman.

The nature of women's engagement with the Communist Party shifted considerably in the 1930s, and Elaine's work with the ILD exemplified the change. Communist ideology had always acknowledged that women's unpaid labor in the home served the aims of capitalism, as Engels had written in his *Origins of the Family*, but the solution to the problem was oriented toward better wages for male heads of households rather than empowering women to enter the workforce on an equal footing with men. Similarly, while women's roles in industrial labor had always been a concern of the party, the necessity of women taking factory jobs represented the ills of the capitalist society where men could not earn an adequate amount to support their families. And, before the 1930s, women did not play much of a role within the party leadership.

In the 1930s, women's presence within the party increased dramatically. The Comintern had urged the CPUSA to establish women's bureaus as early as the 1920s, but the CPUSA did not focus on that effort until the 1930s. By the end of the 1930s, women would constitute nearly 40 percent of the membership of the CPUSA.[5] The party afforded women more avenues for activism than they had had in other parties and organizations during the decade. Women were drawn to the CPUSA after the women's movement in the United States splintered following the passage of the Nineteenth Amendment, which granted women the vote in 1920. The suffrage movement had galvanized women from very diverse backgrounds into a common cause. Once that goal had been achieved, the women's movement lacked cohesion. The CPUSA welcomed those women who were seeking a place to put their time and energy into addressing workers' rights and civil rights more broadly, as historians such as Susan Ware and Rosalyn Baxandall have shown.[6] While the number of women within the CPUSA rose and women did have open avenues of participation, the party still had a sexist working atmosphere and a ceiling beyond which women rarely rose within leadership.

The CPUSA's decision to actively include roles for women coincided with Elaine's turn to labor activism. Her competence and skills within the ILD were recognized early within the organization and she was quickly given additional responsibility. She worked side by side with many other women. She definitely did experience gender discrimination from the leadership at times, but mostly she was able to pursue her work and commanded much respect. As Baxandall has written, "in spite of male chauvinism, the CPUSA empowered women. Women were exposed to international politics, had opportunities to travel to attend conferences and meetings, and were exposed to political debate, community activism, ideology, and a diverse group of people and projects. . . . [The party] provided new horizons for women usually confined by family and community."[7] Elaine seized this opportunity. Rather than remain in Los Angeles, married to Ed, who had not supported her career aspirations, and where she was bound by motherhood and domesticity, she ambitiously moved to San Francisco, taking on a larger role within the San Francisco ILD and fulfilling it with gusto. Certainly, it was an unusual move for a woman of Elaine's generation to leave her daughter in the care of her parents to pursue her career. After a very productive period throughout the 1930s, she would never rise much higher within the party than the ILD, although the reason may have been less a matter of structural limitations from the CPUSA, and more a result of other major events that would unfold in her life, for World War II would change everything for the Yonedas. In the meantime, Elaine made a powerful impact on the landscape of labor organizing stretching from her home base in San Francisco to Sacramento, the Central Valley, Sonoma County, and Eureka.

10

In San Francisco, Elaine's title in the ILD was district secretary. She was responsible for raising the bail funds used to get arrested workers out of jail, posting the bail, and arranging for workers' defense at trials. As she had done in Los Angeles, Elaine led the ILD's efforts in national campaigns such as those to free Tom Mooney and the defense of the Scottsboro Nine.

Posting bail occupied much of Elaine's time. Elaine regularly traveled with large amounts of cash on her person. She was ever attentive to protecting these funds, which were hard won through fundraising efforts and badly needed to get people out of jail. In San Francisco, she regularly made the trip from the ILD headquarters on 6th and Market Streets to the Hall of Justice on Kearney and Washington Streets, nearly two miles, to post bail. She went on foot rather than spend any of the precious tender on carfare. On one occasion, she arrived at the Hall of Justice with $2,000 to post bail for two arrested longshoremen. She was met by the San Francisco red squad, who arrested her on the charge of vagrancy, with bail set at $1,000. Vagrancy laws, which allowed police to arrest a person who appeared to have no visible means of support, were often used as a generic form of suppression for everything from street activism to prostitution—Elaine herself would go on to be arrested for vagrancy on numerous additional occasions.[8] Rather than use the cash on hand to bail herself out, she called someone in from her office to help her argue that it made no sense to arrest someone for vagrancy when they had $2,000 cash on hand. She successfully argued her way out of the situation and posted the bail to release the two maritime workers. When the two released men and other activists who were being held there heard what had happened, they told Elaine that people were calling her the "red angel."[9] The nickname had been coined by one of the policemen, as he told the prisoners, "Don't worry what the bail is, your 'red angel' will be here soon."[10] The moniker would stick for years to come.

Aid and relief for labor prisoners across the country was also an ongoing ILD activity. The Northern California ILD supported more than thirty prisoners in the Folsom and San Quentin prisons, including some who had been incarcerated for years and whose cases garnered national attention, such as Tom Mooney, Warren Billings, James B. McNamara, and Matt Schmidt. A number of these prisoners had been arrested on charges under the Criminal Syndicalism Act of 1919, a sweeping law that was regularly misapplied in order to squelch union activity. The ILD fought for the repeal of this law in California throughout the period, but the repeal did not happen until 1991. Violation of the act was a felony, which in California would result in detention at the high-security prisons of Folsom or San Quentin. If the defendant was an immigrant, they could alternately be deported.

The ILD raised funds to provide each prisoner with $5 cash every month, to be used on incidentals. They also provided them with reading materials—often union newspapers—and ensured that their right to receive mail was being honored. Elaine was diligent in fighting to get visiting rights for herself and others to see the prisoners. She also helped arrange for nationally known luminaries in the CPUSA to come to California to visit the prisoners, including Ella Reeve Bloor and Anna Damon. An ILD group visited the prisons once a month, rotating their visits among the prisoners. For her part, Elaine made weekly visits.[11] Hers was a significant commitment, for San Quentin, located in Marin County on San Francisco Bay, was about twenty miles from the San Francisco ILD office. Elaine did not drive and the prison was not reachable by public transportation, and so she had to ask friends or colleagues to drive her. In addition to the prison visits, the ILD provided relief in the form of caring for the families of prisoners, especially the children. Funds were provided to families, and in cases where children were left without a parent because of incarceration, ILD families would take the children in.[12]

The campaign to free Tom Mooney in particular garnered a lot of noto-riety and lasted more than two decades. Elaine visited Tom at San Quentin as often as she could. She grew to be close friends with Mooney's family, par-ticularly his mother, Mary. The case once again came to national attention in 1933. On a technicality, Mooney's lawyers had successfully argued for a retri-al, which had been scheduled for May in San Francisco. Based on significant attendance at a Free Tom Mooney meeting in Chicago, which indicated to organizers a surge of interest in the cause, they planned a gathering for the May trial date in San Francisco, at Portsmouth Square, just off of Columbus Avenue. Though there was no hope of lifting the previous verdict, supporters saw an opportunity to bring attention to Mooney's unjust incarceration once again, and presumably there would be the chance to see Tom Mooney, since he would need to pass through the square on his way to the courthouse. By 8:30 a.m. on the day of the rally, a large crowd had gathered at Portsmouth Square, which continued to fill with supporters all morning. The crowd shouted, "Free Tom Mooney" and other slogans while mounted police ap-peared among them, with other armed forces stationed in buildings sur-rounding the square, ready to shoot into the crowd if necessary. Uneasy about the size of the crowd, the police quickly decided to put an end to the demon-stration. The mounted police used clubs to beat protesters, and many were arrested. Ultimately, the authorities did not allow Mooney to attend his own trial, citing fears for the violence of the protests—violence that they them-selves had perpetrated. It was a particularly memorable day for Elaine. In the melee, she was pinned against a wall by a horse and experienced quite a scare when she realized that this horse could cause her end.[13]

The day galvanized support for Tom Mooney, who had become a major symbol for the national labor movement, and Elaine was a key organizer of his support. As an ILD pamphlet expressed it, the Mooney campaign was "fought with a bitterness and a fury scarcely surpassed in all the history of the class struggle." The Mooney case had "become the symbol of capitalist terror and suppression of the working class and its leaders."[14]

Later that decade, in 1939, the campaigns to free Tom Mooney and War-ren Billings would come to a successful conclusion. The effort was largely supported by a state senator named Culbert Olson, who argued unsuccess-fully for passage of a pardon resolution in 1937 when the Democrats held a majority in the California Senate for the first time in decades. The Mooney campaign was receiving national attention as well, with U.S. senators and members of Congress pressing for a federal investigation. In the midst of this activity, Olson ran for governor of California in 1938. He promised labor that he would issue pardons for Mooney and Billings in exchange for their support in his election. Olson won the election, and one of his first acts in office was to pardon Tom Mooney.[15] In a dramatic special session broadcast by radio, Olson spoke in the assembly chamber at the state capitol in Sacramento, California, on January 7, 1939. Legislators, attorneys, supporters, and Mooney himself were all present. Olson asked those assembled whether anyone could state a reason why Mooney should not be pardoned. Back in San Francisco, Elaine and Joyce leaned in to listen carefully to the radio. They trembled with excitement, on the edge of their seats—then came the announcement.[16] Tom Mooney would be freed. Though it would take another month to secure a pardon for Billings, there was much rejoicing over Mooney's release, including a massive march in San Francisco to welcome him from San Quentin, where he had been held for twenty-two years.

11

When Elaine arrived at the San Francisco office of ILD in 1933, unionism and labor organizing were heating up across California. The San Francisco ILD office supported all workers in the Bay Area's ports and shipping industry on the coast, as well as agricultural workers from Eureka to Fresno, making Elaine's job quite demanding. The scale of labor activity in the agricultural sector in California in this period was unprecedented.[17] In 1933 alone, more than thirty-seven official strikes, as well as countless informal strikes, took place.[18] The ILD played a major role by assisting local strike committees, instructing them on how to access legal support. ILD staff and volunteers kept rosters of those arrested and helped apprise them of their rights, worked to raise funds and traveled to distant locations to post bail, provided fiscal and emotional support to the families of imprisoned workers, enlisted community support for workers, and generally helped boost morale.[19] Elaine was constantly on the move, between her work in the city itself, her regular visits to San Quentin, and the added burden of traveling to locations such as Sacramento, Salinas, and Sonoma to post bail.

The intense activism of the period was matched by vehement suppression, which at times became quite violent. Conflicts between employers and laborers were particularly rampant in California's Central and Imperial

Valleys, which had grown exponentially and had drawn legions of workers: those escaping the Dust Bowl conditions of the Midwest, African Americans leaving the Jim Crow South, and immigrants from Mexico, the Philippines, Japan, and elsewhere. During the 1930s, agricultural production in the region reached new heights. Growers reaped enormous profits yet paid workers very little. The years of the Great Depression were marked in California by bitter and often violent battles waged between union activists and the Associated Farmers Association of California, a vigilante organization of farmers, business owners, and others who banded together to fight labor organization by any means necessary. The latter's efforts were tacitly supported by the state police and the courts. Sociologist Nelson Pichardo describes the Associated Farmers as "perhaps the most virulent and notorious right-wing U.S. group [in the twentieth century], with the possible exception of the Ku Klux Klan."[20] The Communist Party pledged its support to oppose the Associated Farmers and aid agricultural workers. Meanwhile, the Trade Union Unity League had morphed into the Cannery and Agricultural Workers Industrial Union, which brought under one umbrella previously disparate unions, an effort that also aided in the opposition to the state-sanctioned vigilante violence of the Associated Farmers.[21]

Elaine's work with the ILD countered the vigilantism, the attempts to frame labor activists, and many other forms of anticommunist and antilabor violence. The violence was not confined to the Central Valley but extended into other agricultural regions in the state. Sonoma County, north of San Francisco, was another major agricultural region. Chicken farming, apple growing, and other key farm industries were located there. In 1935 apple workers in Santa Rosa gathered to plan a strike on August 5, when 250 vigilantes descended on the meeting hall and physically attacked the workers. The vigilantes also threatened the Works Progress Administration that if they did not remove any known Communists from their payroll, they too would experience the mob's "wrath." Several weeks later, an angry, large group including vigilantes and law enforcement officers disrupted a union meeting, then proceeded to the homes of a number of labor activists and others known to them to be Communists, among them Sol Nitzberg. The mob demanded that Nitzberg kiss the U.S. flag, but he refused, stating that this was a perversion of the meaning of the flag. Nitzberg and four other men were dragged through the streets, beaten, and tarred and feathered. Nitzberg's home was destroyed.[22]

Anti-Semitism mingled with red-baiting in Sonoma County, which had become home to a group of left-wing, Yiddish-speaking Zionists who had taken up chicken ranching there. Elaine arrived at the scene the day after the attack on behalf of the ILD, which had a Sonoma County branch to which Elaine was regularly invited. On this occasion, she traveled there as a show of support. She assured the community there, who felt themselves to be "at wit's end" about how to respond to the violence. The ILD and the ACLU demanded that "Governor Merriam see that the rights and well-being of those people were protected and that the vigilantes be brought to task."[23] Felony charges were eventually brought but, unfortunately, the perpetrators were acquitted at trial.[24]

In addition to the extreme violence of such an act, what was particularly unusual about this attack is that Nitzberg and Green were not themselves apple workers nor were they strikers—they were labor organizers who had offered to assist the workers. For Elaine, the tar-and-feathering incident "confirmed [her] belief that the ruling class would do anything to frustrate the rights of workers and terrorize the Left. This thing was well planned, with the full approval of Sonoma County leaders. These vigilante actions were happening all over California as capitalists tried to prevent workers from organizing trade unions and winning a living wage."[25]

As she had done in Southern California, Elaine proved herself to be creative and quick-witted in the face of police harassment. Time and again, she would arrive on the scene to post bail, only to encounter vigilantes determined to interfere. In 1933, during a grape workers' strike in Lodi, Elaine traveled to Stockton to post $1,000 bail for an arrested striker. When she got to the courthouse, she was told that she would have to bring the bail money to the home of the justice of the peace. This unusual instruction alerted Elaine to the fact that something was awry—typically, bail would be posted at city hall, and then a receipt would be issued that could be taken to the jailhouse to secure the release of the person who'd been arrested. Though wary, Elaine decided to follow their instructions. Elaine was able to secure a ride in a car with four men from the ILD. They soon realized that the road from Stockton to Lodi, where the justice lived, was blockaded by vigilantes armed with sawed-off shotguns and pickax handles, who were screening anyone coming in—those coming to support strikers would be turned away or arrested. The vigilantes stopped the car from the ILD and demanded to know where they were headed. Elaine quickly understood what was afoot— if she announced that they were going to post bail, their $1,000 cash would be confiscated and their striker would remain in jail. Elaine reached for the hand of the man sitting next to her and explained to the vigilantes that she and this man were going to the home of the justice of the peace to be married, with the other three men as their witnesses. The car was allowed to pass. The justice of the peace was certainly shocked to see them and attempted to turn them away, but Elaine insisted that he accept the bail money and issue them a receipt. On their way back to Stockton, the vigilantes waved to the "newlyweds."[26] Elaine stressed the importance of being alert in such situations.

Of course, the presence of a well-dressed woman also helped in many situations, where she could pass as someone other than a labor organizer. Throughout her life, Elaine would continue to place great importance on her appearance. The emphasis she placed on being fashionable and "put together" clearly had an instrumental purpose as well; in a number of situations, such as this one in Lodi, she was able to pass for someone other than a labor organizer and so escape attack or arrest. Elaine reconciled her love of fashion with her socialism by holding the belief, which she attributed to her parents, that "the lot of the worker was [not] to go around in rags."[27] There was, perhaps, something more at play. While it is certainly the case that Elaine provided immeasurable support to workers throughout this time, she also seemed to take some pleasure in her role in the cat-and-mouse game being waged throughout the state between labor and vigilantes. Elaine loved to tell stories about her ability to outwit her adversaries. She would recount these anecdotes throughout her life. During the 1930s, her stories were prominent in the labor press, particularly in the ILD publication the *Labor Defender*. These pieces, some of which were written by Elaine herself, present in black and white the ill-treatment of unionists who prevailed nonetheless—good guys and bad guys. One senses in Elaine's narration of events a certain glee in the chase itself, above and beyond the goals of the cause. This observation is not to imply that Elaine did not truly and deeply want to address the wrongs being perpetrated against workers. But it's clear at the same time that she enjoyed the spotlight. Seen this way, her emphasis on being well-dressed might be interpreted as a desire to always be camera-ready and, indeed, Elaine appeared in the papers quite often.

While unionists and supporters continued to face violence and terrorism for their organizing work, there was also strife within the labor movement. Specifically, the American Federation of Labor (AFL) strongly opposed radical labor politics and actively suppressed activities such as those of the ILD in support of strikers and other activists. The AFL had achieved moderate, mainstream approval and feared that association with a Communist organization would jeopardize their standing.

The AFL-ILD conflict came to a head in the defense of James Workman, who had been arrested at a strike of the Mine, Mill, and Smelter Workers local in Amador County, east of Sacramento in the foothills of the Sierra

Nevada mountains. Workers had gone on strike primarily to protest hazardous working conditions. When the strike had lasted for four months, the sheriff and vigilantes confronted strikers in what became a bloody exchange. More than thirty workers were arrested. As the ILD would normally do, they sent offers of aid and support for the arrested workers. But the workers rejected the ILD offer—they had been led to believe by their AFL affiliates that they should avoid the aid of such a radical organization. In Elaine's words, "Their minds had been poisoned by the labor fakers."[28] One of the men arrested, James Workman, did accept the ILD's offer to help by posting his bail, which had been set at $500. At the preliminary hearing, the bail was increased to $2,000—more surprising and upsetting to the ILD was that Workman's attorney, retained by the AFL, did not protest this sudden increase in bail.

Despite the group's rejection of ILD support, Workman's family was eager to see him released and accepted the offer—Workman suffered from tuberculosis and was not faring well in prison. Elaine traveled to the county seat in Jackson with cash to bail him out. As always, Elaine required a colleague to drive; this time she rode with Joe White, an African American longshoreman who worked on the San Francisco waterfront. The longshoremen and other maritime workers had organized a caravan, of which White's car was part, to stage a rally at the site of the strike and to provide food and clothing as aid to the strikers and their families. The larger aim was a show of support between the coastal laborers and the inland agricultural and mine workers. Elaine and White split off from the caravan in order to go to the jailhouse to post bail with the sheriff and have Workman released. Their plan was to then bring Workman to the rally site so he could speak to the crowds gathered there. When they arrived at the jailhouse, however, they were told that the sheriff was at the mine where the caravan was heading. Elaine was already feeling suspicious as she and White headed to the mine, and her instincts turned out to be correct. As they arrived at the mine, they could see that the whole thing had been a setup—the caravan was met by "deputized men" who "got out of cars armed with rifles, clubs, pick handles, blackjacks." They attacked the cars that had driven in along the one route in—they couldn't possibly turn around, resulting in many injuries among the strikers and supporters. Because White's car had arrived later, he and Elaine were able to turn around—Elaine did not want to leave the others but feared that if they were to be caught in the melee, the $2,000 cash would be taken. Later, a San Francisco newspaper would report that Elaine had "instigated a stevedore riot in Jackson" and then "escaped in an expensive car driven by a Negro chauffeur."[29] Elaine was able to return a few days later to post Workman's bail.

The conflict between the AFL and the ILD came to blows repeatedly, in Amador County and throughout the state. In a lumber and sawmill strike in Eureka County, the director of the AFL was informing local authorities about Communist activities among the unionists—even members of his own union. While ostensibly supporting its members, the AFL time and again took on the role of informant in its efforts to be legitimized, exposing Communists and generally participating in red-baiting. Further, the ILD felt that if the AFL did not deem a particular strike or another to be important, it would turn a blind eye to the vigilantism and state-sponsored violence and allow the strike to wither and fail. By contrast, the ILD's position was to always provide defense and support to strikers, without questioning the potential of a particular strike to succeed or to gain publicity.

Strife between the ILD and AFL appeared again in Salinas in 1936, during a strike of lettuce pickers there. Two years earlier, Salinas had been the site of a major strike that had pitted Filipino pickers against the AFL. The Filipino workforce had become significant for agricultural production in the Central Valley since the Asia Exclusion Act. When limitations were placed on immigration from other Asian countries, notably China and Japan, Filipinos, who were U.S. citizens as a result of the U.S. colonization of the Philippines, flooded the void in the labor market. Predictably, however, and as continues today, all these immigrant groups were relegated to the most unskilled and physically strenuous aspects of agricultural production; the more highly skilled and high-paying jobs were reserved for white workers. In 1934, when Filipinos organized into a union and struck for higher wages, they were not supported by the AFL, which as a general policy did not support unions of people of color. The result of the 1934 strike was union recognition for the Filipino workers and a modest wage increase. After the strike, the Filipino Labor Union moved its headquarters from Salinas to Guadalupe, California, near Watsonville on the coast. But in Salinas the underlying tensions between the AFL, the white workers, and other immigrant workers had never been resolved. The tensions continued and resulted in a second strike in 1936.

The Executive Committee of the Fruit, Vegetable, and Shed Workers had sent a message to the ILD requesting assistance; Elaine immediately went to Salinas. The Associated Farmers mounted a campaign to bring negative media attention to the ILD's arrival, describing them as Communists and outsiders. The red-baiting produced the desired effects—the AFL distanced itself from the strike entirely and began to doubt its earlier decision to enlist the ILD's help.[30] But one member forcefully voiced his objections and urged the union to accept the ILD's support. Unionist Ray Brannan's wife, Louella "Happy" Brannan, was in jail, and it mattered little to him who it was that could help free her. He stated forcefully, "I don't care whether they are red Russian or purple Russian, or the man from the moon, or green cheese, if they are going to get Louella out of jail, I am going to get their support."[31] When Elaine arrived, she took Ray to the courthouse to post bail for Happy. As she entered the courthouse, a large intimidating deputy sheriff asked who she was. When she gave her name, he shouted back to his colleagues, "Elaine Black is here." This statement produced a number of additional deputies, their guns drawn, and they asked her what she was doing at the courthouse. Ever alert to such harassments, rather than state that she had come to post bail, Elaine asked for information on *how* to post bail in that county, and what the amount would be. Elaine had the cash on hand, but she knew that if that was made clear to these men, she and the funds would soon be parted. Eventually, Elaine obtained the information she needed and followed the instructions to appear at the appropriate office to post bail for Happy.

Elaine returned to Salinas a number of times during that strike. At times she would spend the night, since the town is about 110 miles from San Francisco. Continual harassment accompanied Elaine on every visit, ranging from mild attacks such as newspaper headlines describing the strikers and the ILD as an "army of Communists" to physical violence. On one occasion, Elaine took a train to Salinas and so was there by herself. She was staying in an auto court, a kind of precursor to a motel where guests occupied individual cabins. When she returned to the auto court after working all day, she encountered a group of about twenty Filipino workers. They told her that they were there to protect her, as they had learned that a group of vigilantes was intent on driving her out of town. During another visit, she awoke one morning to find that a noose had been placed on the car that she had arrived in, with a note on it that read "Elaine you are next." Although the farmers did not win that strike, there was at least a congressional investigation of the Associated Farmers and their antiunion activities.[32]

12

While the 1936 Salinas Lettuce Strike had not ended successfully, out of that effort Elaine made a very close friend. Elaine and Happy bonded almost immediately after meeting one another. Happy had been a migrant farm-worker her whole life and her only experience with organized labor was with her own Shed Workers Union, but she joined Elaine on a speaking tour that ranged from San Francisco to Los Angeles. She became an active ILD member. Elaine was impressed by Happy's commitment. "She had been exposed to trade unionism," Elaine related, "and now she was able to, in the civil rights fight, take hold and become part of it—not only for her own defense, but for the defense of others."[33] Acknowledging commitment to helping others was Elaine's highest form of praise, and these words could easily have been used to describe Elaine herself. As soon as she believed that someone was as devoted as she was to defending others, she would become that person's loyal and lifelong friend.

Elaine's friendship with Happy Brannan was exemplary of the many strong female friendships Elaine enjoyed, both with women like herself and with women from different ethnic, religious, racial, and socioeconomic backgrounds. Elaine introduced Happy to the world of labor activism, and their shared commitment became the basis for their friendship, which would span decades. The central criterion that opened Elaine to connect with other women was a deep commitment to defending the rights of workers. Elaine connected easily with women who shared this commitment, regardless of what else they may have had in common. On the one hand, neither Elaine nor Happy had received formal education; on the other hand, Elaine's parents' economic circumstances were very different from Happy's.

Elaine also had friends who hailed from backgrounds entirely different from her own. Anita Whitney was one such friend. Anita was from an elite family that could clearly trace its roots to the *Mayflower*. Born in 1867, Anita was of a different generation than Elaine and from a completely different social milieu. She grew up surrounded by East Coast high-profile political figures, including her uncle, U.S. Supreme Court justice Stephen Johnson Field. Anita was an active suffragist in the years leading up to the passage of the Nineteenth Amendment and a member of the Socialist Party before helping to found the CPUSA in 1919.[34] She would become one of the most famous of Elaine's close friends because of the attention Anita brought to free-speech rights in the landmark case involving her that went to the U.S. Supreme Court. Anita had become deeply committed to helping workers since her days volunteering in settlement houses exposed her to the terrible living conditions in the tenements. Much to her family's chagrin, Anita devoted her life to helping working-class people. She herself never married or had children but lived in an opulent house on Nob Hill in San Francisco, where she regularly hosted Elaine and others.

Anita was very generous when it came to providing funds to post bail; Elaine could turn to her when high bails were set, knowing that Anita would come through. Anita owned a car, and so she would regularly be Elaine's driver to various protests or other ILD work, and at times they were arrested together.[35] Anita was different from the other women Elaine knew—Anita was soft-spoken and very well-read. Comparing her to another powerful woman in the movement, Ella Bloor, Elaine said that Anita "had a very soft voice, not like mine. She was very knowledgeable. When Mother Bloor would come to town—to hear the two of them speak was really a treat. They were really such opposites. Mother Bloor was from the womb of the working class—the so-called rough side of the railroad tracks. Their thoughts and actions were so interwoven—to better the conditions of the workers."[36]

While Happy and Anita were friends with backgrounds that differed from Elaine's, some of Elaine's closest friends shared a background with her. Ida Rothstein and Louise Todd, for example, grew up in families of Jewish immigrants—like Molly and Nathan, their parents had brought their labor activism and radical politics from eastern Europe. Louise was the district organizer for the Communist Party in Northern California, and Elaine got to know her after moving to San Francisco. Of all Elaine's friends, Ida Rothstein (who at times went by the name Ida Roth) was one whose upbringing most resembled Elaine's. A Russian Jewish immigrant, Ida worked in the garment trades early on, in the notoriously poor working conditions such as those that led to the infamous Triangle Shirtwaist Fire in New York City in 1911, in which 146 people had died. Ida became active in labor politics after that and also spent time organizing in the coal-mining industry. She had no formal education—Elaine described her written English as barely comprehensible, but she was a highly effective public speaker. Ida moved to California after separating from her husband in the 1920s; she and Elaine first met in the Southern California ILD office in 1930. Shortly after Elaine moved to San Francisco in 1933, Rothstein also moved north to the San Francisco Bay Area to work for the CPUSA. Ida remained active in the ILD; she and Elaine attended many protests together and were arrested and harassed together. Their shared background was useful in their work—Elaine and Ida spoke Yiddish to one another on phone lines that they knew were tapped by the red squad.[37]

Elaine's connections with these female colleagues were dear to her, and they would sustain her for many years in her personal and professional life. As discussed earlier, the number of women involved in the CPUSA increased dramatically during the 1930s. Elaine exemplified this uptick—during her most active decade in the 1930s, she was surrounded by women who assumed prominent roles and were doing important work on the ground to advance the CPUSA's mission. And yet there was certainly a ceiling in operation here—not really glass, as it was not very transparent. Although numerous women, including Elaine, would assume midlevel leadership roles, few if any rose to the top of the party's organizational hierarchy, and sexism and stereotypical gender expectations were certainly still the norm.

Would we call these women feminists? Their work was not necessarily focused on issues of importance to women in particular, but they certainly did approach their work through the lens of gender, and they clearly had to face down much sexism within their organizations. A number of these women were former suffragists, such as Anita Whitney. Typical of the earlier Progressive Era, they were often elite women who took on the role of "social housekeeper." Ella Reeve Bloor, nationally known Communist activist and friend of the Buchman family, focused specifically on domestic issues and saw motherhood as a way to serve the state. She was widely known as Mother Bloor, a moniker that she herself encouraged. Scholars have debated the meaning of this gendered assignation and the ways that it invokes maternalism as an acceptable rubric under which women could pursue a life of activism. Bloor has been, at times, dismissed in feminist historiography for her essentialized approach to domestic issues. But, as Kathleen A. Brown writes, Bloor's life and role in the Communist Party offer "a case study for the larger issues of both the place of maternalism in the Left and the problematic construction as maternalist of all women's politics which take into account familial issues."[38] Bloor's maternalism may have been a tool that she used to claim a voice; regardless, she was an effective activist and should not be easily dismissed.

Whether women's sense of responsibility was based on their maternal instincts or not, there was a certain elasticity to the available roles for women within the labor movement in the 1930s—a situation that would certainly shift after World War II as women's roles became quite constricted in the 1950s. The labor movements of the 1930s had not yet calcified into established labor unions led mostly by men, prone to corruption, and deeply antiradical as they would be later. In Elaine's time, she had no trouble taking on very prominent roles, in the streets, in city halls and courtrooms, and in national engagement. With very little formal education, Elaine developed impressive skills as a public speaker, and she was never one to shrink from challenging situations.

For many years, people who witnessed Elaine's ability to defend workers suggested that she become an attorney. In 1934 she had been offered a spot in the law school at the University of California, but she had turned it down. On another occasion, during the Criminal Syndicalism Act trial in Sacramento, she was called on to defend an arrested worker, as the other attorneys—Leo Gallagher and George Anderson—were occupied with other cases. She told the judge that she would stand as a friend of the court (amicus curiae) to mount the defense. Elaine brilliantly cross-examined the prosecution's witnesses. A woman from the welfare office had testified that the accused was harassing her, and had disturbed the peace. Elaine elicited another version of the story—that the accused had visited the welfare office on a number of occasions calmly seeking support, but that the woman had "called him a bum" and told him to leave her office. Elaine pointed out that helping this man was her job, so how could he be harassing her by asking for what the office was set up to offer? At this point the judge broke in and said to Elaine, "You gave me your assurance that you were not an attorney. From the way you are questioning this witness I am led to believe otherwise. Just what legal school did you go to?" To which Elaine replied, "I went to the courts. That has been my only legal training—watching, being a defendant, and seeing the violations under various laws."[39]

It may be somewhat surprising that Elaine never seriously considered going to law school. She always seemed to be most at home with grassroots workers' groups, and it may simply be that she didn't think she'd be at home in an institution of higher education. It was a feeling she shared with Karl, as neither of them had had much formal education, although Karl was certainly well-read by virtue of his editorial work and was a prolific writer. By contrast, Elaine never read Communist theory in depth and didn't think of herself or her work as scholarly.[40] At the same time, she did believe it was to the detriment of the ILD's work that there were no women attorneys in the ILD. For her, "the lack of women lawyers was unfortunate because I think that sometimes a little bit of warmth emanates from a woman," and so she clearly did believe that women brought a different perspective to the table.[41] Despite her lack of formal education and her repeated rejection of the idea that she become a lawyer, she was a skilled and eloquent advocate, adept at wielding that law when necessary. She was, for example, very proud of the fact that she could recite the Bill of Rights by heart. In addition to being known as the Red Angel, she was also known to quote from the Bill of Rights or the Constitution out on the streets, when protesters' rights were being violated.

13

In 1934 Elaine would have the opportunity to apply her skills as an advocate and defender of workers in the streets in one of the most important
labor strikes in U.S. history. The San Francisco General Strike, which began
as a strike of maritime workers, brought the entire Bay Area to a grinding
halt for four days. The strike had ripple effects into the Central Valley and
throughout the state and even the nation. Elaine was the only woman to
serve on the executive committee of the General Strike. She had been invited
to serve on the committee while the strike was still limited to the maritime
industries because of her leadership in providing ILD support to striking
longshoremen, seamen, and their families.

The shipping industry was, of course, an important element of the West
Coast economy and had been for many years. But labor conditions for longshoremen were poor. A selection system was in place that was called the shape-
up, wherein each day workers would gather in San Francisco at the Ferry
Building on the Embarcadero and wait to be chosen to work that day. There
was regularly a surplus of labor, so some workers simply were not chosen,
and the system was rife with favoritism and racial and ethnic biases. Even
for those who were chosen, the system meant that the term of employment
was never longer than one day, providing no job security.

After a major strike in 1919, the San Francisco Longshoreman Association, or "blue-book union," was formed as a company-run union. The blue-
book union, which dominated among the West Coast longshoremen into
the early 1930s, did not allow collective bargaining, regularly neglected or
ignored workers' complaints, and was seen as upholding the employers' rights
above those of the workers. A number of small, independent unions, including the International Longshoremen's Association (ILA), attempted to challenge the blue-book union's dominance over the years, with little success.

The passage of Roosevelt's National Industrial Recovery Act in 1933,
which guaranteed workers' rights to collective bargaining and the right to
organize and prohibited employers from forcing workers to pay dues to any
particular union, empowered and emboldened the ILA. On May 9, 1934, the
ILA launched a major West Coast strike. The union had finally enlisted adequate support from dockworkers, whose financial situation had become quite
desperate during the Great Depression. Longshoremen and other maritime
workers walked off the job at every major seaport on the West Coast, demanding an increase in wages, the right to unionize outside the blue book, and a

six-hour workday.[42] The ILD, the CPUSA, and a number of other groups came quickly to the aid and defense of the picketers, who marched daily in front of San Francisco's Ferry Building. The strikers built bonfires and burned blue-book union cards.[43]

The picketers faced regular violence and attempts at suppression from the police. The government and the media depicted the strike as a Communist uprising. Newspapers, in particular, contributed to growing anticommunist sentiment by publishing sensational headlines about labor unrest fomented by a "red menace." The employers brought in as many as 1,000 strikebreakers, or "scabs," during the first days of the strike. But the strike also united many disparate groups and proved durable. The strike continued for days and weeks, successful in large part because of the unprecedented unity of the sailors and other maritime workers, as well as ethnic and national workers, with the longshoremen—even despite the violent suppression.

Elaine swung into high gear, raising and posting bail for strikers, enlisting support from other industries to organize soup kitchens and free taxi rides for strikers, and advising strikers on how to avoid arrest and what to do if arrested. The ILD produced a small leaflet, "What to Do When under Arrest," that included the address of the ILD office and phone number and listed the ways that people could demand their rights when faced with the authorities. Strikers were advised not to provide police with their real name or address. At picket lines, Elaine carried the leaflet and her copy of the Bill of Rights.[44] Particular attention was given to immigrant workers, who were told to be especially careful not to share any information about themselves because they would risk deportation. Basically, the message was to speak absolutely as little as possible to the authorities. In this work, Elaine drew on her own experiences being arrested and observing all the ways that the authorities attempted to curtail even the most basic of rights.

On May 28, nineteen days after the strike had begun, the police attacked strikers on the picket line with tear gas, clubs, and guns. The strikers fought back and violence erupted. One longshoreman, Alfonso Metzger, was shot in the back and then charged with inciting violence, and Elaine defended him in court.

A few days later, the Young Communist League organized a Memorial Day rally in support of the strikers, and this gathering too turned bloody when police tried to stop the gathering.[45] In response to all the police brutality, another massive rally was organized in support of the strike, to be held at city hall. Several thousand people showed up. They marched from the Ferry Building—site of the violence—to the Civic Center, everyone silent for the entire one-and-a-half-mile trek. Elaine was a speaker at the rally. She promised the full support of the ILD through bail relief and legal defense. The public announcement system was not working—some believed it had been purposefully sabotaged. But Elaine's booming voice, coupled with her ease of public speaking, had a significant impact on the gathered crowd.[46]

Elaine made a major impression. Because of her speech and her overall support, she was asked to serve on the strike's executive committee.[47] She was one of those detained that day on what would be the first of her four arrests during the eighty-three-day strike—all on charges of vagrancy. By now, she had become known to authorities, who, never pleased to see the Red Angel, sought ways to retaliate. Her outbursts were beginning to affect subsequent interactions. One judge was heard to say, after he set particularly high bail, that he was doing so because previously in his courtroom Elaine had called him a fascist.[48]

The pace of Elaine's work became quite frenetic during the strike. Between posting bail, raising funds to cover bail, and producing leaflets and other literature to distribute, she was hardly at home. Karl too was busy with organizing, as he worked to gather the support of Japanese American groups for the maritime workers, and reporting on news of the strikes for his paper. During these few months, they hardly saw one another, both arriving home late and too exhausted to even recount their day to one another.[49]

Meanwhile, the strike wore on. Picketers at the Ferry Building carried signs reading "All We Ask Is a Living" and "We Want Full Recognition: ILA."[50] Federal mediation led to an agreement proposed by the Waterfront Employers Association, an organization that represented the shippers and port owners. Although the agreement was signed by ILA president Joseph Ryan, it ultimately failed. Ryan had not sought rank-and-file input—one of the strikers' demands was for full membership participation in decision making.[51] The failed agreement confirmed the longshoremen's distrust of the conservative Ryan, and out of these events, union member and Communist Harry Bridges emerged as the strike leader.[52] On June 17, the longshoremen roundly rejected the agreement and the strike grew. The San Francisco shipping industry was at a complete standstill.[53]

With no clear prospects for ending the strike peacefully or through mediation, the port owners decided to take a forceful stand; they declared that the port would reopen. With the support of San Francisco mayor Angelo Rossi, on July 3, police and railway cars created a barricade to separate the strikers from a lineup of trucks that picked up the shipped goods from the docks and delivered them to the warehouse.[54] The strikers, still on the picket line, were attacked by police with clubs and tear gas; they responded in kind by throwing bricks and other debris. It was a day of violence with no clear end in sight. The next day, the July 4 holiday, an apparent truce seemed in effect but there was an ominous sense that it would be a brief respite.

Early on July 5, Karl dropped Elaine off at a meeting of the strike's executive committee, at Mission and Steuart Streets, not far from the Ferry Building. The purpose of the meeting was to decide how to respond to the attacks of July 3 and also how to support other nonunionized workers who had joined the strike. As Elaine was leaving the meeting, she could smell tear gas in the streets. Suddenly, she heard shots fired. Instinctively, she ran toward the sounds of the gunfire. One of the ILA men recognized her and expressed surprise and shock—those were live bullets! He grabbed her, jumped into a car with her, and headed away from the scene. This was typical behavior for Elaine—if trouble was afoot, she went right for it, drawn to the site of action. As they drove away toward the ILD office, located at that time on Haight Street far from the port, they saw the crowd that gathered on Rincon Hill to observe the confrontation.[55]

Meanwhile, Karl was in the thick of the confrontation. Many had gathered at the picketers' location that morning to support the strikers after the events of July 3. As police began their attack with tear gas and gunfire into the crowd, Karl and others immediately grasped the severity of the situation. People ran for cover behind buildings as shots rang out. As the crowd attempted to disperse, Karl ran up Market Street away from the commotion. He was troubled by nagging thoughts of Elaine's safety. "While I was running up Market Street, my mind was occupied with Elaine, because the police were rushing toward the strike headquarters, throwing tear gas and shooting live bullets."[56] A few hours passed before he learned that she was safe.

Later that day, Elaine received a call at the ILD office and was asked to come to the morgue to identify a body. At first Elaine hesitated; there was no one else in the ILD office and she felt it important to keep the office open. But another call came after five o'clock from a member of the strike committee. Two bodies were at the morgue: one man had died between Steuart and Spear Streets and the other near Steuart and Mission. As they had been instructed to do by the ILD, they had no identification on them, but one had an ILD lapel pin. The strike committee member also relayed that many others had been wounded, and that they really needed her to come down to the

Hall of Justice. When Elaine arrived and the sheet was removed from the body of the man with the ILD pin, she immediately recognized Nicholas Bordoise, though she had known him by a different name. Elaine broke down at the sight of Nicholas's body. The extremity of the situation and the extent of the violence hit home. "I had seen people with gunshot wounds, broken limbs and split heads," she later recalled, "but I had never really seen a cadaver . . . someone who had been murdered in the line of action. . . . There was no other mark of violence on him; he was shot in the back."[57] She had, in fact, had an appointment with Bordoise later that day. "No, it can't be," she repeated over and over again. Elaine knew Bordoise as a member of the Greek branch of the ILD. A part of the Cooks' Union, he was a committed ILD member who helped out in the strike kitchen and sold copies of the *Labor Defender* to the strikers. Elaine contacted the Greek ILD leaders to ask them to notify his family.[58]

July 5 became known as Bloody Thursday because of the extreme violence of the day and the deaths of Nicholas Bordoise and Howard Sperry. By the end of the day, California governor Frank Merriam would send to San Francisco 2,000 National Guardsmen to quell the violence. The day holds such significance for longshoremen that July 5 is still, today, observed by the International Longshore and Warehouse Union as a day of remembrance at which Bordoise and Sperry are honored, and for years until her death Elaine was invited to speak at these commemorations in San Francisco.[59]

The city was stunned by the events of the day. The outpouring of shock was expressed most vividly on July 9, when a funeral procession carried Bordoise's and Sperry's coffins along Market Street, from the Ferry Building to Valencia Street, attended to by thousands and thousands of mourners.[60] Numerous accounts would later recall that the entire procession was conducted in deferential silence. No strike slogans were shouted; the massive crowd reverentially paid homage to the two workers through an absence of words.[61] At the request of Harry Bridges, Elaine rode in a vehicle with Nicholas Bordoise's wife Julia and Tom Mooney's mother and sister, and Bridges asked Elaine to speak at the cemetery where Bordoise was buried.[62] Many who had never seen Elaine express emotions were surprised by her copious tears.[63]

After the funerals of Bordoise and Sperry, sympathy for the longshoremen increased among other unions. The event had an "uncanny power," as labor historian Bruce Nelson writes.[64] Even the newspapers, which had been spreading the idea that the labor unrest was a Communist plot, noted the power of the funeral. An item in the *San Francisco Chronicle* remarked that though they had lived somewhat anonymous lives as blue-collar workers, "in death [Bordoise and Sperry] were borne the length of Market Street in a stupendous and reverent procession that astounded the city."[65]

The idea of holding a general strike began to spread after the funeral, and by July 14, when the San Francisco Labor Council met, the unions voted to all go on strike in support of the longshoremen and maritime workers.[66] On July 16, the general strike began in San Francisco and in Oakland, with 150,000 workers participating. The unions had agreed to continue basic services such as milk delivery, but otherwise life in both cities came to a stop—streetcars were not in operation and only a handful of restaurants remained open. Butchers, launderers, teamsters—workers in a broad range of industries stayed home.

In response to the general strike, authorities unleashed what would later be described as a reign of terror on organized labor, starting on the second day of the strike on July 17. Authorities deputized vigilantes and together with them mounted massive and violent raids on union halls throughout San Francisco. The ILD boarded up the windows of its offices in an effort to protect the space; records and equipment had been moved out earlier.[67] Karl chose to work out of a friend's home that day to get out the next issue of his paper, the *Rodo Shimbun*. This turned out to be a wise decision, for the office was also raided, and Karl would surely have been arrested had he been there.

The newspapers fueled the flames of sentiment against the strikers, once again portraying them as Communist infiltrators who were attempting to take over the city. The xenophobia and racist rhetoric were hardly below the surface in media accounts, as in an item that appeared in the Hearst press, which stated that "throughout the whole of California, an aroused citizenry continued its spontaneous drive against Communism yesterday. San Francisco municipal courtrooms resembled immigration 'melting pots' as a motley crew of assorted Communist agitators, representing almost every race and color, appeared to answer charges of strike violence."[68]

Elaine learned of the violence almost immediately. She received a phone call about a raid on the Unemployed Council office and the Workers Ex-Servicemen's League. She was told that many were being arrested, and could she come help? When she arrived at the Council office, she couldn't believe what she was seeing. She saw that hundreds of people had been arrested, and there was a general sense of mayhem. Kangaroo courts had been hastily assembled and verdicts were being quickly handed out. Jails with inadequate food, showers, and other facilities quickly became overcrowded. Thirty-two strike sympathizers had not yet been sentenced; under advice of the ILD, they had demanded jury trials. They were charged with vagrancy, which they knew was likely to carry $1,000 bail; Elaine quickly realized that the ILD certainly did not have the means to post $32,000 in bail for all of them.[69]

On July 19, Elaine joined organizers John Rogers and Joe Wilson at the home of Harry Jackson on McAllister Street to consider ways to respond to the violence. Could they request a federal injunction to reopen the Maritime Workers Industrial Union hall?[70] As the group discussed their options, Elaine heard thunderous footsteps on the stairs, and then the red squad burst in and arrested all four of them on vagrancy charges. The ILD insisted on bailing out the four organizers, even though the thirty-two previously arrested were still in jail—the organizers were more badly needed on the outside, they argued, as Elaine tried to convince them that she should not be a priority. But Elaine was soon arrested again while attending an organizing meeting in Jefferson Square Park, on three charges—vagrancy, disturbing the peace, and rioting. Her bail was set at $4,000. This time, Elaine convinced her ILD colleagues not to spend precious bail money on her. Three of her friends, Louise Todd, Ida Rothstein, and Anita Whitney, had also been arrested, and Elaine felt strongly that they should be bailed out first, particularly Whitney, who was much older than the other three women. Also, she was keenly aware that the thirty-two who had originally been arrested were still in the same jail. And so Elaine stayed in jail, where she remained after the general strike came to an end on July 20.[71]

The general strike ended by a narrow vote of 194 to 171 by members of the labor council.[72] Though the general strike lasted only four days, it is nevertheless thought to be one of the most extensive and significant general strikes in U.S. history. Accounts differ on the question of whether the strike was "successful," with all sides claiming gains. Longshoremen did experience an increase in wages, but not as much as they had asked for. The ILA became the official union of the longshoremen; by 1937, it would become the powerful International Longshoremen and Warehouse Union, led by Harry Bridges. The fact that a general strike was possible at all owed in part to Roosevelt's unwillingness to intervene in the original maritime strike in light of the mood of the country and the fact that he had recently won his bid for the presidency on the basis of claims of support for workers.[73] But some felt that the general strike diminished the radical strength and purpose of the maritime strike, which had lasted nearly three months because those workers were holding out for more than mere modest gains.[74]

Elaine was still in jail, along with the thirty-two men who'd been arrested on Bloody Thursday. The men were being held in inadequate conditions and on inflated bail. Although Elaine was in the women's section, she could hear, as she described to Karl in a letter, "them shouting for showers, soap, and better food."[75] Meanwhile, the papers claimed that "Red Suspects in City Jail on Hunger Strike . . . Refuse to Bathe."[76]

The men ultimately decided to stage a hunger strike, and Elaine and the other women who were in jail agreed to participate. Attempts were made to lure Elaine and others to eat. One day, they were told there would be a press conference. Eager to bring more attention to their cause, Elaine agreed to join it. The press conference was to be held in a lunchroom. When Elaine arrived, the table was set with "a tablecloth, butterballs in fancy figures, rolls, salads," and sumptuous steaks.[77] There was no press conference—it was all a setup to try to get Elaine to eat. She refused the meal. Later, a policeman stated that he had been a member of the Teamsters union and that he was sympathetic to Socialist causes. He then offered to sneak in some chicken soup for her. Again Elaine refused.[78] The next day, Elaine's mother, Molly, arrived from Los Angeles with seven-year-old Joyce. Joyce had to wait outside the cell while Molly visited Elaine. An officer goaded Joyce, saying to her that she had a jailbird for a mother. Joyce replied defiantly, "No, she's a worker. She's working for you. You'll learn that someday." When he saw her next, the officer said to Elaine, "Gee, you've got a daughter who really isn't afraid of anything." Elaine replied, "Why should she be afraid if she thinks she's right?"[79]

Worried about her daughter, Molly tried to talk Elaine into eating and into allowing the bail of $4,000 to be posted for her. Elaine protested—those funds could be used to bail out as many as four prisoners. Her mother persisted, pointing out that Elaine was set to go on trial within four days and she would need to prepare. Finally, the bail was reduced to $2,200 and, despite Elaine's continued objections, the bail was posted. The papers portrayed the story differently. Carrying the headline "Red Queen Out on Full Bail; Stomach Empty," the San Francisco Examiner accused Elaine of scabbing on her comrades, leaving them to get a meal as she "quit them cold."[80] The remaining prisoners ended the hunger strike a few days later and emerged somewhat victorious—their demands for better conditions were met, but their bail was not reduced.[81]

Trials did begin the following week, the anticipated crowds so large that they were held at city hall. With so many trials going on, Elaine did not have an attorney—Leo Gallagher would be defending Elaine's friends, Louise Todd and Ida Rothstein, in another part of the building. Elaine was nominally on trial for vagrancy, though it was clear to all that that was a bogus charge. As a reporter for the *Labor Defender* who attended the trial wrote,

> Elaine was clearly tried not because she was even suspected of being a vagrant, everybody in the court had known her and her activity in Frisco for years, but only because of her political opinions. Only because her ceaseless activity on behalf of the working class, only because she dared to commit the crime of telling workers what their rights are, how to fight for them, and how to defend themselves in their struggles.[82]

The anticommunist sentiment in San Francisco was running very high. Coincidentally, the American Legion held a parade through Civic Center plaza right in front of city hall. The legionnaires, notorious for fomenting fear of radicalism in support of "Americanism," were promoting "death penalty for 'Reds'" and similar messages.[83]

In the courtroom, Elaine was ever defiant. When asked to salute the flag, she said she would do so only in support of what the flag really meant to her—support for workers' rights and opposition to fascism. Elaine was accused of working for an illegal organization. When she challenged the judge to tell her under what laws the ILD could be considered illegal, the prosecution objected that the question was irrelevant. Nevertheless, Elaine persisted in explaining to all present the workings of the ILD and how it defends those who are simply seeking better working conditions. She also expounded on why employers opposed labor organizing and the need for workers, in response, to be aware of their rights. The prosecuting attorney, referring to Elaine as "Comrade Black," accused her of distributing "subversive literature" that was intended to incite violence and instruct people on how to disobey the police. He then shared the ILD leaflet "What to Do When under Arrest" with members of the jury. The jury deliberated for fifteen minutes and came back with a verdict of guilty. The same reporter from the *Labor Defender* surmised that

> No lawyer could have got an acquittal for Elaine Black because her case was a frame-up and the jury was "picked"; she was sentenced to six months. . . . Elaine Black brought out the working class issues and gave a not-easily [sic] forgotten education to every juror and every listener in the courtroom.[84]

Meanwhile, Gallagher had managed to have Todd and Rothstein acquitted. The story of Elaine's conviction was covered broadly in the newspapers; the novelty of seeing a "woman radical sent to jail" was apparently quite newsworthy, as was the fact that she "fail[ed] as her own attorney."[85] Eventually, a more just outcome did come about. The case was overturned on appeal, the judge noting that the raid of Jackson's apartment had been conducted without a warrant and without cause and that it was unlawful to prosecute Elaine for her membership in the Communist Party or her work for the ILD.

14

Although the strike had concluded and Elaine's legal battles were put to rest for the moment, the ILD's work continued. A central effort through the rest of 1934 and continuing into the next year was the effort to repeal the California Criminal Syndicalism Act. The law had been passed largely in response to anarchist violence of the 1910s; public sentiment had supported its passage after a number of deadly public attacks, including the 1916 bombing at the San Francisco Preparedness Day parade, the event for which Tom Mooney and Warren Billings were convicted on dubious evidence. The Criminal Syndicalism Act rendered illegal acts that were deemed to advocate violence or crimes intended to bring about economic or industrial change. The law was a thinly veiled means by which labor activists could be arrested and leftist activity could be suppressed; the Communist Party had always been the law's particular target. Its detractors identified the law's language as being overly broad and pointed out the high likelihood that it could be used to limit free speech. By far the most famous case involving the act was the arrest and conviction of Elaine's dear friend Anita Whitney, which had occurred in 1919 in response to Whitney's organizing work for the CPUSA. Challenges to Whitney's conviction went all the way to the U.S. Supreme Court in 1927, where the law was upheld in a landmark decision. Justice Brandeis had stated that if "words used are used in such circumstances and are of such a nature as to create a clear and present danger that they will bring about the substantive evils" to the nation, they could be prosecutable.[86] The concept of "clear and present danger" continues to be invoked in debates over free speech today.

Vagrancy was a charge regularly leveled against unionists and radicals as a way to quickly detain them. Charges of criminal syndicalism were liberally applied as well and could lead to significant jail time. The ILD put considerable energy into circulating petitions, seeking to obtain the thousands of signatures that would be needed to put a referendum on the ballot in California to repeal the law. A major test of the Criminal Syndicalism Act presented itself in 1934 in Sacramento. Agricultural workers throughout the state had been striking in sympathy with the General Strike in San Francisco and, as had happened in the Bay Area, were equally met with vigilante anticommunist violence. On July 20, the union headquarters of the California Agricultural Industrial Workers Union in Sacramento was raided; organizers were brutally attacked and twenty-two were arrested under charges of criminal syndicalism. Some charges were dropped, but eighteen defendants went to trial, with Leo Gallagher defending them. The cases did not go to trial until December, and the trials lasted for four months.

Meanwhile, in San Francisco, Elaine served on an interorganizational committee to support those arrested in Sacramento and to use the case to initiate a campaign to repeal the Criminal Syndicalism Act. The campaign began with a statewide meeting in early 1935 with a broad range of participants, including representatives from the AFL, the Veterans of Foreign Wars, Democratic clubs, and various women's groups in addition to the ILD.[87] The ILD printed leaflets with statements signed by the eighteen defendants in Sacramento. Before and after the meeting, Elaine went on speaking tours throughout the state in support of the repeal. Two hundred forty thousand signatures would be needed to obtain a ballot measure in the upcoming election to repeal the act; simultaneously there was a campaign to have the state legislature introduce a bill to repeal it. Although there was much support, the efforts did not succeed in 1935, nor in the next few years as repeal was repeatedly pursued.[88] The act would not be repealed in California until 1991.

Among the many events organized in 1935 in support of the campaign was a Free Speech rally to be held on St. Patrick's Day in San Francisco, at Dolores Park. Elaine was among those scheduled to speak that day, as was Leo Gallagher, who had just returned from Sacramento, where he had defended the eighteen being tried in the Sacramento Criminal Syndicalism case. Just as another speaker, Edward Johnson, went to the podium, the police appeared and began to make arrests. They grabbed Johnson off of the stage. Elaine was aware that, the previous week, the police had arrested some people who had been distributing leaflets and had used the tactic of taking each person arrested into the station singly, which afforded them the opportunity to beat those under arrest without witnesses. Elaine shouted to the crowd to not allow the police to take Johnson in a car by himself—that he might not survive if they did. Elaine was shouting to the crowd, reciting the Bill of Rights and demanding of the police, "Is this Nazi Germany?" Elaine was arrested, along with Leo Gallagher and eight others, on charges of inciting a riot and disturbing the peace. They had not succeeded in stopping the police from taking Johnson on his own; he suffered a near deadly attack.[89]

Soon after the arrests in Dolores Park, on April 1, the jury returned its verdict on the Sacramento syndicalism case that Gallagher had defended. Ten of the defendants were acquitted, but eight were found guilty. The prosecutor, Neil McAllister, had claimed that the defendants were funded by Moscow and that their aim was to overthrow the U.S. government by any means necessary. For evidence, he had supplied copious Communist Party literature. Using inflammatory language, he managed to convince the jury that the safety of the country was in their hands, stating that "the eyes of the nation are on you, asking you, begging you, pleading with you to stamp out this insurrection."[90] In defense, Gallagher explained that the workers' rights to free speech were being severely hampered. His attempts to read from the literature that McAllister had entered into evidence were shot down. The judge, who had previously allowed McAllister to introduce the leaflets and other material, now claimed that the same literature was irrelevant. Overall, the scene in the courthouse was described by reporters present as a "mad spectacle." Unfortunately, the situation seemed to have gotten the better of Gallagher, his interactions with McAllister nearly coming to physical blows.[91]

By this time, Gallagher had become a well-known thorn in the side of judges and prosecutors throughout the state. Though his efforts were often successful and he was described as a very effective attorney, it was widely known that his temper could flare up. This fact, together with his involvement in labor defense, was beginning to take a serious toll on his legal career. In 1932 he had been dismissed from a teaching position he had held since 1923 at Southwestern University Law School because of "labor activities."[92] When Gallagher was arrested in Dolores Park, he and the ILD began to fear that his arrest was part of a coordinated effort to have him disbarred. The prospect of losing Gallagher as a defense attorney was very worrisome to the ILD. Stories published in the labor press, including the Western Worker, lauded Gallagher's contributions. One author wrote that

"Gallagher's long record of self-sacrifice and loyalty to the working class has made him one of the principal stumbling blocks to employers in their attempts to use the courts against labor."[93] The ILD and Gallagher's supporters banded together to do everything in their power to ensure that Gallagher not be disbarred.

Leo Gallagher had long been a friend and colleague of Elaine and Karl's; the two had deep respect for him and, over the years, he would obtain many acquittals for each of them. Elaine had learned much from Gallagher's approach to the law, and she was in awe of his commitment to workers' rights. As she declared, "he was something to behold."[94] When Gallagher was arrested in Dolores Park along with Elaine, she knew that the arrest would be used as an attempt to discredit him. Charges of rioting and "refusing to move on," when levied against an attorney, could constitute "moral turpitude." Elaine's thoughts immediately turned to Gallagher's association with her and Karl, whose cohabitation was illegal in the state of California. Elaine had already overheard mumblings about the nature of her relationship with Karl at the trial in Sacramento. Elaine feared that Gallagher's association with her and Karl would provide further evidence of behavior not befitting a member of the bar.[95] She shared her fears with Gallagher. "You know, Leo, they are trying to bring out that not only are you connected with a bunch of disturbers of the peace, but also that you are connected with lewd and dissolute people. They are going to throw up the fact that Karl and I are living together. Cohabiting and mixed marriage are illegal in this state. I am sure that at one point or another they are going to bring it up."[96] Karl and Elaine conferred with Gallagher and Anita Whitney on the matter, and together they decided that it would benefit Gallagher's case for Karl and Elaine to legally marry before the trial. Legal matrimony didn't matter very much to Karl and Elaine. They had considered marriage in the past but didn't have much motivation to do so—"That piece of paper [wasn't] going to do anything for Karl and me," Elaine had said.[97] But if it would help preserve Gallagher's standing in the legal community, they were more than willing to wed.

In order to marry, Karl and Elaine would need to leave California. The two closest states that allowed interracial marriages were New Mexico and Washington. Whitney offered to lend them the money they would need to travel. Initially, they planned to go to New Mexico, but that plan was soon nixed. As it happened, a miners' strike was happening there. The ILD had sent a letter of support, which Elaine had signed as district secretary. Elaine soon learned that the newspapers in New Mexico had got ahold of that letter and had reported that Elaine Black was on her way to town to make trouble. The last thing Elaine and Karl needed was for their trip in pursuit of matrimony to be mischaracterized as a cover for labor organizing. They did have friends in Washington state, so they decided that would be their destination.

Elaine and Karl borrowed wedding rings from a friend. They boarded the train bound for Washington separately, as though they did not know one another. The Mann Act, which had been passed a few decades earlier, made it illegal for a man to take an unmarried woman across a state line for purposes deemed to be illicit. Again, the two were as careful as possible to avoid problems. They did, however, manage to sneak in a meal together in the dining car.[98] When they arrived in Seattle, they went to city hall and obtained a marriage license, using their legal names—it turned out to be the first time that Elaine heard Karl's legal name, Karl Yoneda. He had regularly used the name Karl Hama to protect his family in Japan, just as Elaine had been using the name Black for years.[99] On November 5, 1935, Karl and Elaine went to an antiwar, antifascist minister and were legally wed. Their vows included the words "to love, honor, and cherish." But they chose to omit the phrase "to obey," reflecting the efforts the two had made to form an egalitarian partnership.[100] How different this marriage would be from Elaine's first, with Ed's expectations of conventional gender roles. The two hoped to spend a few extra days in Seattle with friends, but their brief honeymoon was soon interrupted. Ida Rothstein sent a telegram stating that Gallagher's attempts to get the trial postponed had not succeeded; their case was going to trial on November 9 and they needed to return home as soon as possible.[101]

The joint trial of Leo, Elaine, and two others began on Monday morning, with Elaine representing herself in the courtroom and Gallagher representing himself and the other two defendants. During jury selection, Elaine got into it with the judge. After Elaine asked a prospective juror whether they "would want fascism to come here, that we were on the brink of this unless we fight against violations of our Bill of Rights," the judge angrily "pounded his gavel" and asked Elaine, "How can you say things like that in this court? You know we're not fascist!"[102] Elaine replied that she had not said the court was fascist; rather, she had pointed out that the country was in danger of becoming fascist from the kinds of arrests that had been made and general suppression of workers' rights to meet and discuss organizing. The judge reminded Elaine of the fact that he had signed her petition to free the Scottsboro Nine and had helped her on other occasions when she sought to lower bail. She acknowledged this but retorted that she had also witnessed his racism when confronted with the case of a Filipino defendant.[103] The judge dropped his line of questioning.

The trial moved forward. Assistant District Attorney Leslie Gillen claimed that a "howling, menacing, dangerous mob" had threatened the safety of San Franciscans in Dolores Park that day. The characterization was clearly contradicted by two witnesses who were ministers, who testified that the rally was peaceful. Gillen then attempted to discredit the ministers, stating that they had been known to speak at Communist meetings. Again, the ministers countered, confirming that they had indeed spoken at meetings sponsored by the Communist Party because they supported workers' rights.[104]

As Elaine had predicted, at one point, Gillen turned the topic to Elaine's personal life. Elaine replied angrily, pounding the table, saying to the attorney, "If you know anything about my personal immoral life that has anything to do with the charge of rioting, tell it to this jury!"[105] Gillen dropped the line of questioning. Although she could have taken recourse by explaining that she and Karl were in fact married, Elaine chose a different route—one that pointed out the unjustness of even broaching the subject. But, in the end, it was worth the trouble of going to Washington for the legitimacy of marriage, as Elaine would later say that she couldn't say "whether or not I would have had the guts to [speak to the attorney that way] if I hadn't had this piece of legal paper, which didn't make any difference in our lives, nor our feelings for one another, and our companionship all through the years. . . . It made no difference, I can assure you, but I was able to pound that table . . . and, of course, the district attorney didn't pursue this any further."[106]

In the midst of the trial, just before the day that Elaine and the defense were scheduled to make their closing arguments, Elaine became seriously ill. She was reluctant at first to go to the hospital—there was the trial and also the fact that she and Karl could not afford the hospital bills. Finally, she was convinced to go; friends offered to lend them the money, including the $100 required for admission to the hospital.[107] A postponement to the following Monday was requested and granted. Elaine's doctors kept her under observation, but over the next few days they still did not have a diagnosis. They were using ice in an attempt to lower her fever, and she was being fed intravenously. Ultimately the determination was made that she had acute appendicitis, and she went into surgery on Tuesday. Three weeks later, Elaine was still hospitalized, and the judge began to doubt that Elaine was truly ill, stating that the trial would continue with or without Elaine present. Elaine left the hospital and appeared in court, so obviously unwell that, in the end, the judge apologized for doubting her.[108]

On December 9, Elaine summed up the case, telling the jury that to find them guilty would "be a violation of our Constitutional rights to petition, to protest, to speak." On December 11, the jury returned its verdicts; all four were acquitted. The trial was considered precedent-setting in the use of the vagrancy charge. Everyone was congratulated on the successful conclusion and breathed a sigh of relief that Gallagher could continue defending workers on behalf of the ILD.

15

With the trial behind them, Elaine and Karl settled back into something of a routine. While Elaine continued to work for the ILD, Karl made the decision to become a longshoreman. The decision was based on a number of factors. First, although Karl loved being an editor for a Japanese newspaper, the pay from the *Rodo Shimbun* was meager and irregular. Karl and Elaine were each earning $10 per week, which was inadequate for their needs, simple as they might be—the bills were piling up. Second, Karl and Elaine had decided that they would like to establish a more permanent home in San Francisco, one where Joyce could finally live with them full-time. They also began to consider the possibility of having a child together.[109] If Karl could land a job garnering union wages, they would be on a path to a much more secure financial future. Karl had earned deep respect for the work of longshoremen during the strike, and he had a number of friends who could help him obtain a union card. The work itself would be grueling; he would begin by "packing the hook," or working to load and unload cargo ships. Karl did not leave the world of editorial work entirely, though. The *Rodo Shimbun* transformed into a new, Los Angeles–based Japanese paper, the *Doho*, and Karl contributed occasionally as the San Francisco correspondent.[110]

Karl approached his friend Len Greer and asked how he could go about joining the union. Greer was an African American longshoreman and served on a five-member committee through which all applications for union membership must pass. Karl knew that Len was well respected among his peers. Greer introduced Karl at a meeting on February 5, 1936, describing the assistance that Karl had provided to workers during the maritime and general strikes by urging Japanese workers not to work as scabs, by distributing literature, and by helping source foods for the soup kitchen. Finally, Greer said, "since our union advocates no racial discrimination and we have no Orientals in our ranks, I move we issue a work permit to brother Yoneda."[111] The other committee members began to question Karl in such a way that immediately alerted Greer to the fact that they were reluctant to admit a Japanese American worker into the union. Greer asserted himself again, stating that the union traditionally admits the sons of current members, and so Greer declared, "I adopt Karl right here and now as my son!" After they left the meeting, Greer told Karl, "Sometimes you have to use strong language to call their bluff, especially where racial prejudice is concerned." Karl thus became the first Japanese American member of the longshoremen's union in the mainland United States. He began work the next day. The work was physically challenging, but he took home $45 per week. A few weeks later, Karl and Elaine moved into a much larger and furnished apartment on McAllister Street. That summer, Joyce moved in with them, in time to start the school year in San Francisco.[112]

In 1937 the ILD turned its attention to legislative work for the first time, in the hopes of becoming a lobby for workers' rights throughout the United States. International affairs were also on the agenda, as the ILD noted the rise of fascism internationally. The organization asserted its commitment to "aid the victims of fascism in all lands, the victims of imperial violence in the struggles of the peoples of colonial and semi-colonial countries, and of national minorities."[113] As Northern California ILD district secretary, Elaine regularly attended the ILD's national conventions. At the 1937 convention in Washington, DC, she was elected vice president for the Pacific Coast region. During this period, the ILD worked on repeal campaigns for a number of pieces of national legislation, including a wire-tapping bill, a House resolution aimed at barring Communist Party candidates from running for office, and a so-called Concentration Camp Bill that allowed imprisonment without trial of non-U.S. citizens who could not be deported to their home countries.[114]

In 1939 Elaine ran to be a member of the San Francisco Board of Supervisors. Though she was unsuccessful, she did receive just over 20,000 votes. Her campaign platform reflected the ILD and CPUSA objectives, including the protection of civil rights, opposition to racist discrimination, advocacy for low-cost housing, and adoption of an antiwar stance. Also, Elaine campaigned for free child care for all families, which would enable women to work. In this platform, her campaign rhetoric clearly invoked the standard maternalist language of women as social housekeepers. During one of her many radio talks during the campaign, she stated,

> I think it is safe to say that if any housewife made as big a mess of her kitchen as some politicians have made of our public affairs, she wouldn't keep her husband five minutes. Then why, will you tell me, do these politicians manage to hang onto the public vote? Your civic

government is as important to every family as the kitchen is to the housewife, or a job is to a man—something he cannot afford to neglect or get in a mess.[115]

It seems ironic that a woman who didn't seem to be much attracted to conventional roles for a woman and mother would make this rhetoric the foundation of her campaign. No records exist that would explain whether this was Elaine's choice or a decision by others involved in the campaign.

Elaine was, in many ways, an unconventional mother. At this point and at twelve years old, Joyce had spent far more of her childhood living with Elaine's parents than with Elaine and Karl. Perhaps Elaine simply felt that Joyce would benefit from greater economic security than she and Karl could offer—and, indeed, as soon as they were on more stable financial footing in San Francisco, they did bring Joyce to live with them. Although Joyce lived with them, she sometimes returned to Los Angeles for holidays to see her father. Relations between Ed and Elaine were strained, but they had made custody arrangements that included his ability to spend time with her. He rarely took advantage of the option, however.

Ed and Elaine's arrangements about Joyce were put to a test in 1937 when Elaine traveled to the ILD convention in Washington, DC. The day after her return to San Francisco, Molly called Elaine and told her that Ed had taken Joyce for a few days and had promised to return her the day prior to Elaine's return, but he had not yet appeared. Elaine was not overly concerned; she assumed that Joyce had simply decided to stay with Ed for a bit longer in Las Vegas, where Ed was living and working on the construction of the Hoover Dam. But as summer wore on and school was about to start, Elaine did become anxious, and so she called Ed, who said that he did not intend to bring Joyce back to her mother at all. Elaine immediately enlisted her mother's help and the two of them went to Las Vegas to retrieve Joyce. At first, Joyce greeted them coolly. The two women were alarmed by this, and also by Ed's appearance—apparently his penchant for drinking was not curbed by his supervision of a young daughter. Elaine announced her intention to bring Joyce back to San Francisco, where school was about to start.

Molly and Elaine took Joyce to a nearby restaurant for lunch. They had some time before they would get on the afternoon train back to San Francisco. Molly asked her granddaughter what was going on as soon as they left Ed's house. Joyce explained angrily that Ed had shared with her the agreement between Ed and Elaine. As he had described it to his daughter, he and Elaine had agreed that Ed would have nothing to do with Joyce for a five-year period and then she would spend five years with him and have nothing to do with Elaine. After that, she would be free to decide which parent she wanted to live with. Ed's version was a creative way to explain his absence from Joyce's life for the previous five years, in addition to being a complete fabrication. Elaine and Molly explained to Joyce that none of it was true. Joyce then asked why she had not heard from Elaine during the time she'd been staying with her father. Elaine realized that Ed had kept from Joyce the cards and letters she and Karl had sent and even gave Joyce a gift that Karl and Elaine had sent for her birthday earlier that summer, claiming it was a gift from him. Apparently, Ed would go to great lengths, including lying outright to his daughter, to compensate for his inadequate parenting.[116]

Being shuttled between parents likely took a toll on Joyce, who tried to run away from home several times over the years—to Los Angeles to her grandparents', to her father's, or elsewhere. Joyce and Elaine's relationship does not appear conventional by the standards of the day. And yet those who knew them felt that the two remained close throughout their lives, even though they did not spend many years living together.[117] Elaine seemed to inhabit the role of Joyce's mother somewhat reluctantly, or at least with some degree of indifference.

At the start of Elaine's marriage to Ed, she had not felt ready to start a family. In the progressive circles that she and her parents were a part of, birth control was discussed somewhat openly, albeit within the bounds of marriage. Elaine was able to get a diaphragm, but she had a difficult time with it as a birth control method. Meanwhile, Ed refused the suggestion that he shoulder the responsibility. The first time Elaine became pregnant, her mother suggested to her that she could assist her in finding a clinic where she could have an abortion. Elaine accepted her help, as well as financial assistance to pay the bill. She conceived a second time, still while trying to use her diaphragm, but this time she decided to proceed with the pregnancy, and Joyce was born. She had a difficult pregnancy and a painful delivery— her doctor had recommended a cesarean section, which she would have elected to do but, being under twenty-one years of age, she needed her husband's signature, and he refused, for reasons that Elaine never understood. Elaine had one more abortion after that before she separated from Ed.[118]

Overall, Elaine certainly did not care for being forced into stereotypical expectations of motherhood. Within her professional circles, many did not even know that she had a daughter. At one point, a male colleague in the San Francisco ILD office had tried to diminish Elaine's role in the organization by suggesting that Elaine should go off and have a child—a fairly standard sexist trope used to dismiss women's value in the workplace. Elaine had acerbically responded, "Well, I already have one child, and I am not about to have another at this particular time!"[119] The fact that her colleague was unaware of Joyce's existence is telling, as is Elaine's angry response to the sexist assumption of Elaine's rightful place.

But beginning in the mid-1930s, Elaine and Karl did in fact begin to consider having another child. Pressure to have another child was coming their way from Karl's mother, who hoped to have a grandson in particular. The couple was concerned about the financial ramifications—maintaining the household with Joyce present was already a financial strain. Surely, for Elaine, the decision to have another child at the time must have been affected by her devotion to her work with the ILD, through which she had just begun to receive national recognition. Nevertheless, for three years, they tried to conceive.[120]

Around this time, Elaine received another offer to go to law school. She had been defending some young people who'd been arrested at a Young Communist Day demonstration, typically held on May Day. Afterward, two women judges who had witnessed Elaine in action in the courtroom approached her and said, "You know, Elaine, you are a born Portia," referencing the character from Shakespeare's *Merchant of Venice*, a young woman who has no formal training but is able to eloquently argue a legal case. They asked whether she would consider taking up law as a practice. Elaine replied that she probably was not eligible, as she had not even completed high school—though the lack of a diploma mattered little to her, she assumed that no college would accept her without that credential. But the judges said they could take care of that and even offered to pay her tuition. They did, however, explain that she would have to give up her labor activism. Elaine replied that that would be the central impediment that would always keep her from a legal career. Besides, she added almost as an afterthought, she was too busy at the moment having a family.[121] Thus she announced her pregnancy to her colleagues. The women warmly congratulated her and did not bring up law school again.

16

Prior to Elaine's announcement of her pregnancy, Elaine and Karl's attempts to have a child over those three years had been put on hold. Karl was on his way to Alaska to be the union representative for the Alaska Cannery Workers Union and also to get some work as a longshoreman, and they had decided to wait at least until he returned to try again. Despite their intentions, Elaine learned she was pregnant just before Karl left.[122] Elaine had previously put her career first over Joyce's upbringing a number of times and had decried sexist assumptions about her maternal role. Even when speaking with the two judges who identified her legal talents, she stated her activist work as the first reason that she could not be a lawyer. What was different now? Perhaps she was just ready for a change—her work had already begun to slow down by 1938. Or maybe she wanted to have a baby with Karl—their relationship was so different from the one she had had with Ed, and she was also older and more mature. With Karl, she could be confident that she had a partner who would share in the parenting responsibilities. There is no record to explain the shift, but Karl, Elaine, and their extended families were ecstatic at the news of this impending addition to the family.

The pregnancy was not easy on Elaine—no easier than her pregnancy with Joyce had been. She suffered terribly from morning sickness both times and she would swing between gaining and losing weight. In the last trimester of her pregnancy with Joyce, she had been in and out of the hospital.[123] The difficulties of this pregnancy were exacerbated by her refusal to diminish her ILD work. Her doctor had advised her to slow down because of her medical history but, much to Karl's dismay, she did not do so. During her pregnancy, she continued to attend campaigns to free Mooney and to visit Tom in San Quentin. She also spent time in Grass Valley, between Sacramento and Lake Tahoe, bailing out arrested strikers in a gold-mine strike happening there. When vigilantes harassed a group of striking miners, representatives went to Sacramento, accompanied by Elaine, to demand that Governor Merriam do something about the situation. Merriam had state troopers eject the group from his office. Elaine was thrown against a wall. She was hurt badly enough that she needed medical attention. When she arrived home, Karl could tell immediately by looking at her that she was in bad shape, and he called the doctor, who ordered her on bed rest. Karl was scheduled to leave shortly after for Alaska—he thought he should cancel his trip, but Elaine insisted that he go. To save money, they moved out of their apartment and in with friends—the added benefit would be that their friends could help with Joyce. Elaine kept the full details of her condition from Karl as she didn't want him to be overly concerned—in fact, Karl did not learn until much later that Elaine had spent two months in bed while he was away.[124] Karl returned a few months later and Karl, Elaine, and Joyce moved into an apartment of their own once again, at Grove and Baker Streets, in anticipation of the baby's arrival.[125]

Shortly after the start of 1939, newly inaugurated governor Culbert Olson issued his pardon of Tom Mooney. Elaine was invited to attend. Elaine was not due to give birth until the end of the month, but her doctor was adamant; she could not allow Elaine to make the trip to Sacramento, some ninety miles away. Elaine was able to see Mooney, however, the next day at a victory march for him planned in San Francisco. Elaine and Karl watched the parade begin at the Ferry Building and then, as it headed up Market Street, they took their seats at the city hall reviewing stand. On January 9, two days later, Elaine went into labor. Though they had previously agreed on names, on their way to the hospital, Karl suddenly stated, "If it's a boy, I want him named Thomas Culbert for Mooney and the Governor!" Elaine was dismissive, because she was convinced that the baby would be a girl. Elaine's mind was also occupied by other matters. She had been working right up to this moment—some other ILD workers were out of town, and so she had been on her way to post bail with $1,500 cash on her, and she feared it would disappear to sticky fingers somewhere along the way. Fortunately, she was able to put the cash in the hospital safe.[126] After a very long and difficult labor, Elaine delivered a baby boy on January 10. Four days later, Elaine eventually agreed that, after the events of earlier that week, Karl's idea was a good one. Their baby was named Thomas Culbert Yoneda, though he would be called Tommy for many years.[127] Tom Mooney was one of the first to congratulate the couple. When Karl and Elaine asked him to be Tommy's godfather, Mooney said he'd be honored.[128] Louise Todd would be the godmother.

As the couple checked out of the hospital with Tommy, the hospital's superintendent, a nun, told their doctor, a female obstetrician, that "half-breed births were not welcome at St. Joseph's" and that the doctor should not refer interracial couples to the hospital in the future.[129] In Karl and Elaine's circles, Tommy was a celebrity—he accompanied them to many events, fundraisers, and even protests, always garnering much attention as everyone wanted to see their new baby. But the couple also faced racism, not only at the hospital but at home as well. Karl and Elaine had moved the family once again into an apartment on Golden Gate Avenue, near Broderick Street, not far from Alamo Square Park, because the Grove Street apartment had been very expensive to heat. One week after they had moved into their new apartment, they were told to leave because "three white tenants had circulated a petition," signed by the majority of tenants, "objecting to having a mixed couple under the same roof." Karl and Elaine were angry, but not terribly surprised—already in that one week, Joyce had heard racist comments and someone had vandalized their laundry. The family packed up once again, and moved to yet another apartment, this one near Japantown at Steiner and Geary Streets, where they hoped to avoid any more such incidents.[130]

After Tommy's birth, Elaine did continue working for the ILD, but her level of involvement and activity certainly diminished. From the time that Tommy was five weeks old, he had significant health problems—he was highly allergic to many foods, and he was also asthmatic. Many of the unions had, by this time, developed their own bail defense funds, and so the work of the ILD was shifting to fundraising support, legislative work, and national civil rights campaigns. Although there was still need occasionally for someone to go to Lodi, Sacramento, or elsewhere to bail out an arrested worker, Elaine did not travel as much. Her work was now focused close to home—public speaking engagements and fundraisers mostly, for the ILD. During this period, Elaine became active in the Women's Auxiliary of the International Longshore and Warehouse Union.[131] She retained her title of vice president of the Pacific Coast ILD region, although she would not again travel to a national convention.[132] One significant case that Elaine worked on in this era was the defense of Festus Louis Coleman, an African American man falsely accused of the rape and robbery of a white woman he had encountered in Golden Gate Park.

Tommy's birth had definitely brought about changes in Elaine's life. From the start, she was deeply devoted to his care. Joyce was entering her teenage years and living in San Francisco with Karl and Elaine and also required attention. Karl worked full-time at the docks. After nearly a full decade of exhaustive work on behalf of others, Elaine settled into a life more focused on her home and family. It's not clear whether Elaine planned to return to full-time work when Tommy became a bit older. One month before Tommy's second birthday, the somewhat quiet life that the Yoneda family had finally settled into would be completely upended after the Japanese attack on Pearl Harbor.

Buchman family, Russia, n.d. (Courtesy Labor Archives and Research Center, San Francisco State University.)

Elaine at age two, with her parents Molly and Nathan Buchman in New York City. (Courtesy Labor Archives and Research Center, San Francisco State University.)

Elaine Black, n.d.
(Karl G. Yoneda Papers
[Collection 1592]. Library
Special Collections,
Charles E. Young Research
Library, UCLA.)

Karl Yoneda and Elaine
Black, Los Angeles,
March 1933.
(Karl G. Yoneda Papers
[Collection 1592]. Library
Special Collections,
Charles E. Young Research
Library, UCLA.)

Elaine holding Tommy, with Karl and Joyce, January 1939. (Courtesy Labor Archives and Research Center, San Francisco State University.)

Elaine Black Yoneda, promotion for bid for San Francisco Board of Supervisors, 1939. (Courtesy Labor Archives and Research Center, San Francisco State University.)

Tommy Yoneda waving from the train on the way to the Manzanar Relocation Center, Los Angeles, 1942. (Karl G. Yoneda Papers [Collection 1592]. Library Special Collections, Charles E. Young Research Library, UCLA.)

Karl, Elaine, and Tommy Yoneda at Block 4, Apartment 4, Manzanar Relocation Center. The Yonedas have hung a sign that says "Tommy's Dust Out Inn," as they try to keep their quarters free from the dust that aggravates Tommy's asthma, 1942. (Karl G. Yoneda Papers [Collection 1592]. Library Special Collections, Charles E. Young Research Library, UCLA.)

Luella (Happy) Brannan (*right*) and Joyce Russell, Elaine's daughter (*second from left*), visit the Yonedas at the Manzanar Relocation Center, June 27, 1942. (Karl G. Yoneda Papers [Collection 1592]. Library Special Collections, Charles E. Young Research Library, UCLA.)

Elaine and Tommy visit Karl at U.S. Army camp at Fort Snelling, Minnesota, 1943. (Courtesy of International Publishers, New York.)

Tommy and Elaine milking a goat, Penngrove, Sonoma County, California, 1946. (Karl G. Yoneda Papers [Collection 1592]. Library Special Collections, Charles E. Young Research Library, UCLA.)

Elaine, Karl, and Tommy Yoneda visiting Kazu Hama, Karl's mother, in Hiroshima, Japan, August 15, 1960. (Karl G. Yoneda Papers [Collection 1592]. Library Special Collections, Charles E. Young Research Library, UCLA.)

facing page, bottom:
Elaine and Karl Yoneda, San Francisco, California, n.d.
(Karl G. Yoneda Papers [Collection 1592]. Library Special Collections,
Charles E. Young Research Library, UCLA.)

Bloody Thursday Memorial Service, San Francisco, July 5, 1980. Elaine (*fourth from left*) was a speaker. (Karl G. Yoneda Papers [Collection 1592]. Library Special Collections, Charles E. Young Research Library, UCLA.)

Tom Yoneda, Santa Rosa, California, February 2019. (Photo by author, Rachel Schreiber.)

PART IV

Manzanar

17

Elaine and Karl awoke on a Sunday morning, December 7, 1941, to clear skies and warm sunshine. They made a plan to bring the children to Golden Gate Park after completing some chores. Elaine took care of some laundry, Karl was outside washing their new Studebaker, Joyce was doing homework, and little Tommy was underfoot. Suddenly the radio show Elaine was listening to was interrupted by an emergency announcement: "This morning at 7:55 a.m. Hawai'i time, Japanese warplanes began attacking Pearl Harbor. Many U.S. warships are damaged with heavy casualties." Elaine yelled for Karl to come inside immediately and hear the shocking news.[1] Karl and his colleagues at *Doho*, the Los Angeles–based Japanese-language progressive paper he worked with at the time, had been discussing for some time the probability that Japan would enter the war. But they did not anticipate that it would come in the form of a Japanese attack in Hawai'i.[2]

Elaine and Karl looked at one another and wondered, how will this affect the Japanese American community? There had been rumors for months that an evacuation of Japanese Americans was possible, but what would evacuation mean? Where might they be sent? Karl said he would go to the center of Japantown and find out what he could—Elaine stayed home to watch the children.[3] What Karl immediately witnessed was confusion, and conflicting responses. Passing by the Goshado Bookstore at Post and Buchanan Streets, Karl overheard some Issei gleefully praising Japan's actions, shouting "Hurrah for the Imperial Japanese Army" and "The Imperial Japanese Army will sail into the Golden Gate soon!" Disgusted by this support for the army from which he had escaped conscription, Karl continued and came upon a reporter asking two Nisei members of the U.S. Army, in uniform, if they were ready to fight Japan. "Of course," the GIs replied. Meanwhile, the proprietor of a Japantown hotel, Ichiro Kataoka, was being arrested and taken away by FBI agents.[4] The arrests appeared to be random, with many innocent people being accused of being enemy aliens. Nisei stood around in clusters, whispering to one another, worried about what would happen to their parents who were not citizens—would they be deported?[5] The scene was one of mayhem and much fear.

Karl returned home and called the editor-in-chief of *Doho*, Shuji Fujii, to ask how things were going in Southern California. Fujii told him that telegrams expressing support from the Japanese American community were being sent to various U.S. officials on behalf of the paper. Karl should consider doing the same from the San Francisco office, Fujii told him, and also begin preparing to issue a special edition of the paper. That night, Karl gathered a group of staff from the paper at the Yoneda home, and together they drafted the following message to send to President Roosevelt by telegram:

On behalf of one hundred fifty readers and subscribers in the San Francisco Bay Area of *Doho*, Japanese American newspaper, we pledge full cooperation in all endeavors to secure victory for the democracies. We stand ready to join the ranks of the fighting forces under your command to defeat the vicious military fascists of Japan.[6]

The group vowed to enlist immediately in the military—the time was "opportune" to "join the U.S. Armed Forces to help dismantle the emperor system and its military clique," giving their lives if necessary. As heartfelt as this statement was for Karl, he harbored a nagging concern for his mother, who was living in Hiroshima. "Would I face her as an enemy" were he to join the military, he wondered.[7]

The next morning, Karl went to work as usual. After he left, Elaine prepared to get Joyce to school and feed Tommy his breakfast. Suddenly there was a knock on the door of their apartment. Elaine opened the door to find two FBI agents asking about Karl's whereabouts. Elaine told the FBI agents that Karl was at work, on the dock. The agents replied, "What do you mean, he's working on the docks?" They added a racial epithet, expressing their disbelief that a Japanese American could be a longshoreman. Elaine was bewildered by their response, surprised and dismayed by their overt racism.[8] She went on to say, "You must be looking for the wrong person. Karl is antifascist. He has been clubbed, beaten, and jailed for being an antifascist, and now you come looking for him, instead of looking for the fascists that might be among us?" The agents ignored Elaine and proceeded to search the house. They came upon the Christmas cards that Elaine and Karl had purchased and were preparing to send out—this year's cards supported relief efforts in China for victims of the war between Japan and China. The agents accused Elaine of having these cards as a front to hide their support for Japan.[9]

The agents asked again where Karl was, still unwilling to believe he was working at the docks. Elaine called the dispatch office to find out his precise location and shared that with the agents. She still thought they had simply made a mistake in pursuing Karl. She thought maybe they were confusing him with another Japanese man who had recently moved into their building but had left with no trace on December 7. Elaine told the agents "you're wasting your time" looking for Karl; maybe they should go find this other man? No, the agents assured her, they were seeking Karl Yoneda, also known as Karl Hama.

Though she was surprised by these agents' interest in Karl, Elaine willingly complied with their requests. For so many years she had defied authorities, and even instructed others on how to do so. She was personally aware of the intimidation and harassment tactics that agencies such as the FBI could employ. This case, however, was different; she and Karl had often discussed what a "vicious enemy" the Imperial Japanese Army was. As she would later recall, "I had known what the Japanese militarists had done in Nanking, I knew what Hitler had been doing throughout Europe, and I knew what Mussolini had done to his people, so I was going to cooperate with the FBI at that point if it was to help expose any fascists that might do damage to this country."[10] What Elaine did not know until later was that the FBI had stationed men with machine guns on the roofs of neighboring buildings.[11]

Karl had arrived at work early that day, and his white coworkers greeted him by saying, "Karl, now we're going to fix that J** army but good." Fellow unionists, they were aware of Karl's criticisms of the Japanese government (though they were not above invoking a racist epithet). A few minutes later, at 8:00 a.m. as the "gang" (as each group of longshoremen assigned to day's work were called) was about to start work, FBI agents appeared and began the process of detaining Karl. His supervisor protested. "Hey, you fellows," shouted the gang captain, "Karl is the main fighter in our union against J** militarism. You are arresting the wrong man." But he did not succeed in his effort to stop the agents from taking Karl.[12]

Karl was taken to the Immigration Detention Station on Silver Avenue, on the other side of the city. About fifty men were being held there, and Karl recognized most of them.[13] A businessman whom Karl knew to be a regular reader of the Doho approached Karl and expressed his certainty that Karl had been detained by mistake; he told Karl that he would surely be released soon. Karl realized that he was not the only one there about whom the same could be said—he recognized four Nisei among those detained who shared his political views. He knew that, like him, they posed no possible threat to the United States, including George Hagiwara, whose family had managed the Japanese Tea Garden in Golden Gate Park for three generations.[14] Karl recognized a few ardent pro-Japanese militarists among those in the detention center.[15] The experience began to be very frightening for Karl, as some from this latter group began to accuse Karl of being a spy, saying, "You're in here as a spy; you're spying on us. Wait until the submarines come in here; you'll be the first one machine gunned!"[16] That night, Karl and the other four Nisei clustered their cots into one corner of the center in solidarity, all watchful for potential violence from their fellow detainees.[17]

Karl demanded to be allowed to phone a lawyer, and finally he was able to place a call to ILD attorney George Anderson.[18] Anderson was already aware of Karl's detention. Elaine had been informed around noon that day by a coworker of Karl's that he'd been taken, and the first thing she did was to call Anderson, who immediately began to prepare a writ of *habeas corpus*. Nevertheless, it would be thirty-six hours before Karl was released. A Filipino neighbor drove Elaine to the detention center, where they met Anderson and were able to bring Karl home.[19]

On the way home, Elaine shared some disturbing news with Karl. The previous evening, the California district secretary had called a meeting of the Bay Area Nisei Communist Party, at the Yoneda home. There, the secretary announced that the CPUSA was suspending from party membership "all members of Japanese ancestry and their non-Japanese spouses for the duration of the war."[20] Elaine told him that "it was so sudden and so unreal that no one uttered a word of protest." Karl was "stunned and speechless" by the suspension. "After all, most of us had been party members for more than ten years and had participated in every struggle the party organized or supported. Regardless of age or family status, we were ready to join the war effort." Once home, Karl called another meeting of local Japanese American CPUSA members. The group decided that it would not be in the best interests of fighting fascism to register a complaint at that moment against the suspension. Rather, the group decided to continue as though they were still members of the party; they hoped that later this irresponsible decision would be overturned. Later, Karl would describe the suspension as a "faulty decision" and would express remorse that the group had not resisted it.[21]

After Karl was released from the detention center, he and Elaine again agreed that Karl should enlist in the military and that Elaine would pursue war-relief work. Karl presented himself at the local draft board, only to be told that they had received instructions that all Nisei were to be reclassified as enemy aliens. Karl was extremely disappointed—he insisted that people such as himself, Japanese Americans who understood firsthand the problems with Japanese aggression, would be very useful in fighting this enemy. He was tenacious; he would continue in his efforts to enlist throughout the following year.[22]

Within a matter of days, racist anti-Japanese misinformation and sentiment began to proliferate, in the Bay Area and elsewhere. Some Chinese and Korean Americans began wearing buttons identifying themselves as non-Japanese. In response, the Japanese American Citizens League (JACL) ordered 10,000 buttons that read "I am an American." Crazy rumors were spreading about an impending Japanese invasion of California, and of Japanese spies infiltrating the U.S. military. The December 22 issue of Life magazine even published an illustrated article titled "How to Tell J**s from the Chinese."[23] Karl saw a poster in a store, prominently displayed and for sale, that read "J** Hunting Licenses Issued Here—Open Season Now—No Limit."[24] In contrast to all of these racist responses, including that of the CPUSA, some elements within the labor movement expressed support. At a San Francisco meeting of the Congress of Industrial Organizations that Karl attended, one of the union presidents who was there spoke in support of the Japanese American members of his union and registered his objection to the continued use of the racial epithet to describe Japanese Americans.[25]

Elaine and Karl learned that the JACL in Los Angeles had formed an anti-Axis committee, chaired by a wealthy businessman named Fred Tayama. The committee issued a statement of "unequivocal repudiation of Japan" and support for a U.S. victory. Karl urged the San Francisco Bay Area JACL chapter to follow suit, but they would not. Karl felt that behind their "overcautious approach" was the fact that most members were "conservative, anti-labor professionals." But Karl and his colleagues continued to try to work with the JACL.[26]

Elaine and Karl spent the rest of December and January in much uncertainty. Both were aware that the intense anti-Japanese racism being expressed all around them could easily turn violent. On New Year's Eve, preoccupied with worries for the coming year, they did not raise glasses in a toast to the new year, as had been their custom. Both were consumed with anxiety.[27] Newspaper headlines described Japan's advances and also told of statewide violence against Japanese Americans—at the hands of whites and of other Asian American groups intent on differentiating themselves from Japanese Americans. Karl continued his letter-writing campaign, imploring local officials to reinstate his job, which was crucial to the war effort, and to federal officials, pressing them to see his loyalty to the United States and allow him to enlist in the U.S. military.

Meanwhile, Elaine and Karl noted that both Mexico and Canada had enacted exclusion plans that moved Japanese residents and citizens to the interiors of those countries. They also read an article in the *San Francisco Chronicle* on February 2, 1942, with the headline "S.F. May Ask U.S. to Move J**s Inland," which described a measure being put to the San Francisco Board of Supervisors and modeled after one that had recently passed in Los Angeles.[28] They began to plan for the possibility that they would have to leave San Francisco, and they initiated arrangements to store their belongings with friends.[29]

Elaine and Karl's response to the bombing of Pearl Harbor and the unfolding news of the months that followed as removal appeared to be imminent was shared within their social and political circles of Japanese Americans. As the Communist International had declared the fight against fascism to be one of its central aims throughout this decade, members of the CPUSA—Japanese and non-Japanese—saw the attack on Pearl Harbor as a dangerous advance of the Imperial Japanese Army. Elaine and Karl were certainly aware that, because they were Communists, the U.S. government maintained detailed dossiers on each of them and tracked their radical political and labor work. But they, and other Japanese American Communists, also persisted in their belief that despite their left-wing record, the U.S. government could be convinced that their deeply held opposition to fascism was proof of their support for the United States and their keen desire for an Allied victory. Karl was not alone in believing wholeheartedly that he could demonstrate his American patriotism by aiding the war effort in any way possible, including enlisting.

This was the position taken by many on the far left, principally the Communists, but other groups within the Japanese American community responded differently. Many Nisei understood that, while they thought of themselves as Americans and feared the attack on the United States as much as others did, they would be "on the spot," as a Nisei graduate student at the University of California, Berkeley described their position. The student reported that Nisei on campus after the attack on Pearl Harbor were "painfully aware" that "their faces [were] so conspicuously that of the enemies."[30] They understood implicitly what was about to unfold. Anti-Japanese racism had long been a feature of life in California, due in large part to resentment of the success of Japanese immigrants in the agricultural sector and other industries. It was clear to many Nisei that most white Americans would view all Japanese and Japanese Americans living in the United States through the lens of this racism and that Pearl Harbor would legitimate their desire to see

Japanese Americans removed from the state. They could see that they would all be labeled enemies of the state, regardless of their backgrounds and political opinions.

Meanwhile, the JACL had taken another position. The JACL had decided to adopt a cooperationist stance toward possible removal and exclusion. The organization's leaders had been meeting with U.S. authorities even before the bombing of Pearl Harbor and had suggested that the Japanese American community would organize its own removal out of the military areas if and when that became necessary. JACL leaders believed that there were Japanese nationalists in California who might pose a military threat, and they advanced the idea that Nisei who were American patriots were the best equipped to rout out such renegades and turn them over to authorities. After the war, the JACL would be heavily criticized for its complicity in the exclusion and incarceration, as well as for taking the liberty to speak for the Japanese American community.[31]

Certainly, there were Japanese Americans—Issei and Kibei mostly—who opposed removal. The JACL and the Left would claim that anyone who opposed or resisted removal was pro-Axis and a sympathizer of the Imperial Japanese Army. Karl clearly recalled hearing expressions of pro-Axis sympathy from time to time, such as those he heard on December 7 in Japantown—that the Japanese Army would triumphantly invade California. But there were those, too, who identified in exclusion and incarceration an egregious violation of the civil rights of U.S. citizens, not because they were pro-Axis but simply because they knew that what was happening was wrong and was fueled by racism. Resistance appeared in numerous ways. Some Japanese Americans, if they had the means, simply relocated to other areas of the United States to avoid incarceration. Others changed their identities and claimed to be Chinese or Korean. In one extreme instance, a California man named Fred Korematsu changed his name, went underground, and even underwent plastic surgery in an attempt to make himself look "less Japanese."[32]

This range of responses reflected the fear and chaos of the moment, as well as the lack of clear information. The first few months of 1942 were tumultuous and filled with uncertainty about the future. Sure enough, it would not be long before the U.S. government and military took action.

18

On February 19, 1942, President Roosevelt signed EO 9066, which authorized the military to designate parts of the country as military zones, from which "any and all persons can be excluded." Karl would later say, "I was among the multitudes who did not realize the significance of Executive Order 9066."[33] Roosevelt had been fielding considerable pressure from various sources, including California attorney general Earl Warren (prior to his appointment to a seat on the Supreme Court), Hearst-owned and other West Coast media outlets, military leadership, and other political figures to enable the exclusion of Japanese Americans from the coast. Roosevelt had also heard from groups who opposed a relocation plan. A 1940 study by the military had found that Japanese Americans did not pose a security threat to the United States, and some focused on this report to try to persuade the president that removal was not only unnecessary, but unjust. But, clearly, opponents to relocation did not win the day. In early March, General John DeWitt, lieutenant general in the U.S. Army and commander over the Western region, established two military zones on the West Coast: Military Area One, which included the coastal portions of Washington, Oregon, and California, as well as the southern half of Arizona; and Military Area Two, which included all other areas in those four states.

A few days after the order was signed, a set of congressional hearings commenced to investigate the claims being made that exclusion of Japanese Americans from the West Coast was necessary. The hearings, which had been planned well before EO 9066 was issued, were conducted by the Tolan Committee, headed by Democrat John Tolan of Oakland, California, and held in Seattle, Portland, San Francisco, and Los Angeles. Various liberal politicians had hoped that the hearings would forestall the worst possible outcomes for Japanese Americans. Alas, the timing of the hearings' start made them merely perfunctory. Elaine, Karl, and others saw them as "window dressing" on a decision that had already been made.[34]

Governor Culbert Olson, namesake for Karl and Elaine's son, testified at the hearing in Los Angeles. He had initially opposed General DeWitt's plans for exclusion because he believed that the California agricultural industry would flounder without the (low-paid) labor of Japanese Americans. Eventually he acquiesced to the rhetoric that asserted the importance of exclusion to the military security of California. While Olson asserted his belief that Japanese Americans could indeed be loyal to the United States, he also made the racist claim that it would be impossible to distinguish those who were loyal to Japan from those who might be American patriots, because of their appearance, invoking stereotypes about Asian Americans. Ultimately, he urged those who were loyal to accept the "inconvenience" of exclusion.[35] Elaine and Karl were surely aware of Olson's testimony. Though they may have been dismayed by Olson's racism, in many ways his notion of acceptance was aligned with their own view.

Elaine and Karl attended the hearings in San Francisco.[36] Rather than testify, Karl chose to write a letter on behalf of the *Doho* readership. In his letter, he reiterated support for the U.S. government, going as far as to say that if it were "deemed a military necessity that all [Japanese Americans] should be evacuated from military areas, we are ready to go."[37] Others attested to their patriotism. Three Japanese Americans, Shuji Fujii, Isamu Noguchi, and George Watanabe—all of whom Karl had worked with on various committees and organizations—submitted a joint statement exposing the flawed logic in the assumption that Japanese Americans could not be loyal to the United States, stating that "in testing loyalty, we wish to point out that loyalty is not entirely a matter of citizenship or educational background nor a matter of religious or political affiliation."[38]

Various people also testified to their strong opposition to exclusion and incarceration. Japanese American James Omura vociferously opposed the removal and would become perhaps its most famous resister. In a dramatic and powerful speech, Omura challenged the committee:

> I would like to ask the committee: Has the Gestapo come to America? Have we not risen in righteous anger at Hitler's mistreatments of the Jews? Then, is it not incongruous that citizen Americans of Japanese descent should be similarly mistreated and persecuted? I speak from a humanitarian standpoint and from a realistic and not a theoretical point of view. This view, I believe, does not endanger the national security of this country nor jeopardize our war efforts.[39]

Omura also went on record opposing the position of the JACL and its claims to represent the entire Japanese American community.

How would Elaine have reacted to Omura's testimony? As a Jewish woman and daughter of immigrants who had fled from anti-Semitism, surely the reference and comparison to Hitler would have resonated. She herself had invoked such a comparison earlier in the face of antilabor violence. But Elaine seemed more swayed by the fear that Hitler would prevail and fascism would spread globally. In the face of this fear, she and Karl held to their belief that

Americans should do all they could to fight fascism, even if it meant giving up civil liberties.

Testimonies were also delivered by non-Japanese Americans. In pointed statements that echoed Omura's references to Nazism, Louis Goldblatt, secretary of the California Congress of Industrial Organizations and also a high-ranking official in the International Longshore and Warehouse Union, asserted "that using racial or ethnic characteristics to determine loyalty compromised American values," as historian Ellen Eisenberg noted.[40] Goldblatt asked, where will such a policy end? Isn't such a practice tantamount to what Hitler was doing in Europe? Goldblatt pointed out that pitting groups of Americans against one another may have been just what the Axis powers would like to see happen. He exposed the fact that hatred of Japanese Americans had long been a part of California and West Coast politics; these actions would only fuel and authorize such sentiment in those western states. The federal government should intervene—not by treating Japanese Americans as enemies but by protecting them from regional bias. Finally, Goldblatt pointed out that if groups of Japanese Americans were supporting removal, it was only because they feared becoming the victims of violence.[41]

Of the nineteen Japanese Americans who testified in San Francisco, eleven spoke out clearly against exclusion. Of the non-Japanese Americans who testified, forty-five favored removal and thirty-four opposed it. Many understood that the refusal to make individual assessments of Japanese Americans was a clear expression of deep-seated, West Coast racism against Asians and Asian Americans. Most who testified believed that, at the very least, Japanese Americans should be treated in the same manner as Italian and German Americans, who were being individually assessed for their loyalty to the United States; as a result, very few were incarcerated.[42] The only possible conclusion to draw about why the Japanese American community was being treated differently was racism.

In the days and months after the attack on Pearl Harbor and up to the exclusion and incarceration of West Coast Japanese Americans, a diversity of responses and positions emerged from the Japanese American community in the Tolan Committee hearings, in public and private discussions, and in the media. In fact, divisive and bitter interactions would ensue for decades to come, long after the war, as Japanese Americans sought redress and reparations. The debates would be played out in public exchanges between Elaine, Karl, and others. With the clarity of hindsight, some—including Elaine and Karl—would reevaluate their decision to willingly abdicate their own civil rights and not oppose their own incarceration. But, in 1942, Elaine and Karl earnestly believed that their commitment to fighting fascism and to defeating Hitler, Mussolini, and Hirohito made all other concerns secondary. Both Elaine and Karl had family histories entangled in these struggles. Karl himself, and Elaine's father, Nathan, had both escaped conscription into armies of nations whose governments they opposed. And surely members of Elaine's extended family who had not come to the United States were suffering the cruel oppression of the Nazi regime. Did this fact influence Elaine's support for the United States and Allied forces? They consistently stated their belief that if the Axis powers were not stopped, they might all be "victims of Hitler's ovens," to use words spoken by both Elaine and Karl.[43]

19

Amid this chaotic atmosphere of debate, misinformation, threats of violence, and economic uncertainty, Karl volunteered to go help build the Owens Valley Reception Center, located between the two small towns of Lone Pine and the somewhat ironically named town of Independence, on the east side of the Sierra Nevada near Mount Whitney. The Owens Valley Reception Center would eventually become the Manzanar War Relocation Center. Initially, it was constructed and administered by the U.S. Army's Wartime Civilian Control Administration. By June 1942, it would be transferred to the War Relocation Authority (WRA). Manzanar was unusual in a number of respects. It was the first of the camps to be built. It would also be the only army-administered transfer center that would transform into one of the concentration camps. Elsewhere, there was a clear differentiation between military transfer centers and WRA-administered camps. The distinction was significant because, throughout the war but particularly during the first weeks and months of incarceration, Manzanar's operational realities did not always follow the policies that governed the other camps and decisions could at times appear to be arbitrary.

Why would Karl, and other Japanese Americans, voluntarily go to this remote location? Conflicting rumors and lack of clear information made it hard to determine the best course of action, and many questions remained unanswered. What would become of the property they were leaving behind? When would they next see their families? Removal had not yet been mandated when EO 9066 was issued, but it certainly seemed imminent. The decision to cooperate and indeed to volunteer was due in part to the realities of the situation and in part to a somewhat naive idealism about their role within the larger aims of the war raging around the world. On the one hand, Elaine, Karl, and others understood what they were up against. Elaine would later recall, "it became apparent that we couldn't possibly fight it . . . knowing the forces that the United States had at its command, knowing that the powers that be would think nothing of dispatching a battalion or two with their guns to evacuate the Japanese should there be resistance."[44] They were keenly aware that the anti-Japanese sentiment was a matter of stereotyping, which meant seeing all Japanese Americans as undifferentiated and not understanding who the real enemy was. And they also knew there were precedents in U.S. history in "what had been done to the Indians, the Native Americans, in the 1830 Removal Act and broken treaties. They could take a whole people at the points of guns and drag them away from their homes."[45] On the other hand, as Karl stated in his memoir, looking back on this history,

> We, Kibei, Nisei, and Issei Communists and sympathizers decided not to fight nor speak out against the [ensuing] "evacuation order," even though it violated our Constitutional and basic human rights. Our rationale was that we would lose all rights if the Germany-Italy-Japan fascist Axis powers were victorious. The menace of worldwide fascism was knocking at our nation's doorstep. We had to do everything to insure Allied victory. We had no choice but to accept the racist U.S. dictum at that time over Hitler's ovens and Japan's military rapists of Nanking. We would thrash out the question of our rights after victory.[46]

Elaine's and Karl's statements were, of course, made later, after the war, with the benefit of hindsight and the desire to rationalize a decision that had been made under clouds of great uncertainty.

The decision to go to Manzanar was also the result of some very pragmatic considerations. Karl and the other Japanese American men who volunteered were responding to an offer that promised compensation for their labor at prevailing union wages. Elaine and Karl weighed the perceived advantages very carefully. They both felt certain that they would not be able to stay in San Francisco. If Karl were to be incarcerated, Elaine could not afford their apartment on her own, which was already becoming a financial burden now that Karl was unable to procure steady employment. It was very unclear where Japanese Americans from the San Francisco Bay Area would be sent—the rumors, which turned out to be well founded, were that people might be sent to locations as remote from their homes as Arizona, Idaho, Wyoming, and even Arkansas. Meanwhile, Molly and Nathan had made an offer for the family to move in with them in Los Angeles. Karl could work at Manzanar and would be within driving distance of the family. Nathan offered to drive Elaine there to visit Karl occasionally. In Los Angeles, Elaine hoped to find war-relief work.[47]

Elaine and Karl began to plan the first step, their move to Los Angeles. They had to spread their belongings among friends, for no one household could take everything that they owned.[48] They would leave in early March. Their departure was delayed, however, because their dear friend Tom Mooney, godfather to their son and icon of the labor movement, was in the hospital, and it was clear that he would not live much longer. He died a few days later, and the Yonedas decided to stay for the funeral on March 8, to be held in the San Francisco Civic Center Auditorium. Karl was among the pallbearers, along with the luminaries Paul Robeson, Theodore Dreiser, Harry Bridges, and Upton Sinclair. Harry Bridges delivered the eulogy.[49] Shortly after the funeral, Elaine, Karl, Joyce, and Tommy piled into the Studebaker, loaded with as many belongings as they could carry, and drove south to Los Angeles.[50] Along the way, they pulled off the highway to have lunch near Bakersfield. But when they saw a sign in the window that read "No J**s Served Here," they got back in the car and kept driving until they reached Elaine's parents'.[51] Arriving at the Buchmans' home was a welcome respite from the journey, and from the last few months in San Francisco. Tommy rushed from the car to greet his grandparents, shouting "Bubbe! Zayde!"—the Yiddish names for grandmother and grandfather. Molly was a great Jewish cook, and she had prepared an elaborate meal for them.[52]

The next day, Karl went to the Maryknoll School in Los Angeles to register as a volunteer to go to Manzanar. The Maryknoll organizations were Catholic missions that operated primarily in Asian countries but also throughout the world and with Asian American communities in the United States. Centered on liberation theology, Maryknoll focused on assisting groups that were under duress.[53] Maryknoll had become the liaison to the military in organizing the removal of Japanese Americans in the Los Angeles area. When Karl arrived at the Maryknoll School, he and others were assured by a priest that there would be plenty of paid work for everyone at Manzanar—with pay ranging from $50 to $94 per month, as determined by skill level. Those gathered were instructed to return that Sunday for instructions from the U.S. Army. Karl joined several hundred others on Sunday, and he recognized some old friends among those gathered. They listened as an army captain explained that they should bring only what they could carry. He also assured them that they would all have jobs at Manzanar and that the families they were leaving behind would be "the last ones ordered out of Military Area One." Finally, they were told that their train would leave the next morning from the Santa Fe Railway station in downtown Los Angeles.[54]

The whole family accompanied Karl to the station to see him off on Monday morning, March 23. The scene was chaotic—more than 800 volunteers like Karl, their families and friends, Maryknoll priests and nuns, and reporters and armed soldiers, who were there ostensibly to protect the volunteers. A photo of Karl kissing Tommy appeared in the paper, with a caption that read "A Japanese father is shown kissing his son good-by [sic] as he departed for the valley. About 1000 J**s left today."[55] Karl and Elaine agreed that Karl would call as soon as he could—he could reverse the charges if needed—and that he would write. They also agreed that Elaine would not come visit until she heard from Karl that conditions there would be acceptable for such a visit. Filled with trepidation and anxiety, they said goodbye, not knowing when they would see each other next. Karl watched Elaine, Joyce, Tommy, and Elaine's parents from the window as his train departed, keeping an eye on them until they disappeared on the horizon.[56]

The journey was slow and arduous. The train stopped at every crossing and bridge—the military police accompanying the train would get out and check that it was safe to cross. It's not clear why the train was so heavily protected—those on the train wondered, what did they fear? That such a large assembled group of Japanese Americans would revolt? These were, nominally at least, people who had made the choice to go. But as the men would soon learn upon their arrival, their status as volunteers was illusory. On the train, Karl quickly realized that a range of political positions was represented—not everyone held his views on the need to support the Allies in their fight against fascism. Some men started rumors, saying that "the U.S. will have to pay each of us three thousand dollars after Japan wins the war, that the U.S. would detain us like Indians in camps, and that we would be fed leftover army supplies."[57] Another man started to make negative comments about Roosevelt, at which point a cousin of Karl's told him to stop, lest he be sent to Missoula, Montana, where there was an enemy alien detention camp.[58] Apparently, some on the train perceived Manzanar to be a more desirable destination than other possibilities.

The train pulled into the rail station at Lone Pine at 10:00 p.m., after thirteen hours of travel. The men were taken by army trucks to the camp, where they spent the first night in crowded barracks with no electricity, no sanitary facilities, and windows open to the elements. Exhausted, Karl fell into a deep sleep on an army cot, in a barrack with two of his cousins and seven other men, wearing his clothes from the day's journey.

By the light of day the next morning, the full bleakness of the scene revealed itself to them. Surrounded on one side by the snow-covered Sierra and desert on the other was a rough construction site where barracks were being constructed in a somewhat disorganized manner, in two shifts. The camp was encircled by barbed wire; guards with machine guns staffed eight watchtowers. The winds from the mountains deposited dust everywhere. The administration building, post office, and medical clinic had been built, but for the barracks there were no sanitary facilities. There was one faucet for water, but it had frozen overnight. Karl overheard someone remark, "So this is the American-style concentration camp."[59] When Karl and a group of others went to the office to ask about the construction jobs, the officials stated that they knew nothing about jobs; they had hired a contractor for the construction, and he had plenty of union workers on the job. Indeed, the men who had just arrived could see that construction crews, composed of white men, were already on the scene.[60] The cold realization that they had been lied to settled in. Confusion turned quickly to anger, and someone shouted, "The goddamn lying American government!" Karl sat down and wrote a letter to Elaine, telling her not to visit under any circumstances for at least one month and never to bring Tommy, whose asthma would surely be triggered by the dusty conditions—he feared the conditions might even prove lethal to his small son.[61]

Karl and the others set out to make the best they could of the deplorable situation. The group organized themselves into various tasks—some would take kitchen duty, others would begin to clean the place up and try to make it livable. They also designated a group to meet new arrivals and orient them to the camp. They received little official direction, and rumors began to spread, adding to the maddening environment. Morale was very low, and some began to feel certain that they would spend the remainder of the war in this dusty camp, frigid overnight at the moment, but with the hot summer looming in the not too distant future.[62]

By the time construction was complete, the camp at Manzanar would span about 6,200 acres. By July, there would be more than 10,000 people incarcerated there. Most came from Los Angeles, though some were from Stockton, California, and Bainbridge Island in Washington state. The living quarters occupied about 640 acres, organized in thirty-six residential blocks, each of which included barracks of about twenty by one hundred feet where a family would live in one large space with no partitions. Each block also maintained its own mess hall, laundry room, recreation hall, and a few other facilities. Additional blocks provided staff housing, administrative buildings, a camp hospital, a post office, a church, and one large meeting space. The perimeter of the camp, encircled by barbed wire, also had eight watchtowers guarded by military police.[63]

Manzanar would also be home to an orphanage, where more than one hundred Japanese American children, most of them under seven years of age, were incarcerated. The children had come from three orphanages in California, two in Los Angeles and one in San Francisco. After Pearl Harbor, there was debate about what would happen to these orphans. A number of the Nisei staff at the three orphanages had been arrested and sent to prison camps, such as the one in Missoula, Montana. The remaining Nisei staff had petitioned for exemption to be allowed to remain with the children; they stressed the importance of the children staying with the staff whom they had come to know. They selflessly offered to take the children to Manzanar, which they could see might be their only chance to stay together. After General DeWitt announced the exclusion order, they maintained their position and argued to be allowed to stay with their charges, even in camp. Their request was granted, and the euphemistically named Children's Village was formed at Manzanar, where the staff lived together with their charges.[64]

Manzanar's Children's Village was the only one of its type among all ten of the camps and exemplifies the ways that Manzanar was initially considered to be a kind of test site. Because Manzanar was built first and overseen by the military for a long time, it housed experiments and pilot programs like the Children's Village and policies such as the early program that allowed those incarcerated to go to Lone Pine to the cinema, for shopping, or to a beauty parlor. But Manzanar's unusual status likely also accounts for frequent confusion about its policies and miscommunication between those at camp and authorities elsewhere. For example, Karl and the others were told that they would have union-wage-paying jobs at the camp, but the reality was that the camp administration had already made the choice to hire white union workers. Had they been deliberately duped? It's certainly possible, but it's quite likely that those who had promised jobs were completely out of communication with those already at Manzanar. Similarly, those who volunteered to go to Manzanar had been assured that their families would be the last to be removed from Military Area One. This promise, too, would soon be broken.

20

After Karl had left for Manzanar, Elaine began to settle into life in her parents' home in Los Angeles and was planning to look for a job—but her plan would be short-lived. Six days after Karl left, Elaine and the family sat down to dinner with the radio tuned to a classical music station. Suddenly the symphony was interrupted by the announcement of an order issued by General DeWitt:

> Attention! Attention! All those of Japanese ancestry whose bread-winners are in the Manzanar Reception Center: you are hereby ordered to report to the Civil Control Center at 707 South Spring Street tomorrow from 8:00 a.m. on for processing to leave for Manzanar by noon, April 2nd, or be in violation of General DeWitt's Civilian Exclusion Order No. 3.[65]

Confusion set in immediately for Elaine. Would this order apply to Tommy? What exactly was meant by "breadwinner"? Elaine had planned to look for a job, and she was living with her parents, who had an income. Not only had the Yonedas been promised that, because Karl had gone voluntarily to build the camp, the rest of the family would be the very last to be ordered to leave Military Area One, but furthermore, that they would be given plenty of notice. April 2 was in a few days—how could they possibly prepare in that short a time? Elaine felt certain that the order did not apply to her, but why would it apply to Tommy, a three-year-old boy, when he was safely settled into a home with three adults? Certainly it was not lost on her either that Tommy was living in the home of three non-Japanese American white adults as well as his white older sister—surely the military could not see Tommy as a threat to national security, could they? Elaine frantically placed phone calls, trying to reach someone in the army, to no avail.

Finally, she reached one of the Maryknoll priests, with whom she had a bizarre conversation. Would the order apply to Tommy? Elaine asked the priest.

"Oh, it doesn't mean you," replied the priest.

"That was not my question," stated Elaine, "my question [is] does it mean this three-year-old . . . does it mean that my child, who is fifty percent of Japanese ancestry, whose father *is* in Manzanar, one of the volunteers? Does it mean him?"

Again the priest responded in the same way, "It doesn't mean you."

Elaine persisted. "That is not my question, Father."

Finally, the priest offered, "Well, we are going by international law. . . . The father's ancestry is what counts."

"But the father was born right here in the state!" Elaine replied indignantly. "If anyone is an alien it is I. I was born in Manhattan. I wasn't born in California. So I'm alien to this state, and it's occurring in this state."

"But it does mean anyone with more than one-sixteenth Japanese blood," replied the priest.

"Well," Elaine shot back, "my child is not going without me."[66]

Elaine arose early and was at the center by 6:45 a.m. the next morning with Tommy, eager to find out more. She had received Karl's letter, but with everything else going on, she had not yet opened it. She hastily put it in her handbag, to be read later. Once at the center, she encountered a large crowd. She also noted that the depot was surrounded by soldiers with guns.[67] She took her place in line, but an army officer and a priest appeared and shouted for Tommy and Elaine to follow them into the building. The men once again tried to convince Elaine that she should not go with Tommy, handing her one application only, for her son. They assured her that there were plans to build a children's village at Manzanar and that Tommy would be well looked after by the nuns who would run it. They also told her that life would be hard there—it would not be easy. But this only infuriated Elaine further. "Is it going to be easy for anyone?" she asked, gesturing to the others who had gathered there. Her loud public-speaking voice began to emerge, as she shouted, "You are not taking this child and putting him in an orphanage. I am not abandoning him on the steps of a church or some other building. He has a home where he'll be cherished and well taken care of. I don't understand this madness. A child who had just turned three and whose father, before many moons pass, will be in the service of the United States Army!"[68] Unnerved, perhaps, by Elaine's booming voice and the scene she was instigating, they acquiesced and handed her a second application.

At one point during her earlier argument with the Maryknoll priest, when he had asked Elaine to confirm that Tommy met the criterion for removal, Elaine—ever the wit—replied sarcastically that Tommy "might even be more [than fifty percent] 'Asiatic' because my parents had come from a region which had been overrun by Genghis Khan and his raping hordes."[69] Both this comment and Elaine's positioning of herself as an alien because she was not from California but from New York were Elaine's attempts to expose the absurdity of these determinations about her family that were based on racist designations. The relationship to what was going on in Europe was not lost on the Yonedas and others, as Hitler and the Nazis were, simultaneously, creating classifications to define who should be considered Jewish by ancestry. The one-drop rule that was being applied to children like Tommy was disturbingly reminiscent not only of contemporary Nazi policy but also of historic classifications of African Americans in the United States.

The U.S. Army's policy on who fell under the exclusion order contained not only these racist designations but sexist interpretations of parental affiliation as well. The army decreed that, in interracial marriages with a white husband and a Japanese American mother, the child could remain in Military Area One with its father. By contrast, the children of Japanese American fathers were incarcerated along with their father, regardless of the mother's race. The gendered assumption was that the father would be the primary influence in a family. The child of a white father might be tainted by close contact with Japanese Americans, whereas the child of a Japanese American father was assumed to have the innate propensity to be a Japanese loyalist. Under this policy, a small but significant population of Filipino, Latino, and white women went to camp to care for their children, as Elaine would do. Later, the army would issue a policy for mixed-marriage leave clearances, whereby non-Japanese American wives could petition to leave camp along with their children, so long as they met other criteria, including having no arrest or FBI records.[70]

It is not clear, under these policies, why Elaine had to argue to be able to go with Tommy to Manzanar. It's possible that it was the result of the condition stated earlier, that Manzanar was the first camp and there were many miscommunications at that early time about the exclusion orders. It is also not clear whether Elaine and Karl were even aware of the possibility of mixed-marriage leave clearances when the policy was issued later that year, in July 1942. Neither made any mention of the policy. It's likely that Elaine would not have been eligible, since she had an arrest record and was being watched by the FBI as well. But had she been aware of the policy, Elaine may have invoked it in order to keep Tommy out of camp. Elaine had always asserted that her priority in insisting on being at Manzanar was her need to care for Tommy. Was it possible that she also did not want to be away from Karl? And even, to some extent, that she was like a moth drawn to the flame of heated situations, as when she ran toward the sound of gunfire on Bloody Thursday?

If Elaine's primary motivation was truly to safeguard Tommy, then it's difficult to understand why she didn't argue more forcefully to be allowed to keep Tommy with her in Los Angeles, rather than insisting that she accompany him to Manzanar. In Los Angeles, she would have been able to care for both her children. Elaine would later look back on that time and say, "There was no thought in my mind of tying up the Army in Federal Court and maybe filing an injunction. It was a time of hysteria. It was a time of not knowing where to turn."[71] Of course, it's not possible to know whether Elaine would have had any success had she attempted to resist General DeWitt's exclusion order. But it's also impossible to imagine that a mother such as Elaine would simply deposit her young son on a train, handing him over to the care of others—even with the assurance of a children's village at the camp. In any case, she did not have much time to make the decision once the exclusion order had been issued. In the hectic situation, she responded in the only viable manner she could see, which was to insist that she go with Tommy to Manzanar. And so Elaine boarded the train bound for Manzanar along with her small son.

On the afternoon of April 1, Karl was cleaning a section of the camp when he was alerted to a group of buses arriving at the gate. Because he was part of the crew that had self-designated to help newcomers get settled, he headed toward the camp entrance. Before he knew it, he heard a familiar voice—Tommy, excited to see his father and running toward him, shouting, "Daddy! Daddy!" There was his son, together with Elaine. Karl was furious! Hadn't Elaine read his letter? Why had she ignored his concerns and brought Tommy to this place? Karl used "a few waterfront words" and asked Elaine, "Are you bringing our son to be killed?"[72] Elaine pulled a sheet of paper from her bag, the notice of DeWitt's exclusion order that required them to come, and told Karl he should read it before saying anything more. They read it together and wept. Elaine recounted her entire ordeal. Karl's anger dissolved as he understood the decision that Elaine had faced and the tenacity with which she had insisted on her right to be with her son and husband.[73]

Elaine joined Karl in the task of trying to make their surroundings more comfortable, or at least habitable. The Yonedas were assigned to a barrack with six other people, including one other white woman who was at camp. Elaine had reason to believe that the woman was a madam who had run a house with many Japanese clients before the war in Los Angeles. When she arrived, she had listed one of the Issei men present as her husband, though it was clear to others that it was not true. Elaine had interacted with prostitutes on the various occasions when she'd spent time in prison. Elaine was concerned that the woman would start a new business right out of the barracks to which they were assigned—she wasn't necessarily opposed to what the woman was doing in principle, but Elaine did not want her family to share living quarters with her. Indeed, this woman was later escorted out of the camp at gunpoint, because she had solicited some of the local white men who were working at the camp.[74]

In short order, Elaine made sure that the Yonedas were reassigned. They were now assigned to Block 4, Building 2, Apartment 2—known more simply as 4-2-2. They shared the space with a seventy-five-year-old man and his fifteen-year-old nephew. The latter two were overflow from the neighboring space, 4-2-1, which held the other members of their family. 4-2-2 consisted of one open room with five cots, initially equipped with straw mattresses. Tommy was allergic to straw, however, so Elaine was granted extra army blankets, which she folded up into a makeshift mattress. Still, Tommy reacted badly to being in such a small space with so much straw. Eventually, 4-2-1 was enlarged and the Yonedas were left to themselves in the remaining space, which measured about twenty by twenty feet—it was something of a luxury to have that amount of privacy, and Elaine, ever vigilant that she might be perceived as receiving special treatment because she was white, was aware that their circumstances provoked some jealousy. But she was willing to accept the resentment, since it was a matter of concern over Tommy's health.[75]

The Yonedas did the best they could to make the space comfortable. Karl built some furniture from scrap wood he gathered, as did others. At first there were no steps to the doors of any of the barracks—Elaine didn't know whether to laugh or cry at the sight of people's creative attempts to enter through doorways that hovered above the ground at the height of most people's shoulders. Eventually, wooden steps were erected at each entrance.[76] The Yonedas were also fortunate because, in contrast to other families who were incarcerated along with everyone they knew, Elaine's parents and many friends who were white and therefore had not been incarcerated could visit and bring them needed items. Elaine wrote her parents and asked for bedsheets, both to sleep on and to create makeshift partitions within their space to allow for at least a measure of privacy.[77] They also were able to maintain subscriptions to various newspapers, including the *San Francisco Chronicle* and the *People's World*, which gave them a window on events beyond camp. Eventually they also received a small electric stove and some extra pots, which enabled them to cook special food for Tommy to supplement what was served in the mess halls.[78]

In addition to straw, Tommy was allergic to wheat, dairy, potatoes, and other foods—much of what was served regularly, he could not eat. Elaine ordered special bread for him, which was sent by post from San Francisco, for the first few months. But as the weather turned hotter, the bread would arrive moldy, so they made do without it.[79] In camp, rice became a central staple of Tommy's diet. When the rare extra ration of sugar would become available, Karl and Elaine would use it to make a sweet rice dish for Tommy, in an attempt to compensate for the fact that the small boy could not enjoy the other treats the camp children occasionally received, such as cake or ice cream.

By far the biggest detriment to Tommy's fragile health, however, was the dust of the Owens Valley. The site of the camp had once been inhabited by Indigenous Peoples who grew apple orchards there, and was therefore named "Manzanar" by the Spaniards.[80] By the middle of the twentieth century it was hard to even imagine that lush fruit trees had once grown here— the valley had become desertified after the Los Angeles Aqueduct was completed in 1913, diverting most of the water from the Owens River to Los Angeles. The result for the inhabitants of the Owens Valley was a complete loss of livelihood, as they saw their once fertile lands become inarable. Much of the population had since left.

With nothing to protect the topsoil, the valley also became subject to intense dust storms. Elaine and Tommy experienced their first dust storm on their second day at camp. Dust would cover and infiltrate every surface, filling the air so thickly that "you'd stand in line and not be able to recognize the person in front of you or in back. You would just get coated. It seemed to adhere and it was thick and rocky sand." Elaine experienced new empathy for the "Dust Bowlers" she had met in her labor work—agricultural workers who had come to California to escape the dust storms of the Midwest.[81] The dust was a serious menace. Many who owned cars had driven to Manzanar so that they could bring as many of their belongings as possible. But they had been required to leave their vehicles outside of the camp's gates for the first few days. By the time they were granted permission to go retrieve items from their cars, just a couple of days after their arrival, they opened the doors to find everything covered in a layer of dust and the vehicles themselves damaged by the storms.

Tommy's health deteriorated quickly in these conditions. He had always had problems with health—in addition to asthma and the food allergies, he experienced severe eczema. Even prior to Manzanar, he had spent a good amount of his three short years in Stanford Hospital. At Manzanar, Tommy was often found in the camp hospital—as Elaine recalled, there were times when he would suddenly lose consciousness. In that first year, the Manzanar camp hospital was makeshift—not a full-fledged care facility.[82] Tommy was regularly dehydrated and required oxygen. Elaine feared that he would fall into a coma, such was the seriousness of his bouts of sickness, which would only years later be fully diagnosed as "internal hives." Karl and Elaine did all they could to keep dust out of 4-2-2 and tried to make it into something of a game—they named their ersatz home "Tommy's Dust-Out Inn" and hung a sign outside bearing this Wild West–sounding moniker.[83]

In addition to doing what they could to make their own quarters more comfortable, Elaine swung into action to implore the camp administration to improve conditions for others as well. The latrines were a particular problem, as there was no privacy, just a group of toilets in a space, though they were separated by gender. However, before the lumber was covered with tarpaper, there were holes and gaps that resulted in a rash of "Peeping Toms, which created some dissatisfaction and upheaval." Elaine felt somewhat accustomed to such circumstances, due to her experiences in prisons, but she could see that the teenage girls were particularly disturbed by the situation, especially when they were menstruating or when a case of the "Manzanar runs" would strike. Elaine marched to the administration building and pounded a desk, saying, "If you don't do something about it and get partitions in there, not only are you going to have mass hysteria, you're going to have mass suicides among the young girls."[84] The camp manager was initially unsympathetic. The latrines had been built to military regulations, he explained. Eventually Elaine convinced him, and partitions were built.[85]

Elaine and Karl lodged other complaints as well. There was a certain amount of mayhem caused by trucks and cars driving through camp with no directions or speed limits. Not only were they endangering the small children, but they also kicked up a lot of dust. They also noticed that the quality of food differed depending on who was assigned to cook duty for each bunk. Block 22 was known, early on, as a block with a particularly good mess hall.[86]

Despite the many privations, life settled into some routines by early summer. Films were occasionally screened in the evenings in the meeting hall. Early on, there were organized trips to the nearby town, Lone Pine, though these were discontinued when the town's inhabitants complained. Elaine took a job in the newly established camp library—she had worked in the small library at the back of her father's shop all those years ago so she had experience. She worked the night shift so that Karl could work during the day and they could take turns watching Tommy—it wouldn't be until much later in the year that schools and a kindergarten were established. Elaine earned a small income of $12 per month for her library work, which she used to buy supplemental food for Tommy and also to buy shoes for the family. Given the conditions at camp, everyone's shoes wore out very quickly.[87]

Elaine developed a few close female friendships in camp, as she had done prior to the war. Some of these friendships had begun outside of Manzanar, and some were developed after incarceration. Taeko Ariyoshi, who married Karl's old friend Koji while in camp, was one close friend. Yo Ukita was another. While Elaine did work many hours, there was also ample time for socializing. Elaine and others would visit each other's "apartments" and share the care packages they had received from the outside.[88] At the same time, however, Elaine's cultural background and personality could be very much at odds with the traditional Japanese roles for women, especially among the Issei. Elaine's outspoken and sometimes gruff nature could put others off in camp, although several young Japanese American women did express admiration for her bold confidence.[89]

21

Karl became active in camp politics, through forms of self-government as well as the more informal alliances that had quickly developed. Most of those incarcerated at Manzanar had come from the Los Angeles area; in keeping with this demographic fact, the spectrum of political perspectives and affiliations closely resembled that of the prewar Japanese American community in Los Angeles. Karl and Elaine identified most closely with those who had not opposed exclusion, making for odd bedfellows, as some of these, including members of the JACL, were individuals with whom the Yonedas had been at odds in Los Angeles. The JACL tended to include business owners; whether overtly antiunion or not, they were often at odds with the labor activists' groups with whom Elaine and Karl were affiliated.

There were those, too, who had strongly opposed and resisted incarceration, and a small handful of those who supported Japan and the Axis powers. Generational distinctions were related to adherence to these positions. The Issei tended to be isolationist because of the intense discrimination they had experienced in the United States, not least of which was their inability to legally apply for citizenship.[90] Many Issei felt keenly the contradiction of the fact that, though their immigration had been encouraged to fill the ranks of agricultural labor, they were barred from U.S. citizenship. This history fed their tendency to distrust the U.S. government.

By contrast, Nisei tended to be the most assimilated and the most trusting of the U.S. government. The children of Issei, they were citizens by virtue of having been born in the United States. Arthur Hansen argues that many Nisei saw themselves as the "selfless inheritors of America's democratic heritage." The JACL was made up largely of this group, and through this perspective "they justified their complicity in the relocation program by the belief that their efforts furthered the democratic cause."[91] JACL members were also likely to believe that cooperation with the government offered the opportunity to prove their loyalty and their capacity to act as Americans. The rhetoric of sacrifice was prevalent at this point in the war for many—everyone was expected to pitch in to the war effort. The JACL position invoked this rhetoric and, moreover, relied on the belief that short-term sacrifices would ensure a democratic and inclusive future, one in which they would play an equal part with others. Third were the Kibei, those born in the United States but who had been educated in Japan. Nisei tended to view the Kibei as "too Japanese." Though of the same generation, Kibei were more likely to be politically aligned with their Issei parents than other Nisei and less likely to be assimilated.

Of course, these overly broad generalizations had exceptions. Karl was one such exception, for though he was Kibei, his involvement with the labor movement in Japan set him apart ideologically from other Kibei; he had distanced himself quite clearly from mainstream Japanese political positions, and he was more assimilated than most Kibei. Indeed, he had married a white woman, a fact that his own brothers-in-law had criticized. Karl's politics made for strange bedfellows—his cooperation and collaboration with the JACL were surprising. Fred Tayama, for example, was a successful restaurateur who had a reputation for antiunion sentiment and for treating his workers badly. Indeed, the paper that Karl wrote for, *Doho*, had published articles decrying Tayama's antilabor practices.[92] And yet Karl expressed appreciation for Tayama's work with the JACL anti-Axis committee in Los Angeles prior to incarceration, and at Manzanar they became allies.[93]

Another commonality between Karl, other Japanese American leftists, and JACL members was that, because they had volunteered to go to Manzanar, they had arrived there first, ahead of other groups who came later after EO 9066. Put simply, the more one expressed opposition and resistance to the exclusion orders, the more likely one was to avoid going until absolutely necessary. Because the JACL and other cooperationists arrived first, and also because of their endorsement of the exclusion orders, this group held disproportionate influence in the early days of the camp. They often got the plum jobs and occupied roles that granted them a closer relationship with administrators and authorities.

Karl, for example, was able to put his editorial experience to good use, and he helped to establish the *Manzanar Free Press*, the first issue appearing on April 11, 1942. The *Manzanar Free Press* established the formal public sphere at camp; hence its editors initially held a lot of influence and political clout. Editorials were aimed at convincing those at Manzanar of the necessity of an Allied victory and loyalty to the United States and the necessity of fighting pro-Japan propaganda. The *Manzanar Free Press* editorial board also believed its duty was to convey the policies of the camp to those incarcerated there, to maintain peace and order. For these reasons, the paper was often viewed as a mouthpiece for the JACL and the camp administration. The *Manzanar Free Press* board did push back against camp administration at times—in particular, they argued for, and were granted, permission to publish a Japanese-language section, which had initially been forbidden. In addition to these types of pieces, the *Manzanar Free Press* also published articles on more mundane topics and even sponsored a garden contest.[94]

Shortly after Karl arrived, the administration set up a system of committees and appointments among the internees to act as liaisons for complaints and grievances. Karl and his circle welcomed the opportunity to participate in what was described to them as "self-government," and Karl was appointed the leader for Block 4, or "blockhead," as they were jokingly described. Meetings were held regularly, moving freely from English to Japanese, where Karl would listen to people's concerns and then relay them at the Block Leaders Council.[95] Those who had resisted exclusion and incarceration refused to take part in anything organized by the camp administration—whether it be self-government, paid employment working for the administration, or writing for the paper. Further, as time went on, active resistance was mounted by some in this group, which resulted in altercations that were regularly verbal but eventually became violent.

In July Karl took part in the formation of the Manzanar Citizens Federation, which operated in some ways like the JACL outside, as an advocacy group that interfaced with the camp administration. In fact, many of the Manzanar Citizens Federation leaders had been active in the JACL. The first meeting was conducted on the evening of July 20, 1942. Despite the 102-degree heat, more than 500 people showed up to hear presentations on various topics: how to improve camp conditions, how to educate citizens for leadership, effective ways to contribute to war efforts from camp, and postwar preparation for those incarcerated. A motion was presented to request that the U.S. government allow select Nisei to enlist in the armed forces.

More than 200 people signed a petition to that effect that was initiated that night and that would eventually be sent to President Roosevelt.[96]

The first meeting of the Manzanar Citizens Federation drew the ire of the camp resistance, among the most vocal of whom were Ben Kishi and Joe Kurihara. The two men heckled Karl as he spoke at the meeting on that hot July night. They shouted at him, "You *inu* (dog), spy, FBI informer and traitor. [Japan] will win, and hang you."[97] This was not the first time Karl had drawn such accusations—as early as the first night that he had been detained after the bombing of Pearl Harbor, people had accused him similarly. Was there any truth to these claims? Was Karl a spy or an informer?

At Manzanar, Karl and other cooperationists regularly wrote letters to the War Relocation Authority, informing them of "anti-American" behavior. While they had not opposed exclusion, they had argued all along for separate camps for those who were loyal to the United States and those whom they described as pro-Axis. The decision about which camp someone might choose should, in their opinion, be voluntary. It was a matter of urgent security. As Karl wrote to Dillon Myer, the national director of the War Relocation Authority, on August 10, 1942, "the government [must] provide every protection for those who are loyal to this country (regardless whether native or foreign born) and their families. As long as loyal Americans and pro-democratic persons are forced to stay in the same camp with pro-Axis elements their very lives are endangered."[98] Regional Director E. R. Fryer responded to Karl in September, writing

Dear Mr. Yoneda,

Although I acknowledged verbally Sunday the many fine reports I have received from you, I wish to take this opportunity to confirm, in writing, my appreciation for your continued interest in the Japanese-American problem and the work of the War Relocation Authority.

The wheels of Government are necessarily slow, but, in my judgment, they are, insofar as they relate to the Japanese-American problem, rolling in the right direction. Your reports are serving to point up thinking on the many faceted problems growing out of evacuation.[99]

Clearly, Karl and the WRA officials had been corresponding regularly, and it is reasonable to assume that the fact was known among the camp resistance. The camp was like a small town. Its inhabitants operated the camp services, including the post office—and they probably read incoming and outgoing mail, which the army did scrutinize. Keeping such an ongoing exchange secret would be unlikely.[100] In this sense, Karl *was* informing the WRA of opposition activity at camp, and the accusations against him were not unfounded.

The question of whether Karl and others should be described as informers or patriots could depend, though, on one's perspective. Another question could be asked: Were those who opposed Japanese American cooperation with the U.S. government during exclusion and incarceration heroes or fascists? Elaine and Karl painted these groups with a very broad brush, seeing them all as pro-Axis and anti-American. More realistically, there could be no simple answer to this question. There was a range of ways that people in camp resisted and demonstrated their opposition to incarceration—they ranged from more passive means, such as not participating in the self-government bodies that were established or not taking war-relief jobs in camp, to outright violence. It is important to respect and account for all the ways that people expressed opposition to the injustices they were experiencing. As Tad Uyeno wrote years later,

> The dissidents in camp I [call] "rebels," for the lack of a more definitive term. They were anti-administration, anti-JACL, anti-Establishment, in general. They protested their confinement in a concentration camp, first for being evacuated from their homes on the West Coast and then thrown into a desert prison camp. Whether or not they were "active pro-Japan supporters" as the metropolitan Los Angeles newspapers called them, I cannot say. But "rebels" they were.[101]

To describe as anti-American everyone who resisted the violation of their rights and the upending of their lives was not only overly broad, it was also instrumental in the efforts of cooperationists, who were intent on differentiating themselves and proving themselves to be patriots.

22

From the start, there were those who opposed the fact that the JACL and others, including Karl, had assumed leadership in camp and had become the voice of all those incarcerated at Manzanar to the camp administration. Over the ensuing months, several actions on the part of the camp administration and the federal WRA fomented this discontent, including barring non-U.S. citizens from camp leadership positions (leaving many Issei ineligible), demanding that all public meetings be held in English, disallowing Kibei from camp leave policies, and more.[102] Over time, opposition to such administration actions found several outlets, including the formation of a Kitchen Workers Union led by Harry Ueno, head of the Block 22 mess hall, and a full-fledged underground resistance movement. The latter operated under several names, including the Southern California Blood Brother Corporation and the Black Dragons.[103]

Karl and Elaine first encountered the Black Dragons in early May. The men, mostly Kibei, worked with trash collection and on repair crews, which gave them access to a garbage truck that they drove around camp adorned with a black pirate flag and another flag bearing the name "Black Dragon Association."[104] Over the ensuing months, the Black Dragons harassed Karl, Elaine, the Manzanar Citizens Federation, and anyone they believed to be supporting the U.S. war effort, in ways that became increasingly menacing and eventually bloody. In the eyes of the Yonedas, the Black Dragons were a group of menacing pro-Axis thugs who spread misinformation around the camp, including claims that the Japanese army would soon arrive in California and that the Allied forces had not, in fact, bombed Tokyo.[105] The Yonedas held very stark views; they tended to see black and white rather than nuance, and they saw anyone who mounted active resistance to being at Manzanar—whether in the form of civil disobedience or acts of outright sabotage—as members of the Black Dragons.

But Elaine and Karl were also viewed through a similarly simplistic lens. Over time, they both came to be held in deep contempt by those who had opposed Japanese American exclusion and incarceration. As Arthur Hansen has written, for the camp resistance, Karl "was a quintessential deviant, representative of all those characteristics the subculture abhorred."[106] Not only his cooperationist stance and allegiance to camp authorities but his past as a Communist was interpreted as an affront to Japanese cultural values and social cohesion. It certainly didn't help that Karl was married to an outspoken white woman. Even the manner in which they conducted their relationship was the source of derision, as Karl was often seen providing childcare to Tommy and doing the family's laundry, upsetting the expectations for gendered familial roles. Meanwhile, Harry Ueno's influence was growing—he was the hero to Karl's antihero.[107] Hansen notes that it is important to understand these polarizations as cultural as well as political, and they had their roots in similar factions that had developed among the Los Angeles Japanese

American community before the war. Divisions were, understandably, exacerbated in the conditions of living in such close quarters with inadequate services and severely limited civil liberties, and over time they would continue to be enflamed. Regardless of one's perspective, though, it is indisputable that Elaine and Karl were subject to harassment, threats, and violence.

War-relief work at Manzanar was one arena that brought debates and controversies over incarceration to a head. In June a factory was opened at Manzanar to produce camouflage netting for the U.S. military. Only U.S. citizens were eligible for the jobs, though few Issei would have accepted the jobs anyway.[108] Elaine eagerly volunteered, leaving her librarian job behind. Through this work, she felt that she "was doing something that . . . was going to help beat that damn enemy that I wanted to see eradicated and never able to raise its head again."[109] The work itself was grueling, not because it was difficult but because it was tedious, hot, and involved toxic materials. The orders would be given, along with the materials, to produce nets with various camouflage schemes—snow, desert, or whatever was needed. Strips of burlap were provided that had been treated with various dyes. The workers wore gauze masks in an attempt to avoid the fumes. The 120-degree weather made the work that much more difficult—workers took salt pills in an effort to avoid dehydration. Elaine was adept at the work, perhaps from her experience as a seamstress.[110] She quickly rose in the ranks and began earning $16 per month as a pattern maker—more than she had made in the library.[111]

The opening of the camouflage factory enraged the camp resistance, who posted flyers throughout the camp when the opening was announced, urging people not to work in the factory. Once the factory opened, its workers were harassed regularly. According to Karl, Ben Kishi and others egged on some teenagers, who began to throw rocks at the workers. Elaine was targeted several times and suffered from bruised legs and even came home once with a bloodied forehead. Karl and others had had enough. In addition to these assaults, Karl and Tokie Slocum had been sitting outside the Block 4 office one day when a group whom they identified as Black Dragon members swerved their truck to where the two men were sitting—had they not jumped out of the way, Karl was sure they would have been hit as the truck indeed ran over the steps where they had been sitting. Together with Koji Ariyoshi and Tom Yamazaki, Karl marched over to the administration building to lodge a complaint and demand that these "fascist hoodlums" be removed from the camp. Though they would later be forced to confront the violence directed toward Karl and others, at this point the administration did not seem overly concerned. Assistant camp manager Ned Campbell replied to Karl and the others, "You are all Japanese and will have to live together."[112] The racist assumption that Japanese Americans were undifferentiated persisted.

The hot summer wore on. Elaine's parents and Joyce came for visits, as did a few other friends. Elaine tried to get permission for her parents and Joyce to spend the night at camp so that they wouldn't have to drive from Los Angeles and back in one day, but her request was denied. A measles epidemic spread through the camp and, in early July, Tommy contracted the disease and was checked into the hospital. Tommy was often in the camp hospital, which was not well equipped, but Elaine appreciated the devotion of the doctors and nurses who worked there. July 15 was Karl's birthday—Elaine was able to buy some treats for the forty or so people who came to their "apartment" to celebrate. These included "[soda] pop, some Koolade [sic], crackers, cookies, cheese, peanut butter, deviled ham and tongue."[113] Elaine and Karl continued to write letters and circulate petitions to allow any citizen—including Japanese Americans—to join the military. They also pressed for the opening of a second front, in Asia.[114] Elaine and Karl made a point of obtaining absentee ballots and voting by mail in the California elections held that summer. On July 27 Elaine developed a burning rash on her forearms from working with the netting material, for which she would eventually be hospitalized.[115]

July 27, 1942, was also Joyce's fifteenth birthday. Elaine marked the day, as she did every year. To this point, she had still spent fewer birthdays with her daughter than she had without her. A photograph taken exactly one month earlier shows Elaine, Karl, and Tommy with Elaine's friend from the days of Central Valley organizing, Happy Brannan, and Joyce, who were visiting them in the camp. The group is assembled for the photo in the scrubby desert at the edges of camp, the high mountains looming in the background. Karl is in the center, his arms on the shoulders of his small son. Happy is to his left, Elaine to his right. Joyce's hand is on her mother's shoulder, and she peers toward the camera from between her mother and stepfather. Elaine and Happy are the only two who even attempt a smile. Joyce's expression is neutral. Elaine's daughter, her first child, appears in this photo much as she does throughout Elaine's story—present, but in the background, absent any indication of her affect. Elaine's daughter's hand on her shoulder seems to indicate affection, but Joyce is nevertheless sidelined in this story. By contrast, Tommy is front and center. He stands resolutely, a small child who in some way seems to be aware that his presence is the reason that this story has unfolded in this way.

Two key events occurred on August 6. First, that morning Karl heard the announcement that Colonel Kai Rasmussen of the Military Intelligence Service Language School was coming to Manzanar and would be interviewing candidates at 10:00 a.m. At last! An opportunity appeared to be opening to allow Nisei to enlist. Karl was interviewed, along with others, in Japanese and told that a more formal recruiting team would be sent soon. Elaine and Karl's moods brightened at the prospect that Karl would, finally, be able to help fight in the war. In total, ninety men were interviewed. A few Kibei hung around outside the door, glaring at those who entered.[116]

That evening, the Manzanar Citizens Federation held its second meeting, with more than 300 people in attendance. Tensions were high because of the presence of the camouflage net factory and the visit that morning of the army recruiter. After the meeting started, Joe Kurihara made a motion, suggesting that the name of the Manzanar Citizens Federation be changed to the Manzanar Welfare Federation because those at camp "were being reduced to welfare recipients whose citizenship meant nothing." Many agreed with Kurihara's statement—his motion was defeated, but by a very narrow margin. The meeting moved on to the agenda at hand, which was to approve the proposed bylaws and agenda for the Manzanar Citizens Federation. Again, Kurihara raised objections, moving that the bylaws and agenda were pro-American. As Karl would later recall, "the meeting that night was a bloodless battle of words and ideas between the pro-Japan elements and the pro-democracy advocates."[117] Camp sentiment seemed to be shifting away from support for the cooperationists who had early on taken a lead role in the self-governing bodies.

In response to their defeat at that second Manzanar Citizens Federation meeting, a group of Kibei, led by Kurihara and Ben Kishi, obtained permission to hold a follow-up meeting about their concerns a few days later. Again, more than 300 people were present, but even more stood outside, hearing the speeches over loudspeaker. The camp police were present, indicating that it was no secret that the meeting would be tense. Karl was invited to speak and had accepted; it was under this pretext that Ned Campbell had given permission for the meeting to take place. Karl would later regret his decision, once he understood that he had been set up for a barrage of criticism. Kurihara and Kishi opened the meeting, speaking in Japanese. A group of others spoke and presented two motions, both of which passed: to stop work on the camouflage nets and to pledge noncooperation with the camp administration. Finally, it was Karl's turn to speak, but he did so to shouts of "FBI dog" and "traitor to Japan." At that point, Kishi was told by authorities to adjourn the meeting, and camp police escorted Karl back to 4-2-2.[118]

Factional disputes within Manzanar were intensifying and, at last, the administration was taking notice. On August 10, 1942, Karl and other Manzanar Citizens Federation leaders met with Camp Director Roy Nash, and together they agreed to several terms that the Manzanar Citizens Federation group believed would ensure calm. Nash agreed to "1) ban all meetings in Japanese that lacked simultaneous translation; 2) to call in the FBI to investigate the known pro-Japan militarist elements; 3) to ask Dillon Myer, National Director of the War Relocation Authority, to establish a Hearing Board in every camp to screen out the disloyal elements and remove them to a separate camp; and 4) to provide more defense work in the camp at prevailing wage rates."[119] Meanwhile, Elaine, Karl, and others continued to regularly have epithets hurled at them when walking around camp. Karl was called "*inu*," "FBI dog," and "Korean dog" and Elaine was called "*keto baba*" or "old foreign hag." Even little Tommy did not escape the name-calling. Moreover, in a new election, Karl was ousted from his post as block captain, replaced by H. Higuchi, an Issei who had a history of siding with the camp resistance.[120] By this point in the summer, Karl was disliked by many at camp. Because Elaine was regularly in lockstep with Karl, the opprobrium extended to her as well. The early authority that Karl, the JACL, and other cooperationists had enjoyed at Manzanar had quickly faded away.

23

The antagonisms continued; meanwhile Karl continued to find ways to support the war effort. In late August, as part of the Work Furlough Committee of the Manzanar Citizens Federation, he took part in a campaign that collected nearly 800 signatures among those incarcerated at Manzanar stating their willingness to participate in the Food for Freedom Campaign. The campaign addressed the desperate need for farmworkers to ensure the wartime success of crops throughout Idaho, Montana, Utah, and elsewhere. These parts of the country had been severely depleted of workers after the removal of Japanese Americans, who had comprised a significant majority of farm labor in the region. The Work Furlough Program also paved the way for the military's eventual acceptance of Nisei enlistees. In some ways, it was used as a testing ground for Niseis' claims that they wanted to support the war effort and as a testament to their patriotism.[121]

The U.S. government agreed to the leave program, and in total several thousand workers left camps on temporary work permits.[122] A particular focus was on sugar beets, not only because there was a shortage of sugar but the crop was also used in the production of military explosives.[123] The Work Furlough Committee provided for men in the camps who were willing to go on furlough to work the fields where assistance was needed. Eight hundred men and women left for Idaho from Manzanar in September to top (remove the leaves from) sugar beets. Many more would follow—including Karl later that year, in October, under a one-month labor contract. Those who signed up to go were subjected to threats from members of the Black Dragons, who asserted that anyone who supported the U.S. war effort would surely be punished when the Imperial Japanese Army won the war.[124]

Karl would have joined an earlier group to Idaho, but in mid-August Elaine received word that Joyce had run away from Molly and Nathan's home in Los Angeles. She received a frantic and urgent request from Molly to help her find the teenager. Elaine applied for a leave, which was granted to her. She traveled to Los Angeles with two camp officials and from there took the train to San Francisco. The rumors began flying immediately that Elaine was leaving Karl and that she was invoking her privilege as a white woman to leave camp.[125]

While looking for Joyce in San Francisco, Elaine took advantage of the time to visit old friends. She was given some gifts that she would bring back to camp, including a Victrola and a record album of Paul Robeson's. Elaine's former neighbor, who had driven Elaine to pick up Karl from the detention center back in December when he had first been arrested at the waterfront, drove Elaine to the Tanforan evacuation assembly center, where she visited friends who had not yet been assigned to camps. They compared notes on their experiences—Elaine described life at Manzanar, and her friends conveyed the uncertainty of being held for months in horse stables. She also spoke to the National Lawyers' Guild, who asked her about statements she had made saying that life in the camp was not terrible.[126] In response, Elaine told them,

> I had hoped there would be more war work, so that we could finish the war in a hurry and do away with Axis. I also told them that we couldn't equate these camps to the Hitler camps and their ovens; they weren't anything like that. There was restriction. I felt that they should pay union wages for union work. There should be clothing allowances, and things like that, but I said, "We can't condemn them altogether."[127]

Many were surprised that Elaine would still not speak out against exclusion and incarceration and that she would minimize the poor living conditions at Manzanar.

It took Elaine and Molly three weeks to find Joyce. It's not clear where they looked or how they found her. When they did find her, she was "shacked up with a sailor," as the family described the situation when telling the story for years to come.[128] Though only fifteen years old, Joyce had lied and told the man that she was older. She was put in a juvenile hall for evaluation. Molly stayed in San Francisco until Joyce was released and took her back to Los Angeles on September 26.[129] Once again, Joyce's grandmother was more of a parent to her than was Elaine, who returned to Manzanar on September 15, stopping off first in Los Angeles to visit other relatives.[130] Was Joyce a cause of concern for Elaine? Elaine herself had been a rebellious teenager and young adult, and so perhaps she related to her daughter's quest for independence. Her leave to San Francisco seemed to be for her as much a break from life at Manzanar and a time to check in with friends as it was a time to be worried about the direction of her daughter's life.

Back at Manzanar, Elaine resumed her job in the camouflage net factory, but she soon had to take a leave from the job because Tommy had become quite ill. She had thought she would return to the job once Tommy recovered some, but then Karl decided to join the contract workers in Idaho. He had been reluctant to do so, because he expected the army recruiters to return and he definitely wanted to be there upon their return. But his friend Koji convinced him to come join him, and so Elaine quit her job to take care of Tommy full time. Soon Elaine had a new job, working in the kindergarten that had been set up—it was adjacent to the nursery school where Tommy could spend his days, and so Elaine could keep an eye on him.[131]

Karl left for Idaho on October 6. Once he arrived, Karl went to the sheriff and demanded protection—the sheriff assured Karl that local farmers would view them as patriotic and not harm them. Contradictory reactions to their presence were felt all around, however. On the one hand, the owners of the farm, the Cobbs, took Karl and a few others out for a steak dinner and a movie. On the other hand, a crew member was refused a haircut in town and, when the group had arrived earlier at the Reno Railway station, they overheard women in USO uniforms making disparaging, racist remarks. Nevertheless, overall those from Manzanar were happy to be earning more money than they could in camp and to be enjoying a brief respite from the far less pleasant housing circumstances back at camp. Karl and others enjoyed meeting hundreds of Nisei men and women who were commuting from nearby Minidoka Relocation Center to work the fields as well. Once the contract was completed, the group stopped on the way back in Bishop, California, for breakfast, about fifty miles north of Manzanar. The waitress initially refused their business, telling the bus driver, "We don't serve J**s." The driver was able to convince her that those on board had just come from contributing to the war effort, and eventually they were served in the restaurant.[132] The conflicting attitudes toward Japanese Americans persisted; their labor was valued as a contribution to the war effort, but many saw them as an enemy and a threat.

Karl was back at Manzanar by November 18. Elaine had urged him to hurry back because there was word that the recruiters might be coming back to Manzanar soon.[133] Life continued in the camp—Elaine worked at the kindergarten when she could, but Tommy suffered from many bouts of illness during this period, and so Elaine was often home with him. Now that Elaine was not working on net production, and moreover often spent whole days in 4-2-2 caring for Tommy, harassment against them diminished. A new beauty salon opened and Elaine had her hair done there.[134] Meanwhile, Elaine got word from her parents that Joyce had once again disappeared from Elaine's parents' house. When she was found, it turned out that she had gotten married, having given her age as twenty.[135]

On November 23 Karl received word from the camp administration that the recruiters from the Military Intelligence Service would be back at camp within the week. Karl sent a telegram to Koji, who was still in Idaho and who was as eager as Karl to enlist, urging him to return to Manzanar immediately. When Koji arrived, Karl spent many hours helping his friend brush up on his Japanese-language skills. Both men knew that language proficiency would be important to the Military Intelligence Service, since they needed translators for the intelligence work; Koji had grown up in Hawai'i and spoke what Karl described as a kind of "pidgin-Japanese." Meanwhile, the Black Dragons posted flyers urging people not to volunteer for the U.S. military.[136]

The recruiting team arrived, and about fifty Nisei and Kibei men lined up at the recruitment hall. Physical, oral, and written tests were administered to them. Although Karl had no previous military experience, his language proficiency yielded him a very high score.[137] Fourteen of these men, including Karl and Koji, qualified and were immediately sworn in as buck privates.[138] The Yonedas were elated, as were Elaine's parents, who had come to visit because Elaine had told them there was a chance Karl would be leaving soon.[139] The family had a small celebration. Sometime after midnight, after everyone had settled into bed for the night, Karl realized that some people were lurking about outside their barrack. He immediately sent one of the boys from the adjoining barrack to notify a friend, who showed up with a baseball bat. The pair sent the would-be attackers away. Karl complained to the camp police, who promised support. For the next few nights, a group of friends took turns staying with the Yonedas, concerned for their safety.[140]

Karl left Manzanar on December 2, headed for training at Fort Snelling. It had been nearly one whole year since the bombing of Pearl Harbor and a little more than eight months since Karl had first arrived at Manzanar. Friends and family gathered to say goodbye and wish them well. Tommy yelled out, "Daddy, take me with you, I'll help you shoot Nazis!"[141]

Karl and the thirteen other recruits traveled first to Los Angeles, then to Minnesota, accompanied by two army sergeants. In Los Angeles, Karl's in-laws and other white friends showed up at the train station to send him off with best wishes. Karl and Koji were able to spend an evening with the Buchmans and enjoy one of Molly's home-cooked meals. On their way to the train station, they stopped at a five-and-dime store to pick up some toiletries. The saleswomen were surprised to see them—"Look," said one, "here come a bunch of J**s!" Karl and Koji had not yet received their uniforms. It took some time to convince the police and FBI agents who had arrived that they were members of the U.S. Army, skeptical as those officials were that the U.S. military would allow Japanese Americans to enlist and, perhaps, doubtful of the capacity for Japanese Americans to be patriotic. Eventually, they convinced everyone and the FBI agents escorted the two privates to the train station.[142]

While Karl was on his way to Fort Snelling, Elaine had made the decision that she and Tommy would not accompany Karl to Minnesota. Instead, she applied for a permit to leave camp and take Tommy with her to San Francisco because of concern for their safety after the threats against the families of those who had enlisted. She met with Ned Campbell, who asked her, "Why don't you go to Minnesota?" Pressing her further, he asked why she was always "trying to put stumbling blocks up," referring to Elaine's penchant for not accepting things as they were. Elaine replied, "Look, Tommy and I weren't going to come to *this* place. Those were not our plans. My plans do *not* include following my husband into army camp! I want to do war work! I want *out*! I want a place where I know my son can have adequate housing and care."[143] Clearly, Elaine had had enough of Manzanar. Tommy's health had continued to worsen, physically as well as psychologically—he experienced a lot of stress from his father leaving. He was constantly in and out of the hospital with diarrhea, fever, and dehydration. Elaine was also convinced that Karl would be assigned overseas in short order, and she did not see the wisdom of making the long trek to Minnesota where she knew no one. Surely, Elaine reasoned, Karl's enlistment should be proof of their loyalty to the United States and the least they could get in return was permission to leave camp. But the most pressing argument and, as it turned out, the most convincing was the need to escape the escalated threats of violence against the Yonedas. The administration began the process of applying for a permit for Tommy to leave. The first step was to have his photograph taken. Elaine was told that the permit would take a minimum of thirty days to process; she rightly feared that a month would be too long for them to avoid any violence.[144]

24

On December 4, Fred Tayama returned to Manzanar after he had attended the national JACL convention in Salt Lake City. He was there in his capacity as the representative of Manzanar. The next day, Tayama was severely beaten and subsequently hospitalized. Some in the camp resistance movement were angered that Tayama would be put in the position to speak for everyone at camp, and they were further angered that he had been allowed to leave camp for the conference. Many had always found Tayama to be ostentatious about his wealth. More egregious, he was believed to have collaborated with the FBI on the arrests they had made in Los Angeles after the attack on Pearl Harbor.[145]

Camp authorities arrested three Kibei for the assault, including Harry Ueno, president of the Kitchen Workers Union at the camp. Ueno was taken to the jail in nearby Independence, California. There was already a sense of unrest at Manzanar. Many were enraged that the military had enlisted fourteen camp residents who subsequently departed. Recruitment had taken place at other camps as well, and recruits at other locations, including the Jerome Relocation Center in Arkansas and Poston Relocation Center in Arizona, saw violence as a result. Other Nisei pushed back against the JACL's participation in the enlistment of Japanese Americans, stating that they would consider joining the military if their rights as U.S. citizens were first returned to them.[146]

The authorities were clearly aware of this anger toward the new recruits, who were escorted out of camp by military police officers (MPs) under cover of darkness to avoid any problems. Ueno's arrest was, for many, a last straw. Ueno had filed accusations against some camp administrators who were believed to have been selling food that was intended for camp—meat and sugar—on the black market for their own profit. Ueno's supporters claimed that Ueno's accusations were the real cause of his arrest and removal from camp, not the beating of Tayama, especially when there was no incontrovertible proof that Ueno was involved.[147]

Early the next day, December 6, about 200 people gathered at Block 22 in Ueno's mess hall to strategize on how to compel the authorities to return Ueno to Manzanar. They discussed several options, including staging a kitchen strike, or even a general strike of all services at camp. They planned a second meeting for later that day, at 1:00 p.m. By that time, word had spread, and a huge crowd appeared for the second meeting—by some accounts, there were as many as 2,000 people assembled and the group had to move outside. Impassioned speeches were delivered by Joe Kurihara and others, mostly in Japanese.[148]

Elaine noticed the gathering as she was taking Tommy to the administration building to check on Tommy's leave permit. She stopped to listen. She couldn't understand much, since the speeches were in Japanese, but she distinctly heard the name "Yoneda" spoken multiple times. She asked someone she knew what was being said and was told that the speaker had clearly said, "If Karl Yoneda was here we would kill him!"[149] She was told that Kurihara and others had developed a death list, on which were the names of the enlistees as well as other cooperationists, including Tayama and Tokie Slocum.[150] Then Satoru Kamikawa, a reporter for the *Manzanar Free Press*, told Elaine, "Get back to your apartment as quickly as possible, don't even go out for meals. They almost killed Fred Tayama last night and they are aiming to get even with Karl though he has temporarily escaped from their grip by going into the U.S. Army! They say and keep pointing out that Yoneda's son and wife are still here and we'll get him through them. Please go—go fast!"[151]

Elaine grabbed Tommy. They first ran to the camp police and demanded protection, which they were promised. They then rushed back to 4-2-2, and Elaine locked herself and Tommy in. They remained indoors all day, skipping the evening meal. Yo Ukita, a devoted friend, came over and brought them some food. She wanted to stay with them but she couldn't, she explained, because her father forbade her from doing so because of threats the family had received about associating with the Yonedas. Outside there was growing commotion. Sometime after dinner, Elaine could hear the constant loud banging of kitchen implements coming from the Block 4 mess hall and shouts of "Strike! Strike!"[152] After midnight, Elaine realized that her neighbors, the Itos, whose barrack faced her own, were crying loudly, evidently in much anguish. Elaine instructed Tommy to be still and not turn on any lights and then went over to see what was going on. "I heard the horrifying news that their youngest son, James . . . was shot and killed by an MP as he headed to his administration night job."[153] The Itos asked Elaine to leave, fearful that her presence would attract attention from the crowds.[154]

About 4:00 a.m., Elaine decided she must do something. The additional protection she had requested had not materialized. She dressed Tommy hurriedly, creating the appearance that he was a girl by tying a scarf on his head, and the two ran toward the administration building. An MP stopped them, demanded to know what they were doing, and shone a flashlight in Elaine's face. Surprised to see this white woman, he listened to her explanation. "I'm married to a soldier but not anyone stationed here. He's in Minnesota. I want to go to the administration building. I want protection for our son. He's been threatened all day, and there have been men gathering around our barrack. . . . I asked for police protection but I haven't gotten it." Finally, Elaine and Tommy were escorted into the building, where they were surprised to see about sixty people on cots that had been set up. Apparently, they too had feared for their safety and the administration had offered them shelter. On seeing Elaine and Tommy, Ned Campbell said, "Oh, I forgot to send you protection." Elaine answered acerbically, "You forgot. Thanks."[155]

A few short hours later reveille was sounded. It was now December 7, 1942—the one-year anniversary of the bombing of Pearl Harbor, and Manzanar had erupted into a full-scale revolt. Elaine and the others who were gathered in the administration building did not yet know the full scope of what had been going on in the camp.

The previous day, after the speeches that had sent Elaine and Tommy back to their block, the demonstrators had formed a five-person committee to negotiate with the camp administration. The administration agreed to bring Ueno back to camp but said they would hold him in the camp jail. In return, the committee agreed not to hold further demonstrations. But the five men were unable to control the crowd, and by that evening, the rally had grown to thousands more. The crowd broke up into groups to attack those on the death list and a group to break Ueno out of the camp jail. Violence ensued. The camp administration had brought MPs in, who were now using tear gas and, for reasons that would never become clear, shooting into the crowd to try to control the chaos. In addition to the murder of James Ito the night prior, Jim Kanagawa, a twenty-one-year-old man from Tacoma, had been badly injured and would die a few days later in the camp hospital, having been caught in gunfire not directed toward him. Nine more were seriously wounded.[156]

Elaine didn't know these details and also did not yet know that newspapers had reported the events of the previous thirty-six hours, publishing sensational stories about a "Manzanar Riot."[157] The *San Francisco Chronicle*, for example, carried a front-page story describing the events as a "pro-Axis uprising" that was allegedly staged as an "anniversary celebration of the Pearl Harbor attack."[158] Karl saw one of these headlines shortly after he arrived at Fort Snelling, and Elaine's parents read what had happened in their paper in Los Angeles. Their concern for Elaine and Tommy grew as they wired the camp but got no news in return.[159] When Elaine did learn that the events had made it into the papers, she requested that a telegram be sent to her parents, letting them know that she and Tommy were okay.[160]

Elaine and the others who had slept in the administration building were moved over to the MP section of the camp, where they spent the day and ate their meals. At night, they were brought back to the administration building, still set up with cots for them, as there wasn't adequate space in the MP area to house them all. Elaine alternated between concern for her friends whom she did not see among those gathered—particularly Koji's wife, Taeko Ariyoshi, who was pregnant—and concern for Tommy, who had just gotten out of the hospital. "The dust was raging," recalled Elaine, "and it got very, very cold."[161] After three days of being shuffled back and forth in this way, Elaine was driven to her barrack by armed guards to gather some belongings—she and Tommy, along with the others who had been under protection, were to be evacuated from the camp.

On December 10, 1942, the group that was evacuated from the camp was relocated to an abandoned Civilian Conservation Corps camp in Death Valley. The living conditions were quite poor—buildings were in a state of disrepair, with broken windows and no intact sanitary facilities. But the group, which had bonded during their ordeal, was happy to be away from Manzanar and the violence. They cleaned up their quarters as best they could.[162] Elaine urged the administration to speed up the process for Tommy's travel permit—his health was deteriorating further in Death Valley, and Elaine was more than ever eager to get back to San Francisco. Others had left. Some family members of the recruits had gone with them to Minnesota; others went wherever else they had family. Elaine learned that someone else's permit had been rushed through, while Tommy's still sat on the desk of the camp administrator. Finally, on December 15, Tommy's permit came through. Elaine prepared to take him to San Francisco.[163]

Elaine would have one final insulting encounter with the camp administration before leaving. Ned Campbell met with Elaine, together with

E. R. Fryer, regional director of the War Relocation Authority, to give Elaine her validated permit, which was accompanied by detailed instructions. Elaine was required to submit a report each month "attesting to the fact that Tommy had or had not been in any fight because of his ancestry [and] had done nothing to endanger national security." Tommy had recently turned four years old, and Elaine thought it laughable that the authorities could really fear that her small son was capable of "endangering national security." Even more outrageous, Tommy was "always to be with his mother or a Caucasian escort." Elaine could not keep quiet in relation to this last requirement, which, in addition to being absurd, was impractical, and Elaine feared she was being led into a trap.

"What does this mean?" Elaine asked Campbell, pointing to the phrase "Caucasian escort."

"Why are you raising obstacles? Why don't you just take it and let it be?" replied Campbell.

"I'm not raising obstacles. I don't want to get entrapped." Elaine reminded Campbell that she intended to find a job and explained that her closest friends in San Francisco were her Filipino neighbors, who very well might be the ones to watch Tommy during the day. "If Tommy [were to spend time] with any of our Chinese, Filipino, or Negro friends, would he be in violation of his right to be in Military Area One?" asked Elaine.

Campbell pressed further, "you always ask unnecessary questions."

Elaine replied, "Not unnecessary; I'm just trying to avoid any misunderstandings that might lead to his return to a concentration camp." With that, Fryer tore up the instructions, and said never mind. But he did make her promise to report any address changes and file monthly reports on Tommy's behavior.[164]

On December 17, Elaine left Death Valley, stopping in Lone Pine first to buy new shoes. She and Tommy boarded a bus for Los Angeles, even though she had not yet been in touch with her parents. She reached them at a stop in Saugus, California, and they met her and Tommy at the Los Angeles bus station. The next day she wrote in her diary "Still shaky, but thrilled."[165] At last, Tommy, Elaine, and Karl had all left Manzanar.

PART V

San Francisco and Penngrove

25

Elaine and Tommy returned to San Francisco after spending some time with her parents. She found them a room to live in, which was not easy in the current housing shortage—over the previous year, people had streamed into California for the plentiful wartime jobs. The room was in a mansion owned by a longshoreman; a friend of Karl's had been planning to use it as an office, but he agreed to rent it to Elaine. There was a shared kitchen that she could use. Elaine was able to find work in a Hills Brothers coffee plant, "working the belt line," jarring coffee. The workers rotated through the various positions so they wouldn't repeat the exact same tasks all day.[1]

Karl and Elaine wrote to each other nearly every day. Elaine was always sure to include some of Tommy's drawings. But Elaine did not share with Karl the full extent of Tommy's health problems, for she did not want to worry him. During the year after they left Manzanar, Tommy spent more time in hospitals than out of them, mostly at the Stanford University Hospital. In addition to his allergies, the doctors suspected that he had rheumatic fever, and he was diagnosed with internal hives. The commute to see him put an additional strain on Elaine, although it did alleviate her childcare issues. Slowly, Tommy's nightmares and fears eased. By February, Elaine did share with Karl that Tommy "no longer cries or gets scared when Manzanar is mentioned. . . . He used to tell me . . . that he did not like Manzanar because there were Nazis there."[2]

Early in spring, Karl learned that he was entitled to a four-day furlough at Easter, and so he wrote to Elaine and asked whether she would bring Tommy to Minnesota for a visit. The costs of such a trip would be a challenge, but the Red Cross did offer loans for families to travel to see those in the military. Karl inquired about a loan from his captain. "Your wife, Elaine Black, is a well-known Communist," was his captain's reply, and the request was denied—the captain was not keen on having Elaine on site, for fear she'd stir up trouble. Elaine was able to borrow the money from a friend instead, but she faced another challenge. She did not have enough leave time from her job at Hills Brothers; if she left, she could not be certain her job would be there upon her return. Elaine decided to take the risk, for she wasn't thrilled with her position at Hills Brothers—she would prefer to do office work, which she had experience with, and she still hoped to work in a more directly war-related industry.[3]

Finally, in April, the arrangements had been made and Elaine and Tommy took the three-day train ride to Minnesota. She had obtained permission to take Tommy out of state from the military, to whom she continued to send reports about Tommy's behavior.[4] On the visit, they saw Karl in uniform for the first time—how proud they were! The three posed for a photograph together. The dust and worry of the time in Manzanar appeared to have been washed away. The threesome appears young and vibrant in the photograph, all smiling confidently. In photographs from Manzanar, Elaine regularly appeared in a simple shift; here, she is dressed as sharply as before the war, with a smart dress and jacket, lipstick perfect, and a stylish hat tipped jauntily to the side. Little Tommy is in a boy's version of his father's uniform. Elaine and Karl are triumphant; they had finally succeeded in convincing the military of their patriotism and seem nearly relieved to be able to contribute to the war effort in this way, as a family.

The family spent four happy days together. Karl and Elaine didn't have any sense of when they would see each other next, so they made the most of their time.[5] After she arrived home, Elaine wrote to Karl, saying, "I shall cherish our furlough, it was memorable for me also and your closeness warmed me and will keep me warm until we can be together again and raise our darling son together in a democratic world."[6]

Back in San Francisco, Elaine was able to find a new job with the United Electrical Radio Workers Union, which had contracts with General Cable, General Electric, Westinghouse, and others. The contracts were war-related, and Elaine would be doing clerical work in the union office—familiar ground, and less physically demanding than the factory work had been. The position had an additional advantage—though it was in Oakland, a fairly distant commute from San Francisco, a childcare center had been established just three blocks from the office for mothers who were engaged in war work. Her hours started a bit later, which meant she would have time to drop Tommy off before arriving at the office.[7] It was not an easy life—Elaine worked long days, and by the time she and Tommy got home and had dinner and she had tucked Tommy in for the night, Elaine had just a few hours to read the paper, listen to the radio, or write to Karl. She also regularly took some work home with her, for which she was paid overtime rates.[8]

26

Karl's studies in the Military Intelligence Service at Fort Snelling
were drawing to a close. He graduated on June 18, 1943, and was then sent to
Camp Shelby, Mississippi, for basic training. This was Karl's first visit to the
U.S. South, and he was shocked by the world of Jim Crow that he encountered, from his very first train trip to Mississippi. He and his fellow Nisei soldiers had settled themselves in on a train car when an MP came through
their car and instructed them to move to the "Whites Only" car. One of Karl's
friends said, "We are not white, can't we stay here?" The MP replied, "This section is for 'Colored Only.' Now move. That's an order!" Karl would recall later
that "during our short stay in Mississippi, we had a glimpse of the oppressed
lives of Negroes and poor whites to whom we talked. They were civilian main-
tenance crews, who had never seen 'yellow' men before and were bewildered.
They asked, 'Why are you fighting for Roosevelt's country?'" As a CPUSA
member, Karl had participated in campaigns to champion the rights of African Americans in the South and had met several luminaries of this community who had come through San Francisco. But this firsthand encounter with
southern race relations brought realities of American racism into sharp relief.
While in the South, he and his fellow Nisei soldiers learned that they were
not "colored," but were they white? As they prepared to go fight for the United States, they read in the papers of signs posted in a California town that read,
"We don't want J**s back here ever!" Somehow, they decided, they had to put
these complex questions and anxieties aside and focus on getting on active
duty.[9]

Once Karl and the others had returned to Fort Snelling after they completed their basic training, the long wait to be assigned commenced. In mid-
August Karl received a furlough to San Francisco, and was overjoyed to see
not only Elaine and Tommy but many of his old friends as well. By December 7, 1943, the second anniversary of the bombing of Pearl Harbor, Karl
had still not received his assignment. Karl and his fellow Nisei soldiers
became jittery and began to wonder whether the army did really intend to
assign them at all. Finally, on December 15, there was some progress—they
received their movement orders. The first step was to pack up and go to Camp
Anza near Los Angeles. After nearly one year waiting for this time, Karl
wrote, "it is impossible to describe our sense of overwhelming relief and the
ensuing hustle and bustle in preparation to get going." Of course, being
assigned to Camp Anza had an added benefit: being on the outskirts of Los
Angeles meant that Elaine and Tommy could visit more easily. The family

spent time together during Christmas at Molly and Nathan's home. Karl got to enjoy Molly's Jewish cooking once again.[10]

On January 12, 1944, Karl sailed from the United States on a ship bound for Calcutta, India. After a long voyage, he was flown to New Delhi, where he received his instructions to join the Office of War Information Psychological Warfare Team. He would be stationed in the village of Ledo, at the edge of Assam tea plantations in India. Ledo was the starting point for the Ledo Road, built by the military during the war to convey supplies to China via Burma. He met the other linguists attached to his unit—soldiers fluent in Chinese and Burmese, including the two Burmese languages of Kachin and Shan.[11]

Karl's first assignment was to write a Japanese surrender leaflet, which was then air-dropped into Burma. He also started and edited a Japanese-language war newspaper, *Senjin Shimbun*, which was used to provide the Allies' version of war news to the Japanese. Another project was the writing and production of flyers aimed at wounded Japanese soldiers. They had heard from prisoners of war that Japanese soldiers were dying from lack of medical care. The flyers included photos of Japanese prisoners of war being treated well by Allied forces and encouraged wounded Japanese soldiers to surrender, as they would receive full medical care from the Allies as mandated by international law.[12]

In July Karl and others were sent to Myitkyina, site of what would be an important Allied victory in opening the Ledo Road. It would be Karl's assignment closest to the front. Here he beheld his first view of a battlefield strewn with dead soldiers—Japanese and American. The sight made an indelible impression. Karl's assignment was broadcast duty. "One of my Caucasian GI escorts hoisted a loudspeaker up about ten feet into the foliage of a teak tree facing the enemy line located behind a bamboo grove five hundred yards away."[13] Through this loudspeaker, the U.S. Army broadcast Japanese music to arouse the interest of its listeners and then had soldiers such as Karl read prewritten messages encouraging surrender. Ironically, though, those who wrote these messages were forbidden to include any antiemperor statements. Rather, the rhetoric of the messages appealed directly to the Japanese soldiers' loyalty, while encouraging them not to die needlessly, with statements such as "Those who truly understand loyalty to the Emperor—those who understand filial piety and love of the real Japan, those who have pity for their parents and love for their wives and children—they must not die!" Finally, Karl was right at the front lines, encouraging the enemy to surrender, yet he was frustrated by his instructions not to state his beliefs, opposing fascism and the Imperial Japanese Army. Karl also evidently understood that his missions included some measure of futility. As he would later recall, "Though this method resulted in few direct surrenders, those soldiers who did surrender to us said, 'The [radio] programs were a breath of fresh air to all listeners and the flyers were very useful for toilet needs.'"[14]

Conditions were not easy in Burma. Karl's work was propaganda, which he conducted in the trenches alongside combat soldiers.[15] Insects were ubiquitous—Karl suffered from mosquito and leech bites. Worse, he contracted malaria and had to be hospitalized. At the same time, Karl began to suspect that Tommy was not doing well at home. While Elaine was keeping the worst of Tommy's health news from him, her letters contained fewer and fewer of Tommy's drawings and scribbled messages, which aroused Karl's concern.[16]

In the early part of 1945, "good news became the order of the day," as Karl learned of one Allied victory after another and the end of the war appeared imminent. Then, "on August 6 cheers broke out in our compound upon hearing the news of the complete destruction of Hiroshima by something called an 'A-bomb.' Along with the rest of the world, little did we realize the horrendous deadly force that had been unleashed upon humanity. Great shock and concern rushed through me—my beloved mother lived in Hiroshima! Why did it have to be Hiroshima?"[17] As a member of military intelligence, he knew that peace talks were underway. He and others felt that it was clear that the Allies were headed to victory and that the war was winding down. In the face of the possibility for a more peaceful resolution with Japan, were the bombings of Hiroshima and Nagasaki necessary? Elaine would later say about the bombing, "the fairy tale we are told to this day that it saved so many American lives is a fairy tale."[18] The complex emotions Karl must have felt over the next two months, before he would learn that his mother had survived, are hard to fathom. It was not until he was on his way to being shipped stateside from Karachi, India, that he received a Red Cross telegram notifying him that his mother, Kazu, was not only alive, but had, miraculously, not suffered any injuries.

It would not be until years later, when he and Elaine visited Kazu in Japan, that he would learn the full details of her experience. As it turned out, Kazu had taken a job doing janitorial work at a shipyard on the far outskirts of Hiroshima. It was a long and arduous commute from where she was living, in a poor section of the city. The wartime economy was quite difficult, so it was worth her long journey and the hard work the job required. In the end, it was the distance that saved her. By chance, she had left for work extra early on the morning of August 6. When the bomb was dropped, Kazu experienced "a strong light [that] flashed through the sky, followed by a terrific wind spreading pieces of human remains and other debris against the building." The shipyard was far enough away from ground zero, however, that the only damage sustained by the shipyard buildings themselves were shattered windows. "Very soon, a dark cloud covered the sky and black rain started to fall. Hundreds of half-naked people, some with horrible burns on their bodies, walked around the yards, like a parade of ghosts, all pleading for water. It was hell created on earth." Several days passed before Kazu could return to her home, where she found absolutely no trace of her house or her belongings. Eventually, she determined that she should make her way to her brother's farm, in the town outside Hiroshima where she was born. Her brother's family had not heard from her and had assumed that she had not survived the blast. One day, while one of her cousins was working in a field, he saw what he believed to be a ghost coming toward him. There was Kazu, walking up the road toward the farm. He soon realized that she was not a ghost and ran to embrace her. Kazu stayed on the farm for a year before returning to Hiroshima.[19]

August 15 was V-J Day, and demobilization followed, a process that would take many months, as millions of GIs were eager to return home. Karl spent time first in Calcutta, then in Karachi, before it was his turn to board a ship bound for the United States on October 13. He arrived in New Jersey on November 3 and from there was flown to Camp Beale, about fifty miles north of Sacramento. November 11 was Armistice Day, and Karl received his honorable discharge papers. As he walked out of the camp's gates, he saw "my two most shining stars, Elaine and Tommy, together with Happy Brannan. . . . We ran towards each other, embracing in big hugs and long kisses and joyful, flowing tears. Happy got her car, loaded my heavy duffle bag into it, and drove us home. It had been a long road to start our family life together again."[20]

Overall, Karl had positive feelings about his role in the war and his contributions. He would continue to feel, throughout his life, that the propaganda campaign had aided in the defeat of the Axis powers. Moreover, he drew another satisfaction, and lesson, from his time in the army. "The memory of associations with hundreds of Chinese, Burmese, Kachin, Shan, Hindu, Gurkha, Sikh, Punjabi, POWs, GIs, and stateside civilians [taught me] one of life's greatest lessons: When the task is to fight injustice, people of all races and ethnic backgrounds can stand united in a common cause."[21] Was it a contradiction that he could hold this idealistic evaluation of what had transpired alongside the knowledge of how many innocent lives had been lost in Japan? As he tried to wrap his mind around what kind of country could commit such an atrocity as unleashing atomic weapons, he also tried to imagine what life would be like back in the country that did so, a country for which he had endured incarceration and for which he had donned a uniform and fought. Karl wondered, "Had my government and its capitalist system saved only a limited democracy in a war in which three hundred thousand Americans, including seven hundred Japanese Americans, had died? Would employers, who had raked in millions of dollars in profits from the war, open their gates to returning GIs, including those of us who were of Japanese descent? Would people of Japanese ancestry, who had been confined in the U.S. style concentration camps, be restored their full rights? Would civil and human rights be protected?"[22] These would be the questions that Karl and Elaine would grapple with for the rest of their lives. For the moment, Karl was ecstatic to be home, reunited with Elaine and Tommy, after three years of separation.

27

Tommy was thrilled to have his father safely home—he wanted to be around his father constantly. Elaine finally shared with Karl the full extent of Tommy's physical and emotional health issues while Karl had been gone. For the Thanksgiving holiday, the three traveled to Los Angeles to see family and friends. They visited others from Karl's family—a sister, two cousins, and their families—who had spent three years in different camps. They shared their experiences of starting a new life from scratch. Another of Karl's siblings had decided to take her family back to Japan, a decision that many had made after their years of incarceration and the violation of their civil rights, although many of those would eventually return to the United States.[23]

Karl encountered mixed reactions, returning home as a Japanese American army veteran. In many instances he was greeted with a hero's welcome. And yet, the racism of the prewar era did not magically vanish with the end of the war. A particular challenge was housing. As had been true before the war, Karl and Elaine experienced significant housing discrimination. Karl placed an ad in the *San Francisco Chronicle* that read "Wanted: two-bedroom house or apartment [to be rented] by Japanese American veteran, Caucasian wife, and six-year-old son." He did not receive even one response. For several months, Karl would visit places that had been advertised. He continued to wear his army uniform, but it did not help—as soon as prospective landlords saw him, they would simply shake their head and close the door.[24]

In contrast, Karl was greeted by his CPUSA colleagues with warmth and sincere regret. Shortly after he had arrived home, he visited the California District Communist Party Headquarters, where he was congratulated and thanked for his heroism. There, he learned that 15,000 CPUSA members in total had fought on all Allied fronts. Individually, various friends "acknowledged and deeply regretted the party's serious wartime errors in suspending comrades of Japanese ancestry from membership and in not speaking out against the 'evacuation order.'"[25] Karl was aware that there had been efforts to reinstate Japanese American members and that he would be well received by the San Francisco party members, because Elaine had written him in September and informed him of this move by various party members, including an old friend of hers, Oleta O'Connor Yates, who was then chair of the Communist Party of San Francisco County. Elaine had included excerpts from Yates's report in her letter to Karl, with the following words:

> We believe that it was a mistake to have dropped all Nisei from the Party immediately after Pearl Harbor and that the reasons given were not sufficient to justify the fact. We believe that the Party failed to carry out in practice a program around the problems within the Relocation Centers following the evacuation, and continued its mistakes in not becoming a leading force in fighting for jobs, housing, and security for the Nisei who began to return many months ago. A sharp turn in this approach and outlook is now necessary.[26]

The San Francisco Communist Party hosted a celebration to welcome home returning GIs. Most had not realized the extent to which Japanese Americans had enlisted and participated on the battlefields—more than 6,000 Japanese American men had served in the Military Intelligence Service alone.[27]

Karl turned his attention to finding a job. He planned to return to his longshoreman work at the docks. Elaine had written to Karl prior to his return, saying, "If you want to go back to the waterfront, I'm sure there'll be no problem there and no discrimination either, except from . . . ignorant people who may be members or are probationary members."[28] Elaine's optimism unfortunately did not mirror the reality that Japanese Americans, both veterans returning from the war as well as those returning from camps, faced significant racism in the postwar period, including severe labor discrimination. Reports of Nisei being refused employment were widespread.[29]

Indeed, obtaining employment was not so simple for Karl upon his return. He applied for registered longshoreman status with the International Longshore and Warehouse Union, as he had so many years before, so that he could work at the waterfront and enjoy all the union's contractual benefits. In January, the Waterfront Employers Association turned down Karl's application, despite his six years of experience as a longshoreman before the war. Karl appealed the decision, and eventually an arbitrator ruled that Karl was entitled to be fully registered. The whole process took several months, needlessly keeping Karl from earning wages during that period.

Around the same time, the union's division in Stockton had refused employment to a returning Nisei union member. International Longshore and Warehouse Union director Harry Bridges ordered an investigation, to be mediated by Louis Goldblatt, who had spoken out so eloquently against exclusion and incarceration before the Tolan Committee years earlier. Goldblatt summed up his arguments, saying, "Race discrimination knows no end. It starts off with the Japanese, then the Filipinos, Catholics, Protestants, and pretty soon it will wreck your union."[30] All over the West Coast, as Japanese Americans returned from concentration camps, they faced similar discrimination in housing and in employment. Moreover, many returned to find that their property—real estate, businesses, personal effects—had been appropriated while they had been away. They quickly learned that, although the camps had been closed, their ordeals were far from over.

Karl was lucky to have a progressive-minded union backing him, and so he was able to reclaim his union status and his job. After going back to work on the docks, however, he soon found that, after five years away that included three years in the army, he was no longer up to the physical demands of the job. After a few weeks, he collapsed on the job and was sent to the navy hospital in Oakland for treatment. There, he learned that his bout of malaria and other health issues overseas had left him with a damaged kidney, which would lead later to the entire removal of the kidney.[31] He could no longer work the docks.

28

As Karl and Elaine considered their next move, Elaine's parents urged them to consider chicken ranching. The suggestion wasn't entirely outlandish. Sonoma County, north of San Francisco, was described in this period as the world's egg basket. By the 1940s, a sizable community of Jewish Socialists and Communists had formed in the county, and in the early twentieth century a community of radical Russian Jewish immigrants had gathered there after escaping the pogroms.[32] With no background in farming, these Zionists took on chicken ranching, with the expectation that they would eventually bring these skills to a new Jewish state. Molly and Nathan had many friends there. Numerous times when they had visited Karl and Elaine in San Francisco, they had all gone together to Petaluma to visit her parents' friends and an aunt and uncle of Elaine's who had a summer cabin on the Russian River.[33] Elaine was also familiar with the community from the tar-and-feather case she had worked on with the ILD before the war. Karl and Elaine reasoned that the fresh air and rural life might be a boon to Tommy's health. Elaine's parents assured the couple that their friends were earning a decent living on their ranches and that surely the work wasn't as hard as being a longshoreman. Elaine would later recall, "Little did we know what we were getting into."[34]

Molly and Nathan contributed some funds and, with the addition of a GI loan, Karl and Elaine bought a six-acre ranch in Penngrove, just north of Petaluma, and moved there in April 1946. Molly and Nathan joined them to help out. They initially bought 6,000 meat birds. At the height of the ranch's production, they raised 30,000 meat birds per year and collected eggs from an additional 1,000 hens.[35] They developed their knowledge in a trial by fire, having arrived with no knowledge whatsoever of how to raise chickens. Early mistakes led to some disastrous financial outcomes, but eventually they learned the trade. They earned a modest living, but both Elaine and Karl found the work to be grueling, physically demanding, and intellectually unsatisfying. They also could not have known that they became chicken ranchers in the waning years of the era when small chicken ranchers reigned. Feed prices skyrocketed after the war, and within a few decades, the entire industry would be industrialized and mechanized.

Nevertheless, the Yonedas stayed in Penngrove for more than thirteen years. The demands of the ranch took most of their time, and they also were very focused on family life in this period. Tommy was in school. Joyce was living in San Francisco with her husband, and they visited her regularly on trips to the city. They did continue to participate in politics, but to a lesser extent than they had before the war. Much of the political work involved extending their radical circle from San Francisco out to rural Sonoma County. In 1947 Elaine helped found a branch of the California Labor School in Sonoma. The California Labor School began in 1942 in San Francisco as the Tom Mooney Labor School, a project of the CPUSA to provide cultural, political, and organizing instruction. The California Labor School was supported by several labor unions, and after the war it was accredited to provide GI instruction. Over the years, a significant number of left-wing luminaries taught at the California Labor School, including Oleta O'Connor Yates, Tillie Olson, Erik Erikson, Maya Angelou, Muriel Ruykeser, and others. The regular faculty from the school in San Francisco would come out to teach classes in Sonoma County, most often in Petaluma.

Elaine also continued with the ILD, which had changed in form. In 1946, the ILD merged with the National Federation for Constitutional Liberties and the National Negro Congress, was renamed the Civil Rights Congress, and committed itself to addressing racial injustice in the United States. Elaine was the first chairperson of the Sonoma County chapter. Much of the congress's work was devoted to the legal defense of African Americans in the South, but it also defended the rights of Communists and other political dissidents.

Elaine and Karl were involved in other groups as well, including the Jewish Cultural Club and the PTA of Tommy's school. It is interesting that, despite ideological differences before the war, the JACL became an organization of focus for Elaine and Karl, and they helped found a Sonoma chapter. Elaine founded a chapter of the Kaiser medical group, which would go on to provide health insurance to more than one hundred chicken ranchers. Karl was county director for the *People's World*. The Yonedas hosted the annual Sonoma County fundraiser for the paper, a chicken barbecue—of course!—at their ranch. The fundraisers were usually held in July, which coincided both with Karl's birthday and with that of their dear friend, Anita Whitney.[36] Because of this extensive community of leftists in Petaluma and Sonoma County more broadly, many nationally known figures in the Communist, progressive, and civil rights movements came through Sonoma and became friends of the Yonedas, including Paul Robeson and Dashiell Hammett. They also maintained connections with long-standing friends from the CPUSA, including Harry Bridges and Oleta O'Connor Yates.

As the 1940s gave way to the 1950s, the Korean War was at its height and the Cold War was heating up. The Communist Party chapter in Sonoma County itself was rather small, but with all the leftist activity that had been going on there for decades, the area was targeted by the FBI during the McCarthy era. The Yonedas knew of at least three families of chicken ranchers who chose to leave the area for fear that their known Communist activities would make them a target.

A number of Karl and Elaine's Issei and Nisei friends were deported under the McCarran Act, a law passed in 1950 that required Communist organizers to register with the federal government and allowed the detention of those deemed by the government to be subversive as well as the deportation of immigrants accused of participating in Communist or other radical activities.[37] Years later, in the 1960s, Karl and Elaine would participate in, and raise funds for, a successful campaign mounted by the International Longshore and Warehouse Union to repeal the McCarran Act.[38] Under a related piece of legislation, the Smith Act, in 1951 Karl's dear friend and army colleague who had been at Manzanar with the Yonedas, Koji Ariyoshi, was arrested along with six others in a trial that would gain much notoriety. Ariyoshi had founded the *Honolulu Record*, a radical paper that advocated for unionization and racial equality in Hawai'i, where he was living at the time. He and the six others were charged with being members of the Communist Party.[39] The International Longshore and Warehouse Union and various civil rights groups protested their convictions, which fortunately were tossed out on appeal at a federal court.

Although Karl and Elaine maintained their membership in the Communist Party throughout this time, they seem to have experienced only minimal harassment during the McCarthy era, perhaps because their overall engagement was much less than it had been before World War II. The reason for the change may simply have been that they were much more preoccupied with raising their son and maintaining the ranch. Also, although the party had acknowledged and apologized for the ousting of Japanese Americans and their families during the war, it's possible that the exclusion had left Karl and Elaine with some distaste for party politics, though there is no direct evidence of this on the record. Karl and Elaine did provide material support for those experiencing the direct effects of the House Un-American Activities Committee. In some cases, this meant simply allowing friends who'd been targeted to stay at their home to avoid further scrutiny.[40] In other instances, they helped raise funds for bail and legal fees and other needed support for friends who'd been arrested.[41]

Elaine and Karl had been followed by the FBI for years. Certainly, they had been aware of FBI scrutiny throughout their work with the ILD and the CPUSA in the 1930s. The resources devoted to their surveillance were quite extensive and provide an indication of the copious wasted time and money spent watching suspected subversives from the 1930s through the McCarthy era. FBI agents and paid informants filed regular reports on Karl and

Elaine's comings and goings, attendance at meetings of all kinds, and the associations they had. Some of the reports, particularly those filed by informants, were factually untrue and even comic—such as a report that Elaine was a prostitute. Not only was that idea preposterous, it's difficult to imagine how such an idea would have circulated at all.[42] The surveillance also likely continued throughout Karl's military service. The Military Intelligence Service had admitted a number of Nisei Communists into its service—they had the necessary language skills and knowledge of Japanese culture and, further, the Military Intelligence Service reasoned that, as Communists, they were committed antifascists. But such reasoning did not stop the Military Intelligence Service from keeping close tabs on their activities even while enlisted, in ways that they would not do for other Military Intelligence Service servicemen who were not identified as Communists.[43]

After the war, Elaine and Karl knew that they were being watched, as were most of their friends. In Penngrove, they were certain that their telephones were tapped. An FBI agent appeared at the ranch on one occasion. He approached Karl and said that his name had been given as a reference for a Nisei who was trying to reenlist. Karl knew this was a pretext—they questioned him about Harry Bridges and other topics well beyond the scope of such a reference. Karl was dismissive. He was busy vaccinating baby chicks. Karl responded, "If you want to know why I am sticking this chicken in the ass, I'll tell you. Otherwise I'll meet you in my attorney's office."[44] Though Karl and Elaine may have kept an arm's length away from the whole topic of anticommunism in this period, Karl's reply indicates that they had regained their disdain for authorities.

Tommy experienced the McCarthy era in unique ways. One can only imagine what it would have meant for a boy to grow up with one Russian-Jewish parent and one Japanese parent, both known Communists, during the McCarthy era and the Cold War. Compounding his experience were his own memories of living in a concentration camp, hazy though they were at his age during incarceration. Understandably, Tommy often confused timelines and events in his young mind, such as when he had thought that there were Nazis at Manzanar. And although there certainly was a significant community of leftists in Sonoma County, the rural area also had some elements that were very conservative, politically and socially. When Tommy was enrolled at the local school, the teacher called Elaine in for a conference. The teacher expressed to Elaine her concern that Tommy might experience some difficulties due to his Japanese ancestry. Elaine replied, "Well I believe Tommy will be able to take care of himself, whether he is attacked for his Japanese ancestry or his Jewish ancestry. He's well aware of what fascism is. I think he can handle it."[45] Indeed, Tommy came home from playing at a friend's house one day, a boy from a German family, and said to his mother that they had a swastika over their fireplace. And he got in a fight at school with some boys who had been making racist comments to the one African American boy in his class.[46]

But most disturbing to Elaine and Karl was when Tommy came home from his social studies class one day, when he was eleven, and asked, "Will I have to go into a concentration camp again because my grandparents came from Russia?"[47] It's easy to understand how the details of World War II history, as well as the intersecting identities and experiences of the Yoneda family, could be confusing to a young boy. After the war, when he had been experiencing nightmares from their time at Manzanar, Tommy had once told Elaine that he had dreamt that the Nazis at Manzanar were coming to kill his father.[48]

Still, overall, Elaine and Karl did feel that living in Penngrove was a positive experience for Tommy. For this reason, they committed to stay until he finished high school, even though the chicken business was becoming less and less lucrative and they very much missed city life. Tommy continued to suffer from allergies and asthma, but, in spite of that, he was a straight-A student and an excellent athlete.[49]

While in high school, Tommy received an award from the Petaluma B'nai B'rith chapter, given annually to a graduate of Petaluma High School for academic and athletic achievement. There was some reluctance to give the award to Tommy, which Karl believed stemmed from the fact that his parents were known Communists and an interracial couple. But Tommy was the clear choice in his graduating class, and so he was selected. The ceremony was to be held at the Petaluma Jewish Community Center, which had once been a regular place for meetings and social events held by the left-wing Zionist chicken ranchers of Petaluma. At one point in the heat of the anticommunist fervor of the 1950s, in what would be a very acrimonious move, right-wing community members who favored assimilation had kicked out the Communists and other left-wing groups and barred them from continuing to use the center. Years had gone by, but the left-wing groups had not forgotten the betrayal. Karl and Elaine's friends were among those who still felt embittered by the experience, and they expressed surprise and regret that the Yonedas would agree to go to the Jewish Community Center at all. Meanwhile, the JACL also gave a scholarship award to an outstanding high school graduate. They, too, gave an award to Tommy.[50]

Tommy Yoneda graduated from high school in 1957, with awards from both the JACL and B'nai B'rith as well as a significant scholarship to attend Stanford University. Elaine and Karl no longer earned a living from chicken ranching, and they both commuted to San Francisco for work—Karl worked once again on the waterfront in less physically demanding jobs than before, and Elaine got a job doing office work. Finally, in 1960, they sold the ranch and moved back to San Francisco. Now that Tommy was out of the house and they were back in the city, Elaine could turn her attention once again to activism. She did not, however, have quite the energy of her youth—now in her fifties, her health was not great and old friends noted that she was frailer than she had previously been. Still, her condition did not seem to diminish her terribly.

Elaine was particularly active in the ILWU Women's Auxiliary. Through her work with the auxiliary, she became involved primarily in the disarmament and antinuclear weapons movement, the antiwar movement that was opposing U.S. involvement in Vietnam, and the draft. These three causes would also become a passionate focus for Karl. The two remained committed members of the Communist Party as well.

29

In 1960 Elaine and Karl prepared to visit Japan, together with Tommy. They had the opportunity to attend the Sixth World Conference against Atomic and Hydrogen Bombs, she representing the West Coast ILWU women's auxiliaries and Karl representing ILWU Local 10. Fortunately, the U.S. government had recently stopped asking passport applicants whether they were, or ever had been, members of the Communist Party—though the change did not stop the FBI from tracking Elaine and Karl's international travels.[51] The conference garnered much international attention. Two important resolutions were adopted at the conference, one to work to prohibit the use of nuclear arms and another to urge a pact of nonaggression among Pacific Rim countries.

The trip would also be the first time that Elaine and Tommy would meet Karl's mother, Kazu, as well as members of the extended family.[52] Karl himself had not seen his mother in thirty-two years. After the conference had adjourned, the sponsors organized a tour for the Yonedas of Hiroshima, and there they met Karl's mother and cousin. Karl had gone to high school in Hiroshima, and he felt very attached to the city. Seeing the aftermath of the bombing deeply affected the Yoneda family. The group visited the Peace Memorial Park and museum and met with atomic bomb victims and learned about their postwar lives. Elaine was personally struck by the stories of women who were unable to find husbands because of the fear that survivors would not be able to give birth to healthy children. A group of these women had formed a kind of cooperative that produced leather goods to earn a living. Later, when Elaine returned to the United States, she organized a sale of their crafts through her auxiliary and raised more than $1,000 for them. The Yonedas also visited an orphanage where children whose parents were bomb victims were living. Twenty-one-year-old Tommy was so moved by the experience that he chose to stay on for three weeks as a volunteer. Elaine and Karl left for the United States before Tommy was done volunteering. They implored Kazu to return with them, but she refused—she did not want to be a burden, nor did she want to leave her native Japan after all these years.[53]

Throughout the 1970s and 1980s, Elaine and Karl continued with their antiwar and anti-nuclear-armaments activities. They were also very active in the campaign to repeal the McCarran Act. The campaign, which was largely mounted by the JACL with help from the American Committee for the Protection of the Foreign Born, finally succeeded in 1971, amid a slew of repeals of McCarthy-era legislation. In 1969 the same repeal committee had also supported the Native American Alcatraz Project, an occupation of Alcatraz Island that began in 1969 and lasted for two years as a protest against U.S. policies affecting Indigenous Peoples. The repeal committee collected food and clothing and delivered it to protesters occupying the island.[54]

During this period of peace activism, Elaine and Karl focused much of their attention on two related causes: the movement for redress and reparation for the exclusion and incarceration of Japanese Americans during World War II and the movement for the establishment of a national memorial at Manzanar. Elaine, Karl, and Tommy began making annual pilgrimages to Manzanar in 1953. In 1962 they stopped at Manzanar with Elaine's parents on the way back to Los Angeles from Lake Tahoe.[55] The first organized mass pilgrimage to the site occurred on December 27, 1969, organized by the Asian American Coalition of Los Angeles and the Title II Repeal Committee of San Francisco, the group that sought repeal of the McCarran Act. On that cold day late in December, more than 200 people gathered and reminisced about their experiences there. Karl felt that they shared a common bond, vowing that "it must never happen again to anyone. The 'evacuation' story must become common knowledge."[56]

One month later, in January 1970, the Manzanar Project Committee was formed, led primarily by Sue Kunitomi Embrey, who had been incarcerated at Manzanar. In addition to continuing to help spread information about the camp, the Manzanar Committee's goal was to obtain California State Historic Landmark Status for the site; they would later seek National Park Service designation. Embrey had met Elaine and Karl at the 1969 pilgrimage. Though Elaine and Sue had not known each other during their incarceration, they bonded over sharing their stories and experiences with a television crew that had come to report on the pilgrimage. They became fast friends and would continue to work together until the end of Elaine's life. Embrey recalled Elaine's devotion to preserving the Manzanar site. Elaine wrote letters in support of the campaign, and she and Karl traveled regularly to Manzanar to organize volunteers at the site.[57]

In the early 1970s, the State Department of Parks and Recreation agreed to post a memorial plaque at the site, but controversy over the exact wording delayed installation for more than a year. The department objected to the use of the term *concentration camp* and also to the word *racism* in the following sentence: "May the injustices and humiliation suffered here as a result of hysteria, racism, and economic exploitation never emerge again." Eventually, the Manzanar Committee got their way and the wording was approved. The committee eventually succeeded in their pursuit of national designation as well; in 1985 the camp's site was established as a National Historic Landmark and in 1992 it was designated a National Historic Site.[58] In subsequent years, an extensive visitor center and museum would open, and some of the camp's original buildings were reconstructed.

In 1972 more than 800 people gathered at Manzanar to mark the thirtieth anniversary of the camp's establishment. Karl was one of the speakers. His remarks included the following words:

> Coming back to Manzanar today strengthens my conviction that racism, jingoism, white chauvinism, and greedy profiteering, the basic structure of U.S. imperialism caused incarceration into ten concentration camps of more than one hundred ten thousand men, women, and children of Japanese ancestry without any hearing or trial. . . . Manzanar is everywhere, whenever injustice raises its ugly head. It is the Indian reservations with close to one million Native

Americans still contained in them; it is the ghettoes where thousands
upon thousands of racial minorities are shunted; it is the prisons
where thousands are confined because most of them are poor and of
different color and race.[59]

Karl's wording was strong and direct and seems to be quite unlike his atti-
tude during the incarceration. At the time, he and Elaine had said on many
occasions that they understood the government's choice to exclude Japanese
Americans from the West Coast. *Imperialism* was a word he used to describe
Japan or the Axis powers; never would he have used that word to describe
the United States at that time. Moreover, Elaine and Karl had refuted critics
who had pointed out the privations and lack of rights at the camps, going
on record to say that the living conditions were acceptable. Some had even
seen them—and certainly the JACL—as collaborators who enabled the
incarceration to happen and abetted the camp administration in suppress-
ing dissent. After all, both Karl and Elaine had effectively gone voluntarily—
which certainly was proof that they were not resisting U.S. policy. What had
changed their minds?

Though the record doesn't indicate when or how such a change came
about, there was clearly a change in their thinking in the years since the war
had ended. A retrospective debate about the meaning of the events at Manzanar, particularly during the December revolt, came about in the 1970s
when Tad Uyeno published a fifty-part series, Point of No Return, in *Rafu
Shimpo*. The series prompted Karl and Elaine to write a passionate letter to
the editor in response. In the postwar years, there were those who remembered the actions of Joe Kurihara, Tad Uyeno, Harry Ueno, and the others
who led the Manzanar Revolt as brave acts of resistance and defiance of an
untenable oppression. Karl and Elaine took great issue with that characterization. In a joint letter to the editor, they wrote,

> Tad Uyeno writes "the dissidents . . . called 'rebels,' for the lack of a
> more definitive term. They were anti-administration, anti-JACL. . . .
> Whether or not they were 'active pro-Japan supporters,' as newspa-
> pers called them, I cannot say." Also he calls them "militant minor-
> ity." (Roger Daniels uses the term "left opposition.") Let us examine
> the role of the so-called "rebels," which consisted of between 25 to 30,
> who claimed to be members of the Manzanar Black Dragons or
> Blood Brothers. They constantly disrupted by spreading false
> rumors, physical attacks and threatening the lives of evacuees, thus

keeping the camp in constant turmoil. Were they then truly "genuine protesters" against evacuation or "Kamikaze type supporters of fascist-militarism"? We believe most of that group belong in the latter classification.[60]

The Yonedas found it maddening that Kurihara was being deified—instead, they felt that more tribute should be paid to the hundreds of Japanese Americans who had lost their lives fighting in the U.S. military in World War II, having "volunteered from behind barbed wire."[61]

In the course of these arguments, Karl and Elaine summarized their current stand on the exclusion in fiery terms:

> Although we were guilty in not speaking out against the EVACUATION ORDER, but acquiescing fully, we have NO GUILT OR SHAME in our efforts to defeat the fascist Axis. We were sure there would be ovens in Manzanar and other camps if the MEIN KAMPFERS won the war, that all of us, including all non-white and non-fascists would end up in these ovens. We believe, to this day, most of those "rebels" would have made good "oven-tenders" in such eventuality![62]

Though they did not say it often, this is one of a few instances on the record where Karl and Elaine did say, in retrospect, that they were wrong to not speak out against exclusion. Elaine would similarly state in an oral history interview, conducted in 1974, that she and Karl "should have been a little more vocal in our protest."[63] Still, what she could not tolerate was to remember as heroes the people who perpetrated violence against her family at Manzanar.

Whether through the work Elaine and Karl had done with others who had survived, whether the years that had gone by gave them the full opportunity to consider how their lives would have been different had they not been incarcerated (not least of which would be the effects on their small son), whether the full knowledge of the horrors visited on Japan by the U.S. military that they knew from Kazu, or for other reasons, Elaine and Karl did devote themselves to memorializing Manzanar, and in the process they came to understand and admit that they should not have been so willing to give up their rights and support the racist treatment of Japanese Americans. In the same oral history interview, Elaine was asked, "What does Manzanar symbolize to you, today?" She replied, "It was just another blot on the history of the nation and the powers that rule it. I know to other people it means other things. But to me, it's always meant that we've got to point out that it mustn't happen to people again."[64]

Ensuring that a proper memorial be erected at Manzanar's site was one of the efforts to which Elaine and Karl devoted themselves to ensure that memory. Perhaps, too, they found in that project a path to ease their sense of regret for their own acquiescence.

Further, Elaine and Karl were active in the movement for redress and reparations from the U.S. government. Some had begun to discuss redress as early as during the war and in the immediate postwar period. But first on the minds of Japanese Americans after the war was reestablishing their lives. And they certainly did continue to experience racism and discrimination after the war ended, and so it did not seem likely that such a movement could gain the support it needed. Still, in 1948 the U.S. Congress did pass a limited piece of legislation, the Japanese Americans Evacuation Claims Act, which provided minimal compensation.[65] Elaine and Karl had made a claim under the act for $1,355 in losses; they received only $460. Ironically, their claim was reduced in part because one spouse was ineligible, since Elaine was not Japanese American.[66] By the end of the 1960s, when the antiwar and civil rights movements had gained so much momentum, and a new generation of Japanese Americans had come of age who were more versed in anti-racist activism, the movement for redress became more viable than ever.

In 1970 Edison Uno, a community activist from Northern California, made the first proposal for a movement to gain significant redress at a national meeting of the JACL.[67] At that convention, a committee was formed devoted to this effort, and they continued to put redress on the agenda at JACL meetings for the next decade.[68] These efforts were not limited to the JACL, which of course had its critics. Some were concerned that the JACL's history of collaboration would affect its work and that they would not ultimately seek redress equally for *all* who had been incarcerated. Two additional groups formed, the National Council for Japanese American Redress and the National Coalition for Redress/Reparations, the latter composed of Manzanar committee members who were engaged in the efforts to create a Manzanar memorial. Eventually the three groups did work together.[69]

Karl and Elaine worked to get a redress campaign on the agenda of the International Longshore and Warehouse Union, which had throughout its history taken on civil rights issues. Karl delivered a speech on the subject at the 1979 International Longshore and Warehouse Union Convention.[70] In 1980 the U.S. Congress appointed a committee of nine to the Commission on Wartime Relocation and Internment of Civilians (CWRIC), which would hold hearings throughout the West Coast and in Chicago, New York City, and Alaska, among other locations, to investigate the effects of EO 9066. In 1981 Elaine spoke at the national ILWU Convention in Hawai'i, along with Nikke Bridges, wife of Harry Bridges, in support of the redress campaign. Elaine urged delegates to attend the CWRIC hearings wherever they could.[71]

Elaine and Karl both testified before the CWRIC hearing in San Francisco on August 19, 1981. Elaine's testimony recounted all the events that had transpired from the bombing of Pearl Harbor and Karl's subsequent detention through his going voluntarily to Manzanar, through her choice to accompany her son when he was required to go, to the details of the Manzanar Revolt and her subsequent return with Tommy to San Francisco. She described the psychological effects of incarceration on Tommy—the years of nightmares and anxiety, as well as the fact that his already fragile physical health only worsened from living under such terrible conditions for nearly a year. She concluded by saying that "we must see that it is made impossible for such racist, repressive edicts to be issued and used ever again against any group of people in these United States."[72]

In 1983 the commission delivered its preliminary finding, admitting that the incarceration of Japanese Americans was due to "racial prejudice, war hysteria, and a failure of political leadership," rather than any military or security necessity. On August 10, 1988, President Ronald Reagan signed the Civil Liberties Act of 1988, offering apology and ordering that $20,000 be paid to every surviving person who had been excluded from the western portion of the United States. The reparations were paid out over the course of the next several years.

Elaine's work on the redress campaign would be the last cause to which she would devote herself. How unfortunate, in light of the time she had devoted to the effort, that she did not live to see President Reagan sign the Civil Liberties Act. Elaine had suffered her first heart attack in 1977 and for the next decade or so struggled with health issues. During 1987 and 1988, her health deteriorated. On Wednesday, May 25, 1988, she and Karl were scheduled to attend a campaign rally for Jesse Jackson's bid for the U.S. presidency on San Francisco's waterfront. Karl later remembered that she was very weak that day—she could hardly walk around the block. The two had plans to travel the next day to Lake Tahoe to celebrate their fifty-fifth wedding anniversary. Karl suspected that Elaine would not be up for the trip. Nevertheless, they got up early the next day and Elaine laid out a pretty dress, with matching jewelry, shoes, and handbag in preparation for the five-hour journey. But, as she began to dress, she complained to Karl of chest pains. Karl ran over to her, and she collapsed in his arms, her faint voice saying "I love you" before she lost consciousness. Karl called 911, but efforts to revive her failed.[73]

The tributes to Elaine poured in from the many, many people whose lives she had touched. The family chose to hold a private funeral service in San Francisco.[74] Tommy, now a grown man with two daughters of his own, wrote a eulogy in which he said, "Mother loved people, especially little children, and she loved flowers and plants and rocks. She wanted to see everybody happy, but she would amaze me most with her love of nature. She would hurry off in her high heels right into a wavering field of grass."[75] But, of course, the person who would miss her the most was Karl. In their later years, they were inseparable. Though he knew that her health was failing, and that her death was imminent, it was nevertheless a shock for Karl to lose the love of his life after fifty-five years. The night she died, Karl "couldn't sleep because she wasn't there in the bed. I cried for love."[76]

Elaine had fulfilled many roles to many people over her lifetime. Though she may not have described herself as a feminist, she fought for women's equality and she modeled what a strong woman could do, particularly when supported in equal partnership by a husband who admired and loved her so much. Her greatest satisfactions in life came from standing up to wrongdoers and defending the rights of others. Throughout the 1930s, the most productive decade of her professional labor work, she helped countless people who had been wrongly accused and unfairly treated. In the following decade, she became one of those people, and although it was surprising that she did not defend herself in the way she had defended others, she spent years after the war addressing that injustice retrospectively.

Elaine brought devotion and commitment to her life as a mother, partner, and friend and to her work as an activist, defender of people's rights, and unionist. Arthur Hansen, who had met and interviewed Elaine on a number of occasions, remembered her as a woman who was not afraid to voice her opinions and who always wanted to convince you of something—she was not five feet tall, and she always seemed to be standing on the tips of her toes to speak to you. At the same time, she was always, always, full of joy.[77] Consistent throughout the memorials and statements made by those who knew her, and who mourned her loss, was the warmth and kindness of a woman who could also be fierce and unrelenting in the face of injustice. For this combination, Elaine will be remembered.

Postscript

While conducting the research for this book, I attempted to locate Tommy Yoneda. I encountered a few people who knew him and had addresses for him in the town of Fort Bragg, in the far north of California, but my letters to these locations were returned unopened. On account of his year of birth, I feared the worst. One day I was speaking with Ken Kann about some details in his book about the Jewish chicken ranchers of Petaluma, for which he had interviewed Elaine.[1] Ken said, "Oh yes, I can put you in touch with Tommy, he is living in Santa Rosa, near where he grew up in Penngrove." Through Ken, I was given a phone number for Tommy. With excitement and some trepidation, I dialed the number. I had been researching his mother for years at that point—what would he think of me writing a book about her? But I was eager to speak directly with someone who knew her so well, albeit from the particularly complex vantage point of being her child.

Tommy answered the phone, and I nervously described that I was writing a biography of his mother. He asked me how I got interested in the subject. I explained that I am a historian who studies Jewish women labor activists and also that I am a photographer who was commissioned by the Contemporary Jewish Museum in San Francisco and that Elaine appeared in that project. Tommy asked for more: he wanted to know what motivated me to explore these topics. I talked about my Jewish upbringing, my grandmothers who were immigrants and similar in age to Elaine, and my interest in labor activism. I asked Tommy if I could come to Santa Rosa and interview him.

At that point, Tommy said, "There is something you want from me, so there is something I'd like to ask in return."

"Of course," I said. "Whatever I can do."

"Have you ever heard of a 'JewBu'?" Tommy asked.

I had. Having lived at that point in Oakland, California, for more than a decade, I was familiar with this distinctly Northern California construction to describe Jewish Buddhists. Most often they were liberal Jews who had a strong cultural identification as Jewish but were drawn to aspects of Buddhist practice, such as meditation. Many have found something sympathetic about the concept of *Tikkun Olam*, the Jewish imperative to make the world a better place, and aspects of Buddhism such as the emphasis on nonviolence. The combination was particularly potent for Northern Californians at the height of the anti–Vietnam war movements and the 1960s. During that period, Elaine and Karl fit right in, going to antinuclear and peace demonstrations. Together they formed a dyad that included Judaism and Buddhism, though neither was religious.

Tommy did not conform to the stereotypical JewBu background, but he seemed to delight in the designation. He explained to me, "I am Jewish and Buddhist. Though neither of my parents believed in religion at all and would not step foot into a house of worship, I have found meaning and comfort in my later years in both religions. I like to alternate weekends, going to the neighborhood synagogue one Saturday and to the local Buddhist temple the next week. What I'd like to ask of you is, if you are coming to Santa Rosa, would you come on a Saturday and take me to synagogue? My eyesight's not too keen so I no longer drive, and the taxi is very expensive. Besides, I'd like the company."

So it was that on a Saturday in February 2019, I left Oakland early in the morning, drove the fifty or so miles to Santa Rosa, picked up Tommy, and together with him attended a Shabbat service. It turned out there was a Bat Mitzvah that day. We stayed through the whole service. Tommy listened attentively, at times with his eyes shut. Afterward, Tommy, impressed, commented on the fact that I knew all the prayers. He was less familiar with them, he said, but he liked how the melodies sounded. We then crashed the Bat Mitzvah luncheon. We sat outside, shaded by a tree from the brilliant sunshine, and talked over California's attempts to recreate a spread of bagels, tuna, cream cheese, lox, rugelach, and black-and-white cookies (a noble but not very successful effort).

Afterward, I drove Tom (as I now learned he preferred to be called) back to his house, where we spent the rest of the day looking at family photographs and talking more about his parents and his childhood. Tom is a talker, and he seemed happy to have a listener. He had many stories to tell, and I tried to politely guide the narratives back to the topic of his mother. He shared some random memories, such as remembering his mother hand-cleaning eggs at the chicken ranch before they went to market, which made them fetch a higher price. He remembered playing as a child at the opulent home of Anita Whitney on Nob Hill in San Francisco. He told me about his own family, including his children and grandchildren. He also told me that he still has flashbacks and distinct memories of Manzanar. Lately, he had been seeing a vivid image in his mind of walking up to the camp's entrance, the razor-wire fences with their tops at sixty-degree angles to ward off escape, and armed guards in the watchtower holding rifles with bayonets. "We hold these dramatic moments within our being," said Tom, "and they contribute to our very makeup."[2]

I realized that there was something I wanted from him that was, of course, impossible. I wanted to know his mother through him. I wanted to get some sense of her as a woman. I wanted to know what it was like to sit in a room with her. That didn't exactly happen; nevertheless, it's been a rare and special treat to get to know him. He was able to answer a number of my questions about things that were not among the archival materials. Were they a happy family? (Yes.) I was eager to hear more about Joyce, who was so absent from the record. Tom assured me that she was very much part of the family and that Elaine felt very close to her.

I reflected on what this all meant—how it was that this eighty-year-old man had come to find meaning in religious observance. How his particular experiences, with one Russian-Jewish American parent and one Japanese American parent, having spent eight months as a very small boy in a concentration camp, had shaped him. I remembered that Tom had been awarded college scholarships from both B'nai B'rith and the Japanese American Citizens League, surely not a common combination. Nevertheless, his life seemed to exemplify some of the idiosyncrasies of what it means to be part of the wide-ranging identity we call American.

Some might consider it odd or even problematic to conclude this book about a woman's life with a story about a man, even if he is her son. As a feminist biographer, I have endeavored always to keep Elaine centered in this story. And yet, as is surely clear, Elaine's son was a central guiding force in her life and her story—her north star. I met Tom just a few days before I left California to relocate back to the East Coast, to New York City. My own personal geography overlapped significantly with that of her family. I had been researching Elaine for nearly a decade at that point, and it was shortly after the visit with Tom that I began to put her story down in writing. Occasionally while I was writing there would be a long voice mail from Tom, recounting some new detail he remembered or suggesting new family members for me to speak with. Tom's presence lingers throughout these pages and carries on Elaine's legacy.*

* Since the completion of the writing of this book, Tom Yoneda passed away peacefully on January 28, 2021, in his home. He is survived by his daughters Tamara, Yvonne, Eliana, and his extended family. His memory will surely be a blessing for all who knew him.

Notes

ACKNOWLEDGMENTS

1. *California Dreaming: Jewish Life in the Bay Area from the Gold Rush to the Present*, November 17, 2011–April 28, 2013, accessed July 26, 2020, available at https://www.thecjm.org/exhibitions/33.

2. Fred Rosenbaum, *Cosmopolitans: A Social and Cultural History of the Jews of the San Francisco Bay Area* (Berkeley: University of California Press, 2009).

INTRODUCTION

1. W. J. Hennigan, "Trump Administration to Hold Migrant Children at Base That Served as WWII Japanese Internment Camp," *Time*, June 11, 2019, available at https://time.com/5605120/trump-migrant-children-fort-sill/; Ben Fenwick, "'Stop Repeating History': Plan to Keep Migrant Children at Former Internment Camp Draws Outrage," *New York Times*, June 22, 2019, available at https://www.nytimes.com/2019/06/22/us/fort-sill-protests-japanese-internment.html.

2. See Jo Burr Margadant, *The New Biography: Performing Feminism in Nineteenth-Century France* (Berkeley: University of California Press, 2000); Hans Renders, Binne de Haan, and Jonne Harmsma, eds., *The Biographical Turn: Lives in History* (London: Routledge, 2016); Linda Wagner-Martin, *Telling Women's Lives: The New Biography* (New Brunswick, NJ: Rutgers University Press, 1994).

3. I use the terms *woman* and *women* here to represent individuals who present themselves as such, with deliberate recognition that the term should be expansive and include cisgender as well as transgender women. To fully account for the lives of women, we need to view history through this broader lens of gender and not be tacit

in our assumption of who inhabits this category. To the point, I note here Elaine's self-presentation as a cisgender woman.

4. Judith P. Zinsser, "Feminist Biography: A Contradiction in Terms?" *Eighteenth Century* 50, no. 1 (2010): 43–50.

5. Renders et al., *Biographical Turn*, 7.

6. See Chapter 2 in Karen Brodkin, *How Jews Became White Folks and What It Says About Race in America* (New Brunswick, NJ: Rutgers University Press, 1994). Brodkin's book provides a critical examination of race-making in the United States with attention to gender and class. Her arguments are particularly salient for a family such as Elaine's, who arrived in the United States at a time when Jews were constructed as non-white due to their status as immigrant laborers and how that racial assignment shifted over the course of the twentieth century.

7. Brodkin, *How Jews Became White*, 1–2.

8. Allison Varzally has demonstrated the ways that groups that were disallowed from settling in majority white neighborhoods comingled in those they were relegated to, including Boyle Heights in Los Angeles, which boasted a broad range of migrant and immigrant populations. See Allison Varzally, *Making a Non-white America: Californians Coloring outside Ethnic Lines, 1925–1955* (Berkeley: University of California Press, 2008).

9. One of the first and most important examples of feminist biography is Laurel Thatcher Ulrich, *A Midwife's Tale: The Life of Martha Ballard, Based on Her Diary, 1785–1812* (New York: Alfred A. Knopf, 1990). Ulrich closely reads the diary of Martha Ballard, a New England midwife who kept a thorough but sparse diary from 1785 to 1812. The diary, a truly exceptional primary source, had been dismissed by previous (male) scholars because of its laconic entries, which simply but meticulously note the details of Ballard's career in a sustained way throughout her career through several decades. Through Ulrich's telling, we see Ballard as an itinerant businesswoman who models the ways that women of her era could be central to economic formations and not relegated to the domestic sphere. Two other important examples are Patricia Cline Cohen, *The Murder of Helen Jewett* (New York: Vintage, 1999), and Carolyn Steedman, *Landscape for a Good Woman: A Story of Two Lives* (New Brunswick, NJ: Rutgers University Press, 1986). Cohen writes the story of a murdered sex worker in 1830s New York City by reading against the grain of the lurid newspaper accounts that, until her book's publication, formed the accepted narrative of Jewett's life. Steedman imaginatively constructs a biography of the life of her mother through an experimental narrative that examines her mother's life in relation to her own in order to illuminate the struggles of a working-class mother in Britain in the 1950s.

10. To be fair, Karl was an author and editor, and therefore he appears in more print culture than she does. Nevertheless, even aside from published works, his archive contains more extensive materials and is housed in a prominent research university (University of California, Los Angeles), whereas hers is at a more modest state university (San Francisco State University). Further, Karl was sought after as a speaker and lecturer after the war, a fact that surely reveals a gender bias since Karl and Elaine often traveled to these venues together but she was not the one asked to speak, even though she was known as a forceful orator.

11. Arthur Hansen, "Oral History and the Japanese American Evacuation," *Journal of American History* 82, no. 2 (1995): 625–639; Arthur Hansen, "A Riot of Voices: Racial and Ethnic Variable in Interactive Oral History Interviewing," in *Interactive Oral History Interviewing*, ed. Eva M. McMahan and Kim Lacy Rogers, 107–139 (London: Taylor and Francis, 2013).

12. Hansen, "Riot of Voices," 136.

13. Vivian McGuckin Raineri, *The Red Angel: The Life and Times of Elaine Black Yoneda, 1906–1988* (New York: International, 1991).

14. Raineri, *Red Angel*, xi.

15. Karl Yoneda, *Ganbatte: Sixty-Year Struggle of a Kibei Worker* (Los Angeles: University of California, Los Angeles Asian American Studies Center, 1983).

16. California Historical Society, *Only What We Could Carry: The Japanese American Internment Experience* (San Francisco, CA: Heyday, 2000). The Commission on Wartime Relocation and Internment of Civilians was appointed by the U.S. Congress in 1980 to investigate war crimes perpetrated by the United States against its own citizens during World War II through the incarceration of Japanese Americans. The commission ultimately concluded that "racial prejudice, wartime hysteria, and a failure of political leadership" led to the denial of the rights of citizens. But it was not until 1992 that the U.S. government would issue its formal apology to Japanese American citizens.

17. I am grateful to Ashlynn Deu Pree, Arthur Hansen, Kenneth Kann, Ben Kobashigawa, Paul Spickard, and Tom Yoneda for generously sharing their time.

18. Mark Wild, *Street Meeting: Multiethnic Neighborhoods in Early Twentieth-Century Los Angeles* (Berkeley: University of California Press, 2005). Another work that considers the interracial makeup of Los Angeles as viewed through the lens of public health is Natalia Molina, *How Race Is Made in America: Immigration, Citizenship, and the Historical Power of Racial Scripts* (Berkeley: University of California Press, 2014).

19. Rosalyn Baxandall, "The Question Seldom Asked: Women and the CPUSA," in *New Studies in the Politics and Culture of U.S. Communism*, ed. Michael E. Brown, Randy Martin, Frank Rosengarten, and George Snedeker (New York: Monthly Review Press, 1993), 141–161.

20. Elsa Jane Dixler, "The Woman Question: Women and the American Communist Party, 1929–1941" (Ph.D. diss., Yale University, 1974), available at http://search.proquest.com/pqdtglobal/docview/302771545/citation/1CD61F09D29E4D8 1PQ/1.

21. Kate Weigand, *Red Feminism: American Communism and the Making of Women's Liberation* (Baltimore, MD: Johns Hopkins University Press, 2001). To be clear, this is not to say that the CPUSA was successful in avoiding racism and gender discrimination, but it did attempt in this period to be a more inclusive organization.

22. As stated, the literature is vast. Perhaps the most prolific scholar on the topic is Roger Daniels. To name a few of his key contributions: Roger Daniels, *Concentration Camps USA: Japanese Americans and World War II* (New York: Holt, Rinehart, and Winston, 1971); Daniels, *Prisoners without Trial: Japanese Americans in World War II* (New York: Hill and Wang, 2004), Kindle edition; Daniels, *The Politics of Prejudice: The Anti-Japanese Movement in California and the Struggle for Japanese Exclusion* (Berkeley: University of California Press, 1999). A brief list of additional key

works is the following: Jeffery Burton et al., *Confinement and Ethnicity: An Overview of World War II Japanese American Relocation Sites* (Seattle: University of Washington Press, 2002); Richard Drinnon, *Keeper of Concentration Camps: Dillon S. Myer and American Racism* (Berkeley: University of California Press, 1987); Brian Masaru Hayashi, *Democratizing the Enemy: The Japanese American Internment* (Princeton, NJ: Princeton University Press, 2010); John W. Dower, *War without Mercy: Race and Power in the Pacific War* (New York: Pantheon, 1986); Tetsuden Kashima, *Judgment without Trial: Japanese American Imprisonment during World War II* (Seattle: University of Washington Press, 2004); Greg Robinson, *By Order of the President* (Cambridge, MA: Harvard University Press, 2009); and Michi Weglyn, *Years of Infamy: The Untold Story of America's Concentration Camps* (New York: Morrow, 1976).

23. This is neither to compare this history to, nor to elide, the genocide of Indigenous Peoples in North America, but only to focus the comparative analysis to Japanese Americans on the basis of exclusion, concentration, and incarceration, a comparison put forward by Japanese Americans at the time. On West Coast racism that fueled exclusion and incarceration, see John Howard, *Concentration Camps on the Home Front: Japanese Americans in the House of Jim Crow* (Chicago, IL: University of Chicago Press, 2008); Dower, *War without Mercy*; Lon Kurashige, *Two Faces of Exclusion: The Untold History of Anti-Asian Racism in the United States* (Chapel Hill: University of North Carolina Press, 2016); Geoffrey S. Smith, "Racial Nativism and Origins of Japanese American Relocation," in *Japanese Americans: From Relocation to Redress*, ed. Roger Daniels, Sandra C. Taylor, and Harry H. L. Kitano, 79–87 (Seattle, WA: University of Washington Press, 1991).

24. See Chapter 2 in Arthur Hansen, *Barbed Voices: Oral History, Resistance, and the World War II Japanese American Social Disaster* (Boulder: University Press of Colorado, 2018), Kindle edition.

25. Paul R. Spickard, "Injustice Compounded: Amerasians and Non-Japanese Americans in World War II Concentration Camps," *Journal of American Ethnic History* 5, no. 2 (1986): 5–22.

26. Koji Ariyoshi, *From Kona to Yenan: The Political Memoirs of Koji Ariyoshi* (Honolulu: University of Hawaii Press, 2000), Google books edition; Andrea Warren, *Enemy Child: The Story of Norman Mineta, a Boy Imprisoned in a Japanese American Internment Camp during World War II* (New York: Margaret Ferguson, 2019); James Omura, *Nisei Naysayer: The Memoir of Militant Japanese American Journalist Jimmie Omura*, ed. Arthur Hansen (Palo Alto, CA: Stanford University Press, 2018), Kindle edition.

27. John Okada, *No-No Boy* (Tokyo, Japan: C. E. Tuttle, 1957).

28. Such an approach was taken with Italian and German Americans.

29. See Brian Niiya, "No-No Boys," *Densho Encyclopedia*, available at http://ency clopedia.densho.org/No-no_boys/, and Cherstin M. Lyon, "Questions 27 and 28," *Densho Encyclopedia*, available at http://encyclopedia.densho.org/Questions_27 _and_28/.

30. Alexandra Atter, "Dispute Arises over 'No-No Boy,' a Classic of Asian-American Literature with a Complex History," *New York Times*, June 6, 2019, available at https://www.nytimes.com/2019/06/06/books/no-no-boy-penguin.html.

31. Gerald H. Robinson, *Elusive Truth: Four Photographers at Manzanar* (Nevada City, CA: Carl Mautz, 2002); Linda Gordon and Gary Y. Okihiro, eds., *Impounded: Dorothea Lange and the Censored Images of Japanese American Internment* (New York: W. W. Norton, 2006); Ansel Adams, *Two Views of Manzanar: An Exhibition of Photographs* (Los Angeles: Frederick S. Wight Art Gallery, University of California, Los Angeles, 1978).

32. See, for example, Cara A. Finnegan, *Picturing Poverty: Print Culture and FSA Photographs* (Washington, DC: Smithsonian, 2003); Nicholas Natanson, *The Black Image in the New Deal: The Politics of FSA Photography* (Knoxville: University of Tennessee Press, 1992).

33. Jeanne Wakatsuki Houston and James D. Houston, *Farewell to Manzanar* (Boston, MA: Houghton Mifflin, 2017), Kindle edition.

34. Daniels goes even further by recounting the history of Japanese nationals residing in the United States who were interned by the federal government after Pearl Harbor. Such detentions were indeed carried out according to U.S. laws on internment; by contrast, Japanese Americans removed from Military Area One were not treated in a lawful manner. The contrast makes the application of the term *internment* to U.S. citizens even more egregious. See Roger Daniels, "Words Do Matter: A Note on Inappropriate Terminology and the Incarceration of the Japanese Americans," in *Nikkei in the Pacific Northwest*, ed. Louis Fiset and Gail M. Nomura, Japanese Americans and Japanese Canadians in the Twentieth Century (Seattle: University of Washington Press, 2005), 190–214.

35. See Hennigan, "Trump Administration to Hold Migrant Children"; Fenwick, "'Stop Repeating History.'"

36. Daniels, "Words Do Matter," 201.

37. Raineri, *Red Angel*, 284–289.

PART I RUSSIA AND NEW YORK CITY

1. Kat Eschner, "Friction Matches Were Boon to Those Lighting Fires—Not So Much to Matchmakers," *Smithsonian.com*, November 27, 2017, available at https://www.smithsonianmag.com/smart-news/friction-matches-were-boon-those-lighting-firesnot-so-much-matchmakers-180967318/.

2. Elaine Black Yoneda, interviewed by Arthur Hansen and Betty Mitson, March 2–4, 1974, San Francisco, CA. Oral History #1377a-b, transcript, Japanese Americans Project, Center for Oral and Public History, California State University, Fullerton, #1377a, 2. [Hereafter EBY, COPH interview in notes.]

3. Elaine had a brief first marriage, which yielded a daughter, Joyce. As is demonstrated, Joyce appears to be, as here, a footnote to Elaine's story.

4. Gerald Sorin, *Tradition Transformed: The Jewish Experience in America*, American Moment Series (Baltimore, MD: Johns Hopkins University Press, 1997), 39.

5. Sorin, *Tradition Transformed*, 41.

6. Sorin, *Tradition Transformed*, 40.

7. Vivian McGuckin Raineri, *The Red Angel: The Life and Times of Elaine Black Yoneda, 1906–1988* (New York: International, 1991), 1.

8. Elaine Black Yoneda Oral History, MS 3524, Interview by Lucy Kendall, February 23, 1976–June 24, 1977, California Historical Society, 1. [Hereafter EBY, CHS interview in notes.]

9. EBY, CHS interview, 1.

10. Sorin, *Tradition Transformed*, 48–49.

11. Roger Daniels, *The Politics of Prejudice: The Anti-Japanese Movement in California and the Struggle for Japanese Exclusion* (Berkeley: University of California Press, 1999), 1.

12. EBY, CHS interview, 89.

13. EBY, CHS interview, 3.

14. EBY, CHS interview, 1, 4.

15. Tony Michels, *A Fire in Their Hearts: Yiddish Socialists in New York* (Cambridge, MA: Harvard University Press, 2009), Kindle edition.

16. EBY, CHS interview, 3.

17. EBY, CHS interview, 4, 104.

18. EBY, CHS interview, 100–101.

19. EBY, CHS interview, 2.

20. EBY, CHS interview, 2.

21. Michels, *Fire in Their Hearts*.

22. EBY, CHS interview, 2.

23. EBY, CHS interview, 1.

24. EBY, CHS interview, 94.

25. EBY, CHS interview, 105.

26. Raineri, *Red Angel*, 3.

27. EBY, CHS interview, 91.

28. EBY, CHS interview, 94.

29. Raineri, *Red Angel*, 3.

30. EBY, CHS interview, 90–91.

31. EBY, CHS interview, 91.

32. EBY, CHS interview, 91.

33. As quoted in Raineri, *Red Angel*, 4.

34. Raineri, *Red Angel*, 4.

35. Raineri, *Red Angel*, 4.

PART II LOS ANGELES

1. Elaine Black Yoneda Oral History, MS 3524, Interview by Lucy Kendall, February 23, 1976–June 24, 1977, California Historical Society, 106. [Hereafter EBY, CHS interview in notes.]

2. EBY, CHS interview, 106.

3. EBY, CHS interview, 107.

4. Vivian McGuckin Raineri, *The Red Angel: The Life and Times of Elaine Black Yoneda, 1906–1988* (New York: International, 1991), 8.

5. Allison Varzally, *Making a Non-white America: Californians Coloring outside Ethnic Lines, 1925–1955* (Berkeley: University of California Press, 2008), 32.

6. Raineri, *Red Angel*, 8; EBY, CHS interview, 101.

7. Elaine Black Yoneda, interviewed by Arthur Hansen and Betty Mitson, March 2–4, 1974, San Francisco, CA. Oral History #1377a-b, transcript, Japanese Americans Project, Center for Oral and Public History, California State University, Fullerton, #1377a, 6. [Hereafter EBY, COPH interview in notes.]

8. Varzally, *Making a Non-white America*, 31.

9. Wendy Elliott, "The Jews of Boyle Heights, 1900–1950: The Melting Pot of Los Angeles," *Southern California Quarterly* 78, no. 1 (1996): 1–10.

10. Raineri, *Red Angel*, 10.

11. Raineri, *Red Angel*, 8.

12. EBY, CHS interview, 102.

13. Kathleen A. Brown, "The 'Savagely Fathered and Un-Mothered World' of the Communist Party, U.S.A.: Feminism, Maternalism, and 'Mother Bloor,'" *Feminist Studies* 25, no. 3 (1999): 543.

14. EBY, CHS interview, 6–7.

15. Varzally, *Making a Non-white America*, 3.

16. Varzally, *Making a Non-white America*, 3.

17. Raineri, *Red Angel*, 10.

18. Raineri, *Red Angel*, 10.

19. EBY, COPH interview #1377a, 6.

20. EBY, CHS interview, 8.

21. EBY, CHS interview, 7.

22. EBY, CHS interview, 8.

23. Diana Selig, *Americans All: The Cultural Gifts Movement* (Cambridge, MA: Harvard University Press, 2008), Google books edition.

24. EBY, CHS interview, 7.

25. EBY, CHS interview, 9.

26. Raineri, *Red Angel*, 14.

27. Raineri, *Red Angel*, 14.

28. Article VII, Constitution of the Benevolent Protective Order of the Elk, accessed July 3, 2020, available at https://en.wikipedia.org/wiki/Benevolent_and_Protective_Order_of_Elks. This article was not repealed until 1973.

29. EBY, CHS interview, 9.

30. Raineri, *Red Angel*, 14.

31. EBY, CHS interview, 8–9.

32. Meyer Baylin, Meyer Baylin's Oral History, October 1993, Bancroft Library, 38.

33. EBY, CHS interview, 10.

34. EBY, CHS interview, 10.

35. EBY, CHS interview, 11.

36. Shelton Stromquist, *Labor's Cold War: Local Politics in a Global Context* (Urbana: University of Illinois Press, 2008), 21.

37. EBY, CHS interview, 12.

38. Daniel J. Leab, "'United We Eat': The Creation and Organization of the Unemployed Councils in 1930," *Labor History* 8 (January 1, 1967): 305.

39. EBY, CHS interview, 13.

40. EBY, CHS interview, 24.

41. EBY, CHS interview, 14.

42. EBY, CHS interview, 14.

43. Kevin Starr, *Endangered Dreams: The Great Depression in California*, Americans and the California Dream series (New York: Oxford University Press, 1997), 168–171.

44. Daniel Geary, "Carey McWilliams and Antifascism, 1934–1943," *Journal of American History* 90, no. 3 (2003): 21.

45. Carey McWilliams, "Leo Gallagher," *The Nation*, October 16, 1935, 438.

46. EBY, CHS interview, 14.

47. EBY, CHS interview, 16.

48. EBY, CHS interview, 17.

49. EBY, CHS interview, 17.

50. EBY, CHS interview, 17.

51. EBY, CHS interview, 18.

52. Raineri, *Red Angel*, 37.

53. EBY, CHS interview, 20.

54. EBY, CHS interview, 20.

55. EBY, CHS interview, 22.

56. EBY, CHS interview, 23.

57. EBY, CHS interview, 21.

58. EBY, CHS interview, 24.

59. EBY, CHS interview, 25.

60. EBY, CHS interview, 24.

61. Karl Yoneda, *Ganbatte: Sixty-Year Struggle of a Kibei Worker* (Los Angeles: University of California, Los Angeles Asian American Studies Center, 1983), 41.

62. "Police Have Dampening Influence on Red Demonstration on Main Street," *Los Angeles Times*, February 11, 1930, 10.

63. EBY, CHS interview, 17.

64. Yoneda, *Ganbatte*, 6–7.

65. Erika Lee and Judy Yung, *Angel Island: Immigrant Gateway to America* (Oxford, UK: Oxford University Press, 2012), 111.

66. Yoneda, *Ganbatte*, 9.

67. Yoneda, *Ganbatte*, 3.

68. Lee and Yung, *Angel Island*, 111.

69. Yoneda, *Ganbatte*, 4.

70. Yoneda, *Ganbatte*, 4–5.

71. Lee and Yung, *Angel Island*, 113.

72. Yoneda, *Ganbatte*, 5.

73. Yoneda, *Ganbatte*, 11.

74. Yoneda, *Ganbatte*, 12.

75. Yoneda, *Ganbatte*, 12.

76. Lee and Yung, *Angel Island*, 113. Lee and Yung's account of these events, drawn from Angel Island records, differs slightly from Karl's telling of the same events in *Ganbatte*. Here, I have drawn the likely conclusions from considering both narratives together. For example, Karl omits the discussion of his sister Emi's role.

77. Yoneda, *Ganbatte*, 15.

78. Yoneda, *Ganbatte*, 17.

79. Yoneda, *Ganbatte*, 20.

80. Yoneda, *Ganbatte*, 42.

81. EBY, CHS interview, 17.

82. Yoneda, *Ganbatte*, 42.

83. Yoneda, *Ganbatte*, 45–46.

84. Yoneda, *Ganbatte*, 59.

85. Varzally, *Making a Non-white America*, 109.

86. EBY, CHS interview, 26.

87. Yoneda, *Ganbatte*, 59.

88. Yoneda, *Ganbatte*, 59.

89. Raineri, *Red Angel*, 47.

90. Yoneda, *Ganbatte*, 61.

91. Yoneda, *Ganbatte*, 60.

92. Yoneda, *Ganbatte*, 60.

93. Yoneda, *Ganbatte*, 65.

94. Raineri, *Red Angel*, 47.

95. Yoneda, *Ganbatte*, 61.

96. Raineri, *Red Angel*, 47; Yoneda, *Ganbatte*, 61.

PART III SAN FRANCISCO

1. Karl Yoneda, *Ganbatte: Sixty-Year Struggle of a Kibei Worker* (Los Angeles: University of California, Los Angeles Asian American Studies Center, 1983), 65.

2. Yoneda, *Ganbatte*, 65.

3. Elizabeth Pepin and Lewis Watts, *Harlem of the West: The San Francisco Fillmore Jazz Era* (San Francisco, CA: Chronicle, 2006), 30; Meredith Oda, *The Gateway to the Pacific: Japanese Americans and the Remaking of San Francisco* (Chicago, IL: University of Chicago Press, 2019), 27.

4. David F. Selvin, *A Terrible Anger: The 1934 Waterfront and General Strikes in San Francisco* (Detroit, MI: Wayne State University Press, 1996), 60.

5. Kate Weigand, *Red Feminism: American Communism and the Making of Women's Liberation* (Baltimore, MD: Johns Hopkins University Press, 2001).

6. See Rosalyn Baxandall, "The Question Seldom Asked: Women and the CPUSA," in *New Studies in the Politics and Culture of U.S. Communism*, ed. Michael E. Brown et al. (New York: Monthly Review Press, 1993), 141–61; and Susan Ware, *Holding Their Own: American Women in the 1930s* (Boston, MA: Twayne, 1982), 141.

7. Baxandall, "Question Seldom Asked," 148.

8. Vivian McGuckin Raineri, *The Red Angel: The Life and Times of Elaine Black Yoneda, 1906–1988* (New York: International, 1991), 70.

9. Elaine Black Yoneda Oral History, MS 3524, Interview by Lucy Kendall, February 23, 1976–June 24, 1977, California Historical Society, 34–35. [Hereafter EBY, CHS interview in notes.]

10. Yoneda, *Ganbatte*, 78.

11. Raineri, *Red Angel*, 59; EBY, CHS interview, 33.

12. Raineri, *Red Angel*, 60.

13. Raineri, *Red Angel*, 50–51.

14. Raineri, *Red Angel*, 51.

15. Raineri, *Red Angel*, 153.

16. "The Activist Tom Mooney, on Death Row, Is Pardoned," January 7, 1939, Annotations: The NEH Preservation Project, accessed May 25, 2021, available at https://snaccooperative.org/ark:/99166/w6rf5s84.

17. Kevin Starr, *Endangered Dreams: The Great Depression in California*, Americans and the California Dream series (New York: Oxford University Press, 1997).

18. Raineri, *Red Angel*, 54.

19. Raineri, *Red Angel*, 55.

20. Nelson A. Pichardo, "The Power Elite and Elite-Driven Countermovements: The Associated Farmers of California during the 1930s," *Sociological Forum* 10, no. 1 (March 1, 1995): 25.

21. Raineri, *Red Angel*, 54.

22. Jack Withington, "A Night of Tar, Feathers and Terror," *Jewish American Society for Historic Preservation*, accessed May 14, 2019, available at http://www.jewish-american-society-for-historic-preservation.org/images/A_Night_of_Tar,_Feathers_and_Terror-1.pdf; Kenneth L. Kann, *Comrades and Chicken Ranchers: The Story of a California Jewish Community* (Ithaca, NY: Cornell University Press, 1993); Raineri, *Red Angel*, 119.

23. Kann, *Comrades and Chicken Ranchers*, 2.

24. Withington, "Night of Tar, Feathers and Terror."

25. Kann, *Comrades and Chicken Ranchers*, 110. The quote is from an interview published in Kann's book and attributed to Sylvia Stern Kurokawa. Kenneth Kann has confirmed, however, that the speaker is Elaine Black Yoneda. Kann had changed names to fictional ones when the book was published (author phone interview with Kann, February 5, 2019).

26. Elaine Black Yoneda, interviewed by Arthur Hansen and Betty Mitson, March 2–4, 1974, San Francisco, CA. Oral History #1377a-b, transcript, Japanese Americans Project, Center for Oral and Public History, California State University, Fullerton, #1377a, 73–76. [Hereafter EBY, COPH interview in notes.]

27. Raineri, *Red Angel*, 8.

28. Elaine Yoneda, "Trade Union Defense Builds the ILD," *Labor Defender*, October 1935, 15.

29. Yoneda, *Ganbatte*, 15.

30. EBY, CHS interview, 56.

31. EBY, CHS interview, 56.

32. EBY, CHS interview, 58.

33. EBY, CHS interview, 58.

34. Philippa Strum, *Speaking Freely:* Whitney v. California *and American Speech Law* (Lawrence: University Press of Kansas, 2015), 3.

35. EBY, CHS interview, 82.

36. EBY, CHS interview, 83.

37. EBY, CHS interview, 80–81, 91.

38. Kathleen A. Brown, "The 'Savagely Fathered and Un-Mothered World' of the Communist Party, U.S.A.: Feminism, Maternalism, and 'Mother Bloor,'" *Feminist Studies* 25, no. 3 (1999): 538.

39. EBY, CHS interview, 49.

40. Raineri, *Red Angel*, 95.

41. Raineri, *Red Angel*, 95.

42. Yoneda, *Ganbatte*, 72.

43. Chris Carlsson, "The Waterfront Strike," *FoundSF*, accessed April 5, 2019, available at https://www.foundsf.org/index.php?title=The_Waterfront_Strike.

44. Raineri, *Red Angel*, 68.

45. Raineri, *Red Angel*, 67.

46. EBY, CHS interview, 36.

47. Raineri, *Red Angel*, 63.

48. Raineri, *Red Angel*, 68.

49. Yoneda, *Ganbatte*, 76.

50. See the still photographs and film clips at Carlsson, "Waterfront Strike."

51. Carlsson, "Waterfront Strike."

52. Yoneda, *Ganbatte*, 74.

53. Raineri, *Red Angel*, 68.

54. Selvin, *Terrible Anger*, 142–144.

55. EBY, CHS interview, 37.

56. Raineri, *Red Angel*, 72.

57. Raineri, *Red Angel*, 73.

58. EBY, CHS interview, 37–38.

59. Raineri, *Red Angel*, 73.

60. Mike Quin, "1934 Funeral March: I Was There . . .," *FoundSF*, accessed April 5, 2019, available at https://www.foundsf.org/index.php?title=1934_Funeral_March.

61. Bruce Nelson, *Workers on the Waterfront: Seamen, Longshoremen, and Unionism in the 1930s* (Urbana: University of Illinois Press, 1988), 132.

62. The account of events in the CHS interview is contradicted by another source, which states that Julia Bordoise and the Mooneys were in two separate cars, one at the front of the procession and one at the back. The differing account appears in Irving Bernstein and Frances Fox Piven, *The Turbulent Years: A History of the American Worker, 1933–1940* (Chicago, IL: Haymarket, 2010).

63. Raineri, *Red Angel*, 74.

64. Nelson, *Workers on the Waterfront*, 128.

65. As quoted in Nelson, *Workers on the Waterfront*, 132.

66. Nelson, *Workers on the Waterfront*, 149.

67. Raineri, *Red Angel*, 75.

68. Raineri, *Red Angel*, 94.

69. EBY, CHS interview, 39–40; Raineri, *Red Angel*, 76.

70. EBY, CHS interview, 40; Raineri, *Red Angel*, 80.

71. EBY, CHS interview, 40–41.

72. Nelson, *Workers on the Waterfront*, 150.

73. Selvin, *Terrible Anger.*

74. Carlsson, "General Strike."

75. Yoneda, *Ganbatte*, 77.

76. "Red Suspects in City Jail on Hunger Strike," *San Francisco Examiner*, August 5, 1934, 1.

77. EBY, CHS interview, 43.

78. EBY, CHS interview, 44.

79. EBY, COPH interview #1377a, 72.

80. "Red Queen Out on Full Bail; Stomach Empty," *San Francisco Examiner*, August 10, 1934, 21; EBY, CHS interview, 44–46.

81. Raineri, *Red Angel*, 84.

82. "An Eyewitness," "What Does She Know about Halibut?" *Labor Defender*, October 1934, 8.

83. EBY, CHS interview, 85.

84. "Eyewitness," "What Does She Know."

85. "Woman Radical Sent to Jail," *Reno Evening Gazette*, August 15, 1934; "Communist Woman Found Guilty Here," *San Francisco Examiner*, August 15, 1934. The story was carried by papers in Baltimore, Spokane, St. Louis, Honolulu, throughout California, and elsewhere. Also see Raineri, *Red Angel*, 87.

86. As quoted in "*Whitney v. California* (1927)," The First Amendment Encyclopedia, accessed May 22, 2021, available at https://mtsu.edu/first-amendment /article/263/whitney-v-california.

87. Raineri, *Red Angel*, 100.

88. Raineri, *Red Angel*, 103.

89. Raineri, *Red Angel*, 104.

90. Raineri, *Red Angel*, 106.

91. Raineri, *Red Angel*, 105–106.

92. Raineri, *Red Angel*, 109.

93. As quoted in Raineri, *Red Angel*, 121.

94. EBY, CHS interview, 52.

95. EBY, COPH interview #1377a, 60.

96. EBY, CHS interview, 51–52.

97. EBY, CHS interview, 52.

98. EBY, COPH interview #1377a, 62.

99. EBY, COPH interview #1377a, 61.

100. EBY, CHS interview, 95.

101. EBY, CHS interview, 53.

102. EBY, COPH interview #1377a, 64.

103. EBY, COPH interview #1377a, 64.

104. EBY, CHS interview, 122.

105. EBY, COPH interview #1377a, 62.

106. EBY, COPH interview #1377a, 63.

107. Yoneda, *Ganbatte*, 96.

108. EBY, COPH interview #1377a, 62.

109. Yoneda, *Ganbatte*, 96.

110. Yoneda, *Ganbatte*, 96–99.
111. Yoneda, *Ganbatte*, 97.
112. Yoneda, *Ganbatte*, 96.
113. Raineri, *Red Angel,* 142.
114. Raineri, *Red Angel*, 167.
115. Raineri, *Red Angel*, 165.
116. EBY, CHS interview, 67–70.
117. Tom Yoneda, interview by author, Santa Rosa, California, February 23, 2019.
118. EBY, CHS interview, 135.
119. EBY, CHS interview, 135.
120. EBY, CHS interview, 135.
121. EBY, CHS interview, 66.
122. EBY, CHS interview, 66.
123. EBY, CHS interview, 135–136.
124. EBY, CHS interview, 66.
125. Yoneda, *Ganbatte*, 101.
126. Yoneda, *Ganbatte,* 103.
127. Yoneda, *Ganbatte*, 103–104; EBY, CHS interview, 72–74.
128. Yoneda, *Ganbatte*, 104.
129. Raineri, *Red Angel*, 155.
130. Yoneda, *Ganbatte*, 104; EBY, COPH interview #1377b, 2.
131. Raineri, *Red Angel*, 172.
132. EBY, CHS interview, 194.

PART IV MANZANAR

1. Vivian McGuckin Raineri, *The Red Angel: The Life and Times of Elaine Black Yoneda, 1906–1988* (New York: International, 1991), 179.
2. Karl Yoneda, *Ganbatte: Sixty-Year Struggle of a Kibei Worker* (Los Angeles: University of California, Los Angeles Asian American Studies Center, 1983), 111.
3. Raineri, *Red Angel*, 179.
4. Yoneda, *Ganbatte*, 112.
5. James Oda, *Heroic Struggles of Japanese Americans: Partisan Fighters from America's Concentration Camps* (Hollywood, CA: J. Oda, 1980).
6. Yoneda, *Ganbatte*, 113.
7. Yoneda, *Ganbatte*, 113.
8. Yoneda, *Ganbatte*, 97.
9. Elaine Black Yoneda, interviewed by Arthur Hansen and Betty Mitson, March 2–4, 1974, San Francisco, CA. Oral History #1377a-b, transcript, Japanese Americans Project, Center for Oral and Public History, California State University, Fullerton, #1377b, 5. [Hereafter EBY, COPH interview in notes.]
10. EBY, COPH interview #1377b, 7.
11. Yoneda, *Ganbatte*, 114.
12. Yoneda, *Ganbatte*, 113.
13. EBY, COPH interview #1377b, 20.

14. Yoneda, *Ganbatte*, 114.

15. EBY, COPH interview #1377b, 18.

16. EBY, COPH interview #1377b, 19.

17. Yoneda, *Ganbatte*, 115.

18. Yoneda, *Ganbatte*, 182.

19. Yoneda, *Ganbatte*, 115.

20. Yoneda, *Ganbatte*, 115.

21. Yoneda, *Ganbatte*, 116.

22. Yoneda, *Ganbatte*, 116.

23. "How to Tell J**s from the Chinese," *Life*, December 22, 1941.

24. Yoneda, *Ganbatte*, 116–117.

25. Yoneda, *Ganbatte*, 118.

26. Yoneda, *Ganbatte*, 119.

27. Yoneda, *Ganbatte*, 120.

28. Ron Leavitt, "S.F. May Ask U.S. to Move J**s Inland," *San Francisco Chronicle*, February 2, 1942.

29. Yoneda, *Ganbatte*, 120.

30. J. Oda, *Heroic Struggles*.

31. J. Oda, *Heroic Struggles*.

32. Daniels, *Prisoners without Trial: Japanese Americans in World War II* (New York: Hill and Wang, 2004), Kindle edition. Allison Varzally, *Making a Non-white America: Californians Coloring outside Ethnic Lines, 1925–1955* (Berkeley: University of California Press, 2008), 127.

33. Yoneda, *Ganbatte*, 120.

34. EBY, COPH interview #1377b, 26.

35. As quoted in Lon Kurashige, *Two Faces of Exclusion: The Untold History of Anti-Asian Racism in the United States* (Chapel Hill: University of North Carolina Press, 2016), 178.

36. California Historical Society, *Only What We Could Carry: The Japanese American Internment Experience* (San Francisco, CA: Heyday, 2000), 155.

37. Yoneda, *Ganbatte*, 122.

38. Yoneda, *Ganbatte*, 123.

39. *National Defense Migration. Hearings before the Select Committee on National Defense Migration, House of Representatives*, Seventy-Seventh Cong., 1st sess. (1942) (statement of James Omura, editor of the *Rocky Shimpo* newspaper), available at https://archive.org/details/nationaldefensem29unit/mode/2up.

40. Ellen Eisenberg, *The First to Cry Down Injustice? Western Jews and Japanese Removal during WWII* (Lanham, MD: Lexington, 2008), 71.

41. Robert Shaffer, "Cracks in the Consensus: Defending the Rights of Japanese Americans during World War II," *Radical History Review* 1998, no. 72 (October 1, 1998): 90.

42. Shaffer, "Cracks in the Consensus," 88.

43. Yoneda, *Ganbatte*, 123; EBY, COPH interview #1377b, 168.

44. EBY, COPH interview #1377b, 25.

45. EBY, COPH interview #1377b, 10.

46. Yoneda, *Ganbatte*, 123.

47. EBY, COPH interview #1377b, 27; Yoneda, *Ganbatte*, 122.

48. EBY, COPH interview #1377b, 27.

49. Yoneda, *Ganbatte*, 123.

50. Elaine and Karl state different dates for the move to Los Angeles. Elaine stated that they went directly from the Mooney funeral, whereas Karl remembered driving to Los Angeles a few days later. EBY, COPH interview #1377b, 29; Yoneda, *Ganbatte*, 124.

51. Yoneda, *Ganbatte*, 124.

52. Yoneda, *Ganbatte*, 124.

53. See "Home Page," Maryknoll Fathers and Brothers, accessed May 23, 2021, available at https://maryknollsociety.org.

54. Yoneda, *Ganbatte*, 125.

55. "A Japanse father is shown kissing his son good-by . . .," Karl G. Yoneda Papers, Special Collections, University of California, Los Angeles, box 10, folder 2.

56. EBY, COPH interview #1377b, 35–36; Raineri, *Red Angel*, 206; Yoneda, *Ganbatte*, 126.

57. Yoneda, *Ganbatte*, 126.

58. Yoneda, *Ganbatte*, 126.

59. Yoneda, *Ganbatte*, 127.

60. Yoneda, *Ganbatte*, 127.

61. Yoneda, *Ganbatte*, 127.

62. Yoneda, *Ganbatte*, 127–128.

63. Manzanar Committee, *Reflections in Three Self-Guided Tours of Manzanar* (Los Angeles, CA: Manzanar Committee, 1998); Jeffery Burton et al., *Confinement and Ethnicity: An Overview of World War II Japanese American Relocation Sites* (Seattle: University of Washington Press, 2002), Kindle version.

64. Catherine Irwin, *Twice Orphaned: Voices from the Children's Village at Manzanar* (Fullerton: Center for Oral and Public History, California State University at Fullerton, 2008), 6–8.

65. EBY, COPH interview #1377b, 37; Raineri, *Red Angel,* 207.

66. EBY, COPH interview #1377b, 40.

67. EBY, COPH interview #1377b, 66.

68. EBY, COPH interview #1377b, 44–45.

69. Yoneda, *Ganbatte*, 129.

70. Paul R. Spickard, "Injustice Compounded: Amerasians and Non-Japanese Americans in World War II Concentration Camps," *Journal of American Ethnic History* 5, no. 2 (1986): 5–22.

71. EBY, COPH interview #1377b, 50.

72. EBY, COPH interview #1377b, 51.

73. Yoneda, *Ganbatte*, 128.

74. EBY, COPH interview #1377b, 52–54.

75. EBY, COPH interview #1377b, 57; Yoneda, *Ganbatte*, 131.

76. EBY, COPH interview #1377b, 65.

77. EBY, COPH interview #1377b, 56.

78. EBY, COPH interview #1377b, 73.

79. EBY, COPH interview #1377b, 57–58.

80. *Manzana* is the Spanish word for apple.

81. EBY, COPH interview #1377b, 66–67.

82. Arthur Hansen, interview by author, May 30, 2019.

83. Raineri, *Red Angel*, 210.

84. EBY, COPH interview #1377b, 64.

85. Raineri, *Red Angel*, 211.

86. Houston and Houston, *Farewell to Manzanar*.

87. EBY, COPH interview #1377b, 59.

88. Manzanar authorities and others described the living quarters as apartments. Where the term appears here, it is always in quotation marks to signify the fact that these spaces could hardly be said to resemble the genteel living spaces one associates with the word. Many who were incarcerated at Manzanar objected to the use of the word *apartment* to describe these buildings and used the term only with irony.

89. Raineri, *Red Angel*, 217–218.

90. Hansen interview by author.

91. Arthur Hansen, *Barbed Voices: Oral History, Resistance, and the World War II Japanese American Social Disaster* (Boulder: University Press of Colorado, 2018), 119, Kindle edition.

92. Hansen interview by author.

93. Yoneda, *Ganbatte*, 118.

94. J. Oda, *Heroic Struggles*, 31.

95. Yoneda, *Ganbatte*, 132.

96. Yoneda, *Ganbatte*, 135.

97. Yoneda, *Ganbatte*, 136.

98. Karl G. Yoneda Papers, Special Collections, University of California–Los Angeles [hereafter Karl Yoneda Papers], box 10, folder 6.

99. Karl Yoneda Papers, box 10, folder 6.

100. Hansen interview by author.

101. Tad Uyeno, "Point of No Return" series published in *Rafu Shimpo*, September to November 1973. Quoted in J. Oda, *Heroic Struggles*, 80.

102. Hansen interview by author.

103. Very little appears in the archival record about this group. For Elaine and Karl, they were a very real gang who threatened the physical safety of their family. The term "Black Dragons" does appear in memoirs, articles, and oral histories of a number of people incarcerated at Manzanar. And yet, as historian Arthur Hansen points out, it is the only organization within Manzanar for which there is no written record (in comparison to, for example, the Manzanar Citizens Federation). Whether the Black Dragons was a large, organized group of rebels, whether they truly were actively seeking a Japanese victory over the United States, whether they were a less politically engaged group of ruffians, or whether they were providing noble resistance in unjust times, is not currently known. In these pages I use the phrase "Black Dragons" advisedly, with these caveats in mind, and only when the use of the phrase has been corroborated by more than one person who was incarcerated at Manzanar.

104. Raineri, *Red Angel*, 214.

105. Yoneda, *Ganbatte*, 133.

106. Hansen, *Barbed Voices*.

107. Hansen interview by author.

108. Yoneda, *Ganbatte*, 133.

109. EBY, COPH interview #1377b, 117.

110. EBY, COPH interview #1377b, 113–114.

111. Yoneda, *Ganbatte*, 134.

112. Yoneda, *Ganbatte*, 133–134.

113. EBY, COPH interview #1377b, 131–132.

114. EBY, COPH interview #1377b, 135.

115. EBY, COPH interview #1377b, 138.

116. Yoneda, *Ganbatte*, 136–137.

117. Yoneda, *Ganbatte*, 137.

118. Yoneda, *Ganbatte*, 138.

119. Yoneda, *Ganbatte*, 138.

120. Yoneda, *Ganbatte*, 138.

121. J. Oda, *Heroic Struggles*, 34.

122. Spickard, "Injustice Compounded," 19.

123. Katherine Jellison, "Get Your Farm in the Fight: Farm Masculinity in World War II," *Agricultural History* 92, no. 1 (2018): 5–20.

124. Yoneda, *Ganbatte*, 142.

125. EBY, COPH interview #1377b, 167.

126. There is no clear indication in the records how this meeting came about, or why Elaine would have been questioned in this way.

127. EBY, COPH interview #1377b, 168.

128. Tom Yoneda, interview by author, Santa Rosa, California, February 23, 2019.

129. EBY, COPH interview #1377b, 174.

130. EBY, COPH interview #1377b, 170.

131. EBY, COPH interview #1377b, 75.

132. Yoneda, *Ganbatte*, 142–144.

133. EBY, COPH interview #1377b, 184–185.

134. EBY, COPH interview #1377b, 182.

135. EBY, COPH interview #1377b, 187.

136. Yoneda, *Ganbatte*, 145.

137. EBY, COPH interview #1377b, 188.

138. Yoneda, *Ganbatte*, 146.

139. EBY, COPH interview #1377b, 188.

140. Yoneda, *Ganbatte*, 146.

141. Yoneda, *Ganbatte*, 147.

142. Yoneda, *Ganbatte*, 147.

143. EBY, COPH interview #1377b, 190.

144. EBY, COPH interview #1377b, 191.

145. Arthur Hansen, interview by author, May 30, 2019 (telephone).

146. Eric L. Muller, *Free to Die for Their Country: The Story of the Japanese American Draft Resisters in World War II* (Chicago, IL: University of Chicago Press, 2001), 44.

147. Hansen interview by author.
148. Yoneda, *Ganbatte*, 148.
149. Raineri, *Red Angel*, 222.
150. Hansen, *Barbed Voices*.
151. Quoted in Elaine Black Yoneda, unpublished typescript "Letter to Editor," Karl Yoneda Papers, University of California, Los Angeles, box 11, folder 7. Some dispute this account. According to Arthur Hansen, a death list did exist but there were never any threats against children, including Tommy. Hansen interview by author.
152. EBY, COPH interview #1377b, 198.
153. Raineri, *Red Angel*, 223.
154. EBY, COPH interview #1377b, 200.
155. EBY, COPH interview #1377b, 202.
156. Brian Niiya, "Manzanar Riot/Uprising," *Densho Blog*, accessed May 6, 2019, available at https://densho.org/remembering-manzanar-riot/.
157. The events of December 1942 at Manzanar are described as a riot not only in the media reporting at the time, but in much of the secondary literature on its history. Indeed, Karl and Elaine's accounts use the word *riot*. Arthur Hansen provides a compelling account of how the phrase "Manzanar riot" took hold in the historical record. The use of the term *riot*, argues Hansen, has obscured from view the presence of a resistance movement. The word *riot* connotes a singular, uncontrolled event. By contrast, Hansen proposes that "terming the event the 'Manzanar Revolt' forces us to see it not as an uncaused and inconsequential aberration, but as one intense expression of a continuing resistance movement." The word *revolt* returns agency to those who enacted a campaign of opposition to exclusion and incarceration. See Chapter 2 of Hansen, *Barbed Voices*.
158. *San Francisco Chronicle*, "Manzanar J** Relocation Center under Martial Law: One Killed, Nine Wounded in Pro-Axis Uprising," *San Francisco Chronicle*, December 8, 1942.
159. Raineri, *Red Angel*, 223.
160. EBY, COPH interview #1377b, 205.
161. EBY, COPH interview #1377b, 202–203.
162. Raineri, *Red Angel*, 224.
163. EBY, COPH interview #1377b, 211–213.
164. EBY, COPH interview #1377b, 213–214; Raineri, *Red Angel*, 224–225.
165. EBY, COPH interview #1377b, 214.

PART V SAN FRANCISCO AND PENNGROVE

1. Elaine Black Yoneda, interviewed by Arthur Hansen and Betty Mitson, March 2–4, 1974, San Francisco, CA. Oral History #1377a-b, transcript, Japanese Americans Project, Center for Oral and Public History, California State University, Fullerton, #1377b, 215. [Hereafter EBY, COPH interview in notes.]
2. Vivian McGuckin Raineri, *The Red Angel: The Life and Times of Elaine Black Yoneda, 1906–1988* (New York: International, 1991), 231.
3. EBY, COPH interview #1377b, 218.

4. Raineri, *Red Angel*, 232.

5. Karl Yoneda, *Ganbatte: Sixty-Year Struggle of a Kibei Worker* (Los Angeles: University of California, Los Angeles Asian American Studies Center, 1983), 151.

6. Raineri, *Red Angel*, 232.

7. EBY, COPH interview #1377b, 218.

8. Raineri, *Red Angel*, 234.

9. Yoneda, *Ganbatte*, 151–152.

10. Yoneda, *Ganbatte*, 152–153.

11. Yoneda, *Ganbatte*, 153–154.

12. Yoneda, *Ganbatte*, 155.

13. Yoneda, *Ganbatte*, 156.

14. Yoneda, *Ganbatte*, 157.

15. Yoneda, *Ganbatte*, 156.

16. Yoneda, *Ganbatte*, 158–160.

17. Yoneda, *Ganbatte*, 162.

18. EBY, CHS interview, 161.

19. Yoneda, *Ganbatte*, 180.

20. Yoneda, *Ganbatte*, 165.

21. Yoneda, *Ganbatte*, 163.

22. Yoneda, *Ganbatte*, 164.

23. Yoneda, *Ganbatte*, 170.

24. Yoneda, *Ganbatte*, 170.

25. Yoneda, *Ganbatte*, 169.

26. Raineri, *Red Angel*, 252.

27. Yoneda, *Ganbatte*, 170.

28. Raineri, *Red Angel*, 253.

29. Allan R. Bosworth, *America's Concentration Camps* (New York: Norton, 1967), 211–212.

30. Raineri, *Red Angel*, 252.

31. Kenneth L. Kann, *Comrades and Chicken Ranchers: The Story of a California Jewish Community* (Ithaca, NY: Cornell University Press, 1993), 19.

32. Kann, *Comrades and Chicken Ranchers*.

33. Kann, *Comrades and Chicken Ranchers*, 1.

34. Kann, *Comrades and Chicken Ranchers*, 3.

35. Raineri, *Red Angel*, 255; Yoneda, *Ganbatte*, 171–172.

36. Kann, *Comrades and Chicken Ranchers*, 5.

37. Yoneda, *Ganbatte*, 173.

38. Raineri, *Red Angel*, 278.

39. Cherstin M. Lyon, "Smith Act," *Densho Encyclopedia*, available at https://encyclopedia.densho.org/Koji_Ariyoshi/. Excerpts from Ariyoshi's memoirs, including his perspective on these events, are available on the Center for Labor Education and Research of the University of Hawai'i at Oahu's *Honolulu Record* digitization project, available at https://www.hawaii.edu/uhwo/clear/HonoluluRecord/kojisblog/koji's%20blog.html.

40. Raineri, *Red Angel*, 226.

41. Kann, *Comrades and Chicken Ranchers*, 209–210.

42. Raineri, *Red Angel*, 268.

43. Ben Kobashigawa, interview by the author, San Francisco, California, January 22, 2019.

44. Yoneda, *Ganbatte*, 173; Raineri, *Red Angel*, 262.

45. Kann, *Comrades and Chicken Ranchers*, 3.

46. Kann, *Comrades and Chicken Ranchers*, 4.

47. Yoneda, *Ganbatte*, 173.

48. California Historical Society, *Only What We Could Carry: The Japanese American Internment Experience* (San Francisco, CA: Heyday, 2000).

49. Kann, *Comrades and Chicken Ranchers*, 151.

50. Raineri, *Red Angel*, 262.

51. Yoneda, *Ganbatte*, 177.

52. Raineri, *Red Angel*, 267.

53. Yoneda, *Ganbatte*, 179–181.

54. Yoneda, *Ganbatte*, 197.

55. EBY, COPH interview #1377b, 221.

56. Yoneda, *Ganbatte*, 200.

57. Raineri, *Red Angel*, 278–279.

58. Martha Nakagawa, "Manzanar Committee," *Densho Encyclopedia*, available at https://encyclopedia.densho.org/Manzanar_Committee/.

59. Yoneda, *Ganbatte*, 200–201.

60. Karl Yoneda and Elaine Yoneda, "Manzanar: Another View," *Rafu Shimpo*, December 19, 1973. Quoted from manuscript in Karl Yoneda papers, box 11, folder 7.

61. Yoneda and Yoneda, "Manzanar."

62. Yoneda and Yoneda, "Manzanar." Emphases in original.

63. EBY, COPH interview #1377b, 220.

64. EBY, COPH interview #1377b, 220.

65. Mitchell T. Maki, Harry H. Kitano, and S. Megan Berthold, *Achieving the Impossible Dream: How Japanese Americans Obtained Redress* (Urbana: University of Illinois Press, 1999), 5.

66. Yoneda, *Ganbatte*, 199–200.

67. Mitchell T. Maki, Harry H. Kitano, and S. Megan Berthold, *Achieving the Impossible Dream: How Japanese Americans Obtained Redress* (Urbana: University of Illinois Press, 1999), 6.

68. Yoneda, *Ganbatte*, 198.

69. Alice Yang, "Redress Movement," *Densho Encyclopedia*, available at https://encyclopedia.densho.org/Redress_movement/.

70. Yoneda, *Ganbatte*, 198.

71. Yoneda, *Ganbatte*, 199.

72. California Historical Society, *Only What We Could Carry*, 172.

73. Raineri, *Red Angel*, 269.

74. Katherine Bishop, "Elaine Black Yoneda, 81, Radical Labor Activist," *New York Times*, May 30, 1988, available at https://www.nytimes.com/1988/05/30/obituaries/elaine-black-yoneda-81-radical-labor-activist.html.

75. Raineri, *Red Angel*, 295.
76. Raineri, *Red Angel*, 296.
77. Hansen interview by author.

POSTSCRIPT

1. Kenneth L. Kann, *Comrades and Chicken Ranchers: The Story of a California Jewish Community* (Ithaca, NY: Cornell University Press, 1993).
2. Tom Yoneda, interview by author, Santa Rosa, California, February 23, 2019.

Bibliography

ARCHIVES AND UNPUBLISHED PRIMARY SOURCES

Baylin, Meyer. Meyer Baylin's Oral History, October 1993. Bancroft Library.

Elaine Black Yoneda Collection, Labor Archives and Research Center, San Francisco State University.

Elaine Black Yoneda interviewed by Arthur Hansen and Betty Mitson, March 2–4, 1974, San Francisco, CA. Oral History #1377a-b, transcript, Japanese Americans Project, Center for Oral and Public History, California State University, Fullerton.

Elaine Black Yoneda Oral History, MS 3524, California Historical Society. Series of interviews by Lucy Kendall, from February 23, 1976, to June 24, 1977.

Yoneda (Karl G.) Papers, Special Collections, University of California, Los Angeles.

PUBLISHED SOURCES

Adams, Ansel. *Two Views of Manzanar: An Exhibition of Photographs*. Los Angeles: Frederick S. Wight Art Gallery, University of California, Los Angeles, 1978.

Anonymous. "How to Tell J**s from the Chinese." *Life*, December 22, 1941.

Ariyoshi, Koji. *From Kona to Yenan: The Political Memoirs of Koji Ariyoshi*. Honolulu: University of Hawaii Press, 2000. Google books edition.

Baxandall, Rosalyn. "The Question Seldom Asked: Women and the CPUSA." In *New Studies in the Politics and Culture of U.S. Communism*, edited by Michael E. Brown, Randy Martin, Frank Rosengarten, and George Snedeker, 141–161. New York: Monthly Review Press, 1993.

Bernstein, Irving, and Frances Fox Piven. *The Turbulent Years: A History of the American Worker, 1933–1940*. Chicago, IL: Haymarket, 2010.

Bishop, Katherine. "Elaine Black Yoneda, 81, Radical Labor Activist." *New York Times*, May 30, 1988. Available at https://www.nytimes.com/1988/05/30/obituaries/elaine-black-yoneda-81-radical-labor-activist.html.

Bosworth, Allan R. *America's Concentration Camps*. New York: Norton, 1967.

Brodkin, Karen. *How Jews Became White Folks and What It Says about Race in America*. New Brunswick, NJ: Rutgers University Press, 1994.

Brown, Kathleen A. "Beyond the Great Debates: Gender and Race in Early America." *Reviews in American History* 26, no. 1 (1998): 96–123.

———. "The 'Savagely Fathered and Un-Mothered World' of the Communist Party, U.S.A.: Feminism, Maternalism, and 'Mother Bloor.'" *Feminist Studies* 25, no. 3 (1999): 537–70.

Brown, Wendy. "Tolerance and Equality: The Jewish Question and the Woman Question." In *Going Public: Feminism and the Shifting Boundaries of the Private Sphere*, edited by Joan W. Scott, 15–42. Urbana: University of Illinois Press, 2005.

Burton, Jeffery, Mary Farrell, Florence Lord, Richard Lord, and Tetsuden Kashima. *Confinement and Ethnicity: An Overview of World War II Japanese American Relocation Sites*. Seattle: University of Washington Press, 2002.

California Historical Society. *Only What We Could Carry: The Japanese American Internment Experience*. Berkeley, CA: Heyday, 2000.

Carlsson, Chris. "The General Strike of 1934: Historical Essay." *FoundSF*. Accessed April 7, 2019. Available at http://www.foundsf.org/index.php?title=The_General_Strike_of_1934.

———. "The Waterfront Strike: Historical Essay." *FoundSF*. Accessed April 5, 2019. Available at https://www.foundsf.org/index.php?title=The_Waterfront_Strike.

Cohen, Patricia Cline. *The Murder of Helen Jewett*. New York: Vintage, 1999.

Daniels, Roger. *Concentration Camps USA: Japanese Americans and World War II*. New York: Holt, Rinehart, and Winston, 1971.

———. *The Politics of Prejudice: The Anti-Japanese Movement in California and the Struggle for Japanese Exclusion*. Berkeley: University of California Press, 1999.

———. *Prisoners without Trial: Japanese Americans in World War II*. New York: Hill and Wang, 2004. Kindle edition.

———. "Words Do Matter: A Note on Inappropriate Terminology and the Incarceration of the Japanese Americans." In *Nikkei in the Pacific Northwest*, edited by Louis Fiset and Gail M. Nomura, 190–214. Japanese Americans and Japanese Canadians in the Twentieth Century. Seattle: University of Washington Press, 2005.

Dixler, Elsa Jane. "The Woman Question: Women and the American Communist Party, 1929–1941." Ph.D. diss., Yale University, 1974. Available at http://search.proquest.com/pqdtglobal/docview/302771545/citation/1CD61F09D29E4D81PQ/1.

Dower, John W. *War without Mercy: Race and Power in the Pacific War*. New York: Pantheon, 1986.

Drinnon, Richard. *Keeper of Concentration Camps: Dillon S. Myer and American Racism*. Berkeley: University of California Press, 1987.

Eisenberg, Ellen. *The First to Cry Down Injustice?: Western Jews and Japanese Removal during WWII*. Lanham, MD: Lexington, 2008.

Elliott, Wendy. "The Jews of Boyle Heights, 1900–1950: The Melting Pot of Los Angeles." *Southern California Quarterly* 78, no. 1 (1996): 1–10.

Eschner, Kat. "Friction Matches Were Boon to Those Lighting Fires—Not So Much to Matchmakers." *Smithsonian.com*, November 27, 2017. Available at https://www.smithsonianmag.com/smart-news/friction-matches-were-boon-those-lighting-firesnot-so-much-matchmakers-180967318/.

"Eyewitness, An." "What Does She Know about Halibut?" *Labor Defender* (October 1934): 8.

Finnegan, Cara A. *Picturing Poverty: Print Culture and FSA Photographs*. Washington, DC: Smithsonian Books, 2003.

Geary, Daniel. "Carey McWilliams and Antifascism, 1934–1943." *Journal of American History* 90, no. 3 (2003): 912–34.

Gordon, Linda, and Gary Y. Okihiro, eds. *Impounded: Dorothea Lange and the Censored Images of Japanese American Internment*. New York: W. W. Norton, 2006.

Hansen, Arthur. *Barbed Voices: Oral History, Resistance, and the World War II Japanese American Social Disaster*. Boulder: University Press of Colorado, 2018. Kindle edition.

———. "Oral History and the Japanese American Evacuation." *Journal of American History* 82, no. 2 (1995): 625–39.

———. "A Riot of Voices: Racial and Ethnic Variable in Interactive Oral History Interviewing." In *Interactive Oral History Interviewing*, edited by Eva M. McMahan and Kim Lacy Rogers, 107–39. New York: Routledge, 2013.

Hayashi, Brian Masaru. *Democratizing the Enemy: The Japanese American Internment*. Princeton, NJ: Princeton University Press, 2010.

Houston, Jeanne Wakatsuki, and James D. Houston. *Farewell to Manzanar*. Boston: Houghton Mifflin, 2017. Kindle edition.

Howard, John. *Concentration Camps on the Home Front: Japanese Americans in the House of Jim Crow*. Chicago, IL: University of Chicago Press, 2008.

Irwin, Catherine. *Twice Orphaned: Voices from the Children's Village at Manzanar*. Center for Oral and Public History, California State University at Fullerton, 2008.

Jellison, Katherine. "Get Your Farm in the Fight: Farm Masculinity in World War II." *Agricultural History* 92, no. 1 (2018): 5–20.

Kann, Kenneth L. *Comrades and Chicken Ranchers: The Story of a California Jewish Community*. Ithaca, NY: Cornell University Press, 1993.

Kashima, Tetsuden. *Judgment without Trial: Japanese American Imprisonment during World War II*. Seattle: University of Washington Press, 2004.

Kurashige, Lon. *Two Faces of Exclusion: The Untold History of Anti-Asian Racism in the United States*. Chapel Hill: University of North Carolina Press, 2016.

Leab, Daniel J. "'United We Eat': The Creation and Organization of the Unemployed Councils in 1930." *Labor History* 8 (January 1, 1967): 300–315.

Leavitt, Ron. "S.F. May Ask U.S. to Move J**s Inland." *San Francisco Chronicle*, February 2, 1942.

Lee, Erika, and Judy Yung. *Angel Island: Immigrant Gateway to America*. Oxford, UK: Oxford University Press, 2012.

Maki, Mitchell T., Harry H. Kitano, and S. Megan Berthold. *Achieving the Impossible Dream: How Japanese Americans Obtained Redress*. Urbana: University of Illinois Press, 1999.

Manzanar Committee. *Reflections in Three Self-Guided Tours of Manzanar*. Los Angeles: Manzanar Committee, 1998.

Margadant, Jo Burr. *The New Biography: Performing Feminism in Nineteenth-Century France*. Berkeley: University of California Press, 2000.

McWilliams, Carey. "Leo Gallagher." *The Nation*, October 16, 1935, 912–934.

Michels, Tony. *A Fire in Their Hearts: Yiddish Socialists in New York*. Cambridge, MA: Harvard University Press, 2009. Kindle edition.

Molina, Natalia. *How Race Is Made in America: Immigration, Citizenship, and the Historical Power of Racial Scripts*. Berkeley: University of California Press, 2014.

Muller, Eric L. *Free to Die for Their Country: The Story of the Japanese American Draft Resisters in World War II*. Chicago, IL: University of Chicago Press, 2001.

Nakagawa, Martha. "Manzanar Committee." *Densho Encyclopedia*. Accessed May 12, 2019. Available at https://encyclopedia.densho.org/Manzanar_Committee/.

Natanson, Nicholas. *The Black Image in the New Deal: The Politics of FSA Photography*. Knoxville: University of Tennessee Press, 1992.

National Defense Migration. Hearings before the Select Committee Investigating National Defense Migration, House of Representatives, Seventy-seventh Congress, United States. Congress, House. Select Committee Investigating National Defense Migration (1942). Accessed June 3, 2019. Available at https://archive.org /details/nationaldefensem29unit/mode/2up.

Nelson, Barbara J. "The Origins of the Two-Channel Welfare State: Workmen's Compensation and Mothers' Aid." In *Women, the State, and Welfare*, edited by Linda Gordon. Madison: University of Wisconsin Press, 1990.

Niiya, Brian. "Manzanar Riot/Uprising." In *Densho Encyclopedia*. Densho Blog. Accessed May 6, 2019. Available at https://densho.org/remembering-manzanar-riot/.

Oda, James. *Heroic Struggles of Japanese Americans: Partisan Fighters from America's Concentration Camps*. Hollywood, CA: J. Oda, 1980.

Oda, Meredith. *The Gateway to the Pacific: Japanese Americans and the Remaking of San Francisco*. Chicago, IL: University of Chicago Press, 2019.

Okada, John. *No-No Boy*. Tokyo: C. E. Tuttle, 1957.

Omura, James. *Nisei Naysayer: The Memoir of Militant Japanese American Journalist Jimmie Omura*. Edited by Arthur Hansen. Palo Alto, CA: Stanford University Press, 2018. Kindle edition.

Pepin, Elizabeth, and Lewis Watts. *Harlem of the West: The San Francisco Fillmore Jazz Era*. San Francisco, CA: Chronicle, 2006.

Pichardo, Nelson A. "The Power Elite and Elite-Driven Countermovements: The Associated Farmers of California during the 1930s." *Sociological Forum* 10, no. 1 (March 1, 1995): 21–49.

"Police Have Dampening Influence on Red Demonstration on Main Street." *Los Angeles Times*, February 11, 1930.

Quin, Mike. "1934 Funeral March: I Was There. . . ." *FoundSF*. Accessed April 5, 2019. Available at http://www.foundsf.org/index.php?title=1934_Funeral_March.

Raineri, Vivian McGuckin. *The Red Angel: The Life and Times of Elaine Black Yoneda, 1906–1988*. New York: International, 1991.

Renders, Hans, Binne de Haan, and Jonne Harmsma, eds. *The Biographical Turn: Lives in History*. London: Routledge, 2016.

Robinson, Gerald H. *Elusive Truth: Four Photographers at Manzanar*. Nevada City, CA: Carl Mautz, 2002.

Robinson, Greg. *By Order of the President*. Cambridge, MA: Harvard University Press, 2009.

Rosenbaum, Fred. *Cosmopolitans: A Social and Cultural History of the Jews of the San Francisco Bay Area*. Berkeley: University of California Press, 2009.

San Francisco Chronicle. "Manzanar J** Relocation Center under Martial Law: One Killed, Nine Wounded in Pro-Axis Uprising." *San Francisco Chronicle*, December 8, 1942.

Selig, Diana. *Americans All: The Cultural Gifts Movement*. Cambridge, MA: Harvard University Press, 2008.

Selvin, David F. *A Terrible Anger: The 1934 Waterfront and General Strikes in San Francisco*. Detroit, MI: Wayne State University Press, 1996.

Shaffer, Robert. "Cracks in the Consensus: Defending the Rights of Japanese Americans during World War II." *Radical History Review* 1998, no. 72 (October 1, 1998): 84–120.

Smith, Geoffrey S. "Racial Nativism and Origins of Japanese American Relocation." In *Japanese Americans: From Relocation to Redress*, edited by Roger Daniels, Sandra C. Taylor, and Harry H. L. Kitano, 79–87. Seattle: University of Washington Press, 1991.

Sorin, Gerald. *Tradition Transformed: The Jewish Experience in America*. Baltimore, MD: Johns Hopkins University Press, 1997.

Spickard, Paul R. "Injustice Compounded: Amerasians and Non-Japanese Americans in World War II Concentration Camps." *Journal of American Ethnic History* 5, no. 2 (1986): 5–22.

Starr, Kevin. *Endangered Dreams: The Great Depression in California*. New York: Oxford University Press, 1997.

Steedman, Carolyn. *Landscape for a Good Woman: A Story of Two Lives*. New Brunswick, NJ: Rutgers University Press, 1986.

Stromquist, Shelton. *Labor's Cold War: Local Politics in a Global Context*. Urbana: University of Illinois Press, 2008.

Strum, Philippa. *Speaking Freely: Whitney v. California and American Speech Law*. Lawrence: University Press of Kansas, 2015.

Ulrich, Laurel Thatcher. *A Midwife's Tale: The Life of Martha Ballard, Based on Her Diary, 1785–1812*. New York: Alfred A. Knopf, 1990.

Varzally, Allison. *Making a Non-white America: Californians Coloring outside Ethnic Lines, 1925–1955*. Berkeley: University of California Press, 2008.

Wagner-Martin, Linda. *Telling Women's Lives: The New Biography*. New Brunswick, NJ: Rutgers University Press, 1994.

Ware, Susan. *Holding Their Own: American Women in the 1930s*. Boston, MA: Twayne, 1982.

Warren, Andrea. *Enemy Child: The Story of Norman Mineta, a Boy Imprisoned in a Japanese American Internment Camp during World War II.* New York: Margaret Ferguson, 2019.

Weglyn, Michi. *Years of Infamy: The Untold Story of America's Concentration Camps.* New York: Morrow, 1976.

Weigand, Kate. *Red Feminism: American Communism and the Making of Women's Liberation.* Baltimore, MD: Johns Hopkins University Press, 2001.

Wild, Mark. *Street Meeting: Multiethnic Neighborhoods in Early Twentieth-Century Los Angeles.* Berkeley: University of California Press, 2005.

Withington, Jack. "A Night of Tar, Feathers and Terror." *Jewish American Society for Historic Preservation.* Accessed May 14, 2019. Available at http://www.jewish-amer ican-society-for-historic-preservation.org/images/A_Night_of_Tar,_Feathers_and _Terror-1.pdf.

Yang, Alice. "Redress Movement." *Densho Encyclopedia.* Accessed May 12, 2019. Available at https://encyclopedia.densho.org/Redress_movement/.

Yoneda, Elaine. "Trade Union Defense Builds the ILD." *Labor Defender* (October 1935): 15–16.

Yoneda, Karl. *Ganbatte: Sixty-Year Struggle of a Kibei Worker.* Los Angeles: University of California, Los Angeles Asian American Studies Center, 1983.

Yoneda, Karl, and Elaine Yoneda. "Manzanar: Another View." *Rafu Shimpo,* December 19, 1973.

Zinsser, Judith P. "Feminist Biography: A Contradiction in Terms?" *Eighteenth Century* 50, no. 1 (2010): 43–50.

Index

African Americans, 60–61, 66, 157, 165
agriculture, 65–66, 118, 163–165
Alaska Cannery Workers Union, 95
American Civil Liberties Union (ACLU), 67
American Committee for the Protection of the Foreign Born, 170
American Federation of Labor (AFL), 41, 52, 68–70
American Legion of San Francisco, 84
Anderson, George, 75, 114
Angel Island, 50
anti-Semitism, 14, 22–23, 25, 28–29, 33–34, 66–67
apple growing, 66
Application for Leave Clearance, 11
Ariyoshi, Koji, 140, 145–147, 166
Ariyoshi, Taeko, 134, 151
Asia Exclusion Act of 1924 (Johnson-Reed Act), 52, 70
Asian American Coalition of Los Angeles, 170
Associated Farmers Association of California, 66, 70–71

Baxandall, Rosalyn, 9, 61–62
Bay Area Nisei Communist Party, 114
Baylin, Meyer, 39–40, 42
Baylin, Vera, 39–40
Betsy Ross case, 46–47
Billings, Warren, 63–65

biography: book sources and, 7–8; criticisms of, 4; effect of Yonedas' interracial status on archival material and, 6; feminist, 4–6, 182n9; gender biases and, 6; oral histories and, 6–7; primary sources and, 8; secondary literature and, 8–11
birth control, 94
Black Dragon Association, 139, 144, 146, 196n103
Bloor, Eva Reeve, 35, 63, 74
Bordoise, Nicholas, 79–80
Boyle Heights neighborhood, 5, 8–9, 35–36, 182n8
Brandeis, Louis, 85
Brannan, Louella "Happy," 70–72, 141, 160
Brannan, Ray, 70–71
Bridges, Harry, 78, 80, 82, 123, 163, 165, 167
Bridges, Nikke, 175
Brodkin, Karen, 5
Brown, Kathleen A., 74
Buchman, Al, 25–26
Buchman, Molly. See Kvetnay, Molly
Buchman, Nathan: Bund membership and, 24; in California, 33–36; career in America of, 26–27, 34–35; chicken ranching endeavor and, 164; conscription of, 24; Elaine's marriage to Russell and, 37–38; immigration to United States, 22, 24; Joyce Russell and, 55, 92–93; Karl Yoneda

Buchman, Nathan (*continued*)
and, 54; labor activism and, 27, 35;
marriage of, 28; political environment of
Elaine's childhood and, 14; religion and, 26;
Socialism and, 27; union support and, 27;
visits to Manzanar, 141
Bund (General Jewish Workers' Union),
23–24, 29

California Agricultural Industrial Workers
Union, 85
California Historical Society, Women in
California collection, 6–7
California Labor School, 164–165
California State University at Fullerton
(Japanese Americans Project), 6
Campbell, Ned, 140, 142, 150–152
Cannery and Agricultural Workers Industrial
Union, 66
chicken farming, 66–67, 163–165
Chinese Americans, 115
Chinese Exclusion Act (1882), 25, 49
Civil Liberties Act of 1988, 175
Civil Rights Congress, 165
Cold War, 165
Coleman, Festus Lewis, 61, 98
Commission on Wartime Relocation and
Internment of Civilians (CWRIC), 8, 174–
175, 183n16
Communism, 9, 22–23, 60
Communist Party of the United States of
America (CPUSA): African Americans and,
60–61; Bay Area Nisei Communist Party,
114; "Black Belt Theory," 60; Buchmans
and, 35; Criminal Syndicalism Act and, 85;
expansion and diversity of in 1930s, 60; Ida
Rothstein and, 73; nonwhite workers and,
52; Popular Front strategy, 60;
reinstatement of Japanese American
memberships and, 162; suspension of
memberships of Japanese-ancestry
members and wives after the bombing of
Pearl Harbor, 114; Unemployment Council
of, 48; war effort and, 162; West coast labor
activism and, 2; women and, 2, 9, 61, 73
concentration camps, 12–13, 125, 168, 171
Covid-19 pandemic, 1–2
Criminal Syndicalism Act of 1919, 43, 63,
74, 85

Damon, Anna, 63
Daniels, Roger, 12–13
Darby Hotel, 36–37

Darcy, Sam, 46–47
de Haan, Binne, 4
DeWitt, John, 118, 126–127
Dixler, Elsa Jane, 9
Doho, 91, 111, 119, 135

Eisenberg, Ellen, 120
Elaine Black Yoneda Memorial Book
Committee, 7
Ellis Island, 50
Embrey, Sue Kunitomi, 171
Enemy Child (Warren), 10
Executive Committee of the Fruit, Vegetable,
and Shed workers, 70
Executive Order 9066 (EO 9066), 3, 118, 135

Farewell to Manzanar (Houston &
Houston), 12
Farm Security Administration (FSA), 11
fascism, 2–3, 15, 60, 89, 91–92, 113–114, 119–121
Federal Bureau of Investigation (FBI), 3,
111–113, 129, 143, 148, 165–167
feminist biography, 4–6, 182n9
Filipino Labor Union, 70
Fraternal Order of Elks, 38
From Kona to Yenan (Ariyoshi), 10
Fryer, E. R., 137
Fujii, Shuji, 112, 119

Gallagher, Leo, 43, 47, 53, 74, 84, 86–87, 90
Ganbatte (Karl Yoneda), 7–8
gender: biography and, 3; exclusion orders
and children of interracial marriage and,
129; immigration and, 24; Japanese
American community and beliefs about,
139; Karl and Elaine's public speech after
World War II, 182n10; Kibei response to
Karl Yoneda and, 139; marriage and
expectations around, 38, 48. *See also*
feminist biography; women
Gillen, Leslie, 89–90
Goldblatt, Louis, 120, 163
Goodman, Lillian, 45
Great Depression, 9, 11, 39–40, 60, 66
Greer, Len, 91

Hagiwara, George, 113
Hansen, Arthur, 6–7, 10, 135, 139, 176,
196n103, 198n151, 198n157
Harmsma, Jonne, 4
Higuchi, H., 143
Hiroshima, 16, 159–160, 169–170
Honolulu Record, 166

housing discrimination, 57, 59, 96, 161–162
Houston, James D., 12
Houston, Jeanne Wakatsuki, 12
Hynes, William "Red," 40, 42–43, 46–47

Ichioka, Toshio, 52, 55
immigration: Angel Island and, 50; Asia
    Exclusion Act of 1924 (Johnson-Reed Act),
    52, 70; border separation and, 12; Chinese,
    25, 50; citizenship laws and Japanese
    Americans, 12; of Elaine Black Yoneda's
    parents, 22–25; Ellis Island, 50; Japanese,
    25, 50; Jewishness and, 5; Philippines and,
    70; of Russian Jews, 24–25
imperialism, 171–172
Imperial Japanese Army, 113
Indigenous Peoples, 10, 122
Industrial Workers of the World (IWW),
    37, 39
International Labor Defense (ILD): conflict
    with American Federation of Labor (AFL)
    and, 68–70; Criminal Syndicalism Act and,
    85; Darcy speaking event and, 45–47;
    Elaine Black Yoneda and, 15, 42–48, 55,
    61–63, 97–98, 165; fascism and, 91–92;
    Harlan County (KY) miners and, 45–46;
    Ida Rothstein and, 73; labor prisoners and,
    63; legal aid for strikers and, 2; legislative
    work of, 91–92; Leo Gallagher and, 87; Tom
    Mooney and, 2, 45–46, 63–65; postwar
    mergers and, 165; San Francisco General
    Strike of 1934 and, 76–77, 79, 81–82, 85;
    Scottsboro Nine and, 2, 45–46, 61; Sonoma
    County and, 66–67; women and, 2
International Longshore and Warehouse
    Union, 16, 80, 98, 163, 166, 174
International Longshoremen's Association
    (ILA), 76, 78, 82
International Unemployment Day (March 6,
    1930), 41–42, 46
interracial couples/families: California
    antimiscegenation laws and, 59;
    discrimination from hospital and, 96;
    exclusion orders and, 129; housing
    discrimination and, 57, 59, 96, 161–162;
    legal status of, 54; postwar racism and, 161–
    162; prejudices against, 54
Issei, 117
Ito family, 149–150

Japanese American Citizens League (JACL):
    anti-Axis committee of, 115; campaign for
    reparations for incarcerated Japanese

Americans and, 174; cooperationism and,
    11, 13, 117; enlistment of Japanese
    Americans and, 148; friction with labor
    activists and, 134–135; *Manzanar Free Press*
    and, 136; members of at Manzanar, 134;
    response to racism faced by Japanese
    Americans and, 115; Yonedas' postwar
    involvement with, 165
Japanese American exclusion/incarceration:
    apologies for, 3; arguments against, 119–
    120; Farm Security Administration (FSA)
    photography project and, 11; fears of
    violence as motivation for, 120; Indigenous
    People's experience and, 10, 122, 184n23;
    loyalty oath and, 10–11; in Mexico and
    Canada, 116; non-Japanese members of
    interracial families and, 129; Culbert Olson
    and, 118–119; Omura and, 119; racism in
    arguments for, 9–10, 118–120; reparations
    and, 3, 170, 174–175; resistors to, 119;
    terminology and, 12–14, 171, 185n34;
    understanding of recurring xenophobia
    and, 2; Yonedas' support of, 2–3, 119–121
Japanese Americans: citizenship legislation
    and, 12, 55, 134; cooperationist term and,
    13–14; efforts to allow enlistment of Nisei
    and, 136; employment opportunities and,
    52; housing discrimination and, 57, 59, 161–
    162; labor discrimination and, 162–163;
    oral histories and, 7; postwar racism and,
    161–163; question of loyalty and, 10–11;
    racism and violence faced by after Pearl
    Harbor attack, 115–117; relocation of some
    to Midwest or East, 13; reparations for, 3,
    174; resistance/rebel term and, 14;
    responses to Pearl Harbor attack, 111–113,
    117; service of during World War II, 10,
    146–147, 157–158, 162; as supporters of
    Japanese American exclusion, 3
Japanese Americans Evacuation Claims Act
    (1948), 174
Japanese Americans Project of California
    State University at Fullerton's Oral History
    Program, 6
Japanese Unemployed Council, 52
Japanese Workers' Association (JWA), 52
Jerome Relocation Center, 148
Jewish Americans: chicken farming and,
    66–67, 154; culture in New York, 25;
    discrimination and, 35; immigration and,
    25; racial perception of, 5, 35, 54; religion
    and, 25–26; Socialist circles and, 27;
    Yiddish and, 25

Jewish Cultural Club, 165
Jim Crow laws, 157
Johnson, Edward, 86
Johnson-Reed Act (Asia Exclusion Act of 1924), 52

Kamikawa, Satoru, 149
Kanagawa, Jim, 150
Kanatz, Anna, 49
Kann, Ken, 177, 190n25
Kataoka, Ichiro, 111
Kendall, Lucy, 6–7
Kishi, Ben, 137, 140, 142
Korean Americans, 115
Korean War, 165
Korematsu, Fred, 117
Kurihara, Joe, 137, 142, 149, 172–173
Kvetnay, Molly, 14, 22; *Bund* membership and, 24; in California, 33–36; career in America of, 26–27, 34–35; chicken ranching endeavor and, 164; Elaine's hunger strike and, 83; Elaine's marriage to Russell and, 37–38; immigration to United States, 22, 24; Joyce Russell and, 38, 55, 92–93, 144–145; Karl Yoneda and, 54; labor activism and, 27, 35; marriage of, 28; religion and, 25; return for Russia for nine months of, 28–29; visits to Manzanar, 141

Labor Defender, 6, 68, 83–84
loyalty oath, 10–11

Making a Non-white America (Varzally), 8–9
Mann Act, 88
Manzanar Citizens Federation, 136, 142–143
Manzanar Free Press, 136
Manzanar Project Committee, 13, 170–171
Manzanar Revolt, 3, 10, 16, 149–151, 198n157
Manzanar War Relocation Center: assault of Tayama and, 148; Black Dragon Association and, 139, 144, 196n103; building jobs illusion at, 121–125; campaign to grant national memorial site status and, 3, 16, 170–171; Children's Village at, 126; communication with those incarcerated and, 126, 129; efforts to allow enlistment of Nisei and, 136; Farm Security Administration (FSA) photography project and, 11; interracial families in, 2, 10; Issei vs. Nisei vs. Kibei at, 134–135, 138–139; JACL members at, 134–135; Karl Yoneda's volunteer trip to, 121–125; Kitchen Workers Union and, 139; Manzanar Citizens Federation and, 136, 142–143; *Manzanar Free Press* and, 136; Manzanar Project Committee, 13, 179–180; Manzanar Revolt and, 3, 10, 16, 149–151, 198n157; measles epidemic in, 141; National Historic Landmark and Site designations, 171; policies disadvantaging resistors and, 138–139; racism in treatment of incarcerated, 140–141; resistors/resistance movement at, 134–139, 142–143; rumors about, 124; self-government committees of incarcerated, 136; Southern California Blood Brother Corporation and, 139; terminology and, 12–13, 171, 196n88, 198n157; war-relief work and, 140; Work Furlough Program, 143–144
Maryknoll organizations, 123–124
McAllister, Neil, 86–87
McCarran Act (1950), 166, 170
McCarthy era, 165–166
McNamara, James B., 63
McWilliams, Carey, 43
Merriam, Frank, 80
Metzger, Alfonso, 77
Michels, Tony, 25, 27
Minidoka Relocation Center, 145
Mitson, Betty, 6
Miyatake, Toyo, 11
Mooney, Tom, 2, 45–46, 55, 63–65, 96, 123
Myer, Dillon, 137

Nash, Roy, 142–143
Nation, 43
National Coalition for Redress/Reparations, 174
National Council for Japanese American Redress, 174
National Federation for Constitutional Liberties, 165
National Industrial Recovery Bill (1933), 60, 76
National Industry Recovery Bill, 60
National Lawyers' Guild, 144
National Negro Congress, 165
Native American Alcatraz Project, 170
Nelson, Bruce, 80
Nisei, anti-Japanese racism and, 116–117
Nisei Naysayer (Omura), 10
Nitzberg, Sol, 66–67
Noguchi, Isamu, 119
No-No Boy (Okada), 10–11
Northern California Communist Party, 16

Okada, James, 10–11
Okumura, Saiji, 50
Olson, Culbert, 64–65, 118–119
Omura, James, 119
Only What We Could Carry, 8
oral histories, 6–7
Origins of the Family (Engels), 61
Owens Valley Reception Center. *See* Manzanar War Relocation Center

Pale of Settlement, 21, 23
Pearl Harbor, 2, 9, 15, 111
People's World, 165
Petaluma Jewish Community Center, 168
Pichardo, Nelson, 66
pogroms, 23, 28–29
Point of No Return series (Uyeno), 172
police brutality, 39, 40–42, 46–47, 64, 79–80, 86
Poston Relocation Center, 148
Preparedness Day Parade (San Francisco, 1916), 2, 46

"Question Seldom Asked, The" (Baxandall), 9

race: Buchmans concerns about Elaine and Karl and, 54; effect of interracial marriage on archival materials, 6; Japanese recruits experience in American South and, 157; Karl Yoneda's joining of the longshoremans' union and, 91; labor activism in California and, 35–36; oral histories and, 7; perception of Jewishness in United States and, 5, 54; postwar racism toward Japanese Americans and, 161–163; racism and the internment of Japanese Americans, 4–5, 9–10, 118–119; racism experienced by Work Furlough workers and, 145–146. *See also* interracial couples/ families; Japanese Americans
Rafu Shimpo, 172
Raineri, Vivian McGuckin, 7
Rasmussen, Kai, 141
Reagan, Ronald, 175
Red Angel, The (Raineri), 7
Red Feminism (Weigand), 9
Red Scare, 59
Renders, Hans, 4
resistance (at Manzanar): enlistment and, 146; harassment of war-relief workers and, 140; terminology and, 14; violence after enlistment of some incarcerated, 148; Work Furlough Program and, 144

Rodo Shimbun, 56, 81, 91
Rogers, John, 81
Roosevelt, Franklin, 60, 118
Rossi, Angelo, 78
Rothstein, Ida, 45, 73, 82, 84, 89
Russell, Ed, 15, 37–41, 44, 47–48, 55, 93–94
Russell, Joyce, 15, 38, 55, 83, 91–93, 96, 141, 144–146, 164
Russia, 21–24, 59–60
Ryan, Joseph, 78

Sacco, Nicola, 38–39
Salinas Lettuce Strike (1936), 70–71
San Francisco Bay Area Labor History Workshop, 7
San Francisco Board of Supervisors, 16
San Francisco Chronicle, 151
San Francisco General Strike of 1934, 22, 75–82
San Francisco Labor Council, 80
San Francisco Longshoreman Association, 76
Schmidt, Matt, 63
Scottsboro Nine, 2, 61, 89
Selvin, David, 60
Senjin Shimbun, 158
Shunyo Maru, S.S., 50–51
Silverman, Lillian, 42–43
Slocum, Tokie, 140, 149
Smith Act, 166
Socialism, 23, 60
Sorin, Gerald, 23
Southern California Blood Brother Corporation, 139
Southwestern University Law School, 87
Sperry, Howard, 80
Spickard, Paul, 10
suffragist movement, 74

Tayama, Fred, 115, 135, 148–149
Title II Repeal Committee of San Francisco, 170
Todd, Louise, 73, 82, 84
Tolan, John, 118
Tom Mooney Labor School, 164–165
Trade Union Education League (TUEL), 35, 41, 52
Trade Union Unity League (TUUL), 41–42, 66. *See also* Cannery and Agricultural Workers Industrial Union
Triangle Shirtwaist Fire (1911), 73
Tule Lake Relocation Center, 11

Ueno, Harry, 139, 148–150, 172
Ukita, Yo, 149

United Electrical Radio Workers Union, 156
Uno, Edison, 174
U.S. Army: Hiroshima and, 16, 159–160; Karl
  Yoneda and, 15–16, 146–147, 157–161;
  loyalty oath and, 10; Military Intelligence
  Service, 141–142, 146, 167; Office of War
  Information Psychological Warfare
  Team, 158
Uyeno, Tad, 138, 172

vagrancy laws, 62, 82, 85
Vanzetti, Bartolomeo, 38–39
Varzally, Allison, 8–9, 35, 54–55
Vietnam, 169

Ware, Susan, 61
War Relocation Authority (WRA), 3, 10,
  12–13, 121, 137–138
Warren, Earl, 118
Watanabe, George, 119
Waterfront Employers Association, 163
Weigand, Kate, 9
Western Worker, 87
White, Joe, 69
Whitney, Anita, 72–74, 82, 85, 88, 165, 179
Wilson, Joe, 81
"Woman Question, The" (Dixler), 9
women: Communist Party of the United
  States of America (CPUSA) and, 2, 9, 61, 73;
  International Labor Defense (ILD) and, 2;
  match factories in Russia, 21;
  maternalism and, 74; Nineteenth
  Amendment, 61; suffragist movement
  and, 74; terminology and, 181–182n3.
  See also gender
Woodbury Business College, 36
Workman, James, 68–69
Works Progress Administration, 66
World War I, 29
World War II, 4–5, 13, 158–160. See also
  Hiroshima; Japanese American exclusion/
  incarceration; Manzanar War Relocation
  Center; Pearl Harbor; U.S. Army

Yamaguchi, Einosuke, 52
Yamazaki, Tom, 140
Yates, Oleta O'Connor, 162, 165
Yoneda, Elaine Black: advocacy of for
  prisoners at Manzanar, 133; anti-Semitism
  and, 33; birth of, 25; campaign to grant
  national Manzanar memorial site status
  and, 3, 16, 170–171, 174; chicken farming
  and, 3, 16, 66–67, 163–165; childhood trip

to Russia, 28–29; cooperation with
  exclusion/incarceration and, 2–3, 15–16,
  119–123, 144, 173; courtroom experience
  and, 47, 74–75, 77, 83–84, 89; Criminal
  Syndicalism Act and, 86; Darby Hotel and,
  36–37; daughter Joyce and, 15, 38, 55, 83,
  91–94, 96, 98, 141, 144–146, 164; death of, 3,
  175; divorce from Ed and, 55; Dolores Park
  arrest and trial, 86, 89–90; embrace of labor
  activism, 41; evacuation to Death Valley
  and, 151; FBI search for Karl after Pearl
  Harbor attack and, 112–113; friendships
  and, 70–73; harassment and threats against
  at Manzanar, 139–140, 143, 146–147, 149;
  Hynes and, 40, 42–43; ILWU Women's
  Auxiliary and, 169; International Labor
  Defense (ILD) and, 2, 15, 42–48, 55, 61–63,
  97–98, 165; Japanese American reparations
  and, 3, 170, 174–175; labor prisoner work
  and, 63; leave from Manzanar to find Joyce,
  144–145; Leo Gallagher and, 43, 87–89; life
  in Manzanar and, 130–134, 139–143, 146–
  147; Manzanar Revolt and, 149–151;
  marriage to Ed Russell and, 37–41, 47–48;
  marriage to Karl Yoneda and, 88–89; Tom
  Mooney and, 64–65; motivations for
  fighting to go to Manzanar, 129–130; name
  "Black" and, 40–41; 1934 General Strike in
  the San Francisco Bay Area and, 2; order for
  Tommy to go to Manzanar and, 127–129;
  petition to leave Manzanar with Tommy of,
  147–148; on Point of No Return series, 172–
  173; political activities after chicken
  ranching, 169–170; pregnancy and birth of
  Tommy and, 94–97; privileged upbringing
  and, 33, 37; "red angel" moniker, 63;
  relationship with Karl and, 41, 52–53,
  52–56, 59, 95–96, 155–156; religion and, 26,
  29; run for Board of Supervisors, 92; San
  Francisco General Strike of 1934, 22, 75,
  77–84; school years in California, 33–35;
  socialist lessons of childhood and, 27; trial
  in "Betsy Ross" case, 47; views of resistors at
  Manzanar, 138–139; vigilantism and, 67–69,
  71; visit to Japan, 169–170; war industry job
  and, 16, 156; war-relief work and, 140, 145
Yoneda, Emi, 51–52
Yoneda, Hideo, 49–50
Yoneda, Karl: advocacy of for prisoners at
  Manzanar, 133; Alaska Cannery Workers
  Union and, 95; arrest of after Pearl Harbor
  attack, 112–114; arrest of at February 9,
  1930, demonstration, 49; arrival in United

States and, 50–52; attempts to enlist after Pearl Harbor attack, 114–116; campaign to grant national Manzanar memorial site status and, 3, 16, 170–171, 174; Camp Anza assignment and, 157–158; chicken farming and, 3, 16, 163–165; cooperation with exclusion/incarceration and, 2–3, 15, 119–123, 137–138, 173; early life of, 49–50; Farm Security Administration (FSA) photography project and, 11; harassment and threats against at Manzanar, 16, 139–140, 142–143, 146–147; Hiroshima and, 16, 159–160, 169–170; influences of, 50; as informant, 3, 137–138; International Labor Defense (ILD) and, 53; Japanese American reparations and, 3, 170, 174–175; Karl Hama name and, 52, 88; labor discrimination after the war and, 163; Leo Gallagher and, 87–89; life at Manzanar and, 125, 131–133, 136, 139–143, 146–147; longshoremans' union and, 90–91; Manzanar Citizens Federation and, 136; marriage to Elaine and, 88–89; McCarthy era and, 167–168; news of Hiroshima and, 16, 159; poetry of, 50, 53; on Point of No Return series, 172–173; political activities after chicken ranching, 169–170; racism and interracial marriage of, 15; relationship with Elaine and, 41, 52–53, 53–56, 59,

95–96, 155–156; *Rodo Shimbun* and, 56, 81, 91; San Diego area farm of sister and, 55–56; San Francisco General Strike of 1934, 77, 79, 81; sentence for disturbing the peace and, 53; U.S. Army service and, 15–16, 146–147, 157–161; views of resistors at Manzanar of, 138–139; visit to Japan, 169–170; volunteer trip to build Manzanar, 121–125; War Relocation Authority and, 3; Work Furlough Program, 143–146
Yoneda, Kazu, 49–50, 94, 159–160, 169–170
Yoneda, Tommy: author's interview with, 8, 178–179; birth of, 15, 96; chicken ranching period and, 168–169; childhood health problems of, 97; evacuation to Death Valley and, 151; exclusion order for children of Japanese American fathers and, 117–119; health at Manzanar and, 131–133, 141, 145–146, 147; health problems after Manzanar, 155; on his mother, 175–176; incarceration of, 15; JACL award, 168–169; Karl's return from war and, 161; Petaluma B'nai B'rith award, 168–169; petition to leave Manzanar and, 147–148, 152; role in biography of Elaine, 179–180; threats against at Manzanar, 16, 149, 198n151; visit to Japan and, 169–170
Young Communist League, 77
Young Workers' League (YWL), 37, 39

Rachel Schreiber is Executive Dean of The New School's Parsons School of Design. She is the author of *Gender and Activism in a Little Magazine: The Modern Figures of the* Masses and the editor of *Modern Print Activism in the United States.*